The Sense of the
Sacramental

The Sense of the Sacramental

Movement and Measure in Art and Music, Place and Time

EDITED BY
DAVID BROWN AND ANN LOADES

First published in Great Britain 1995
Society for Promoting Christian Knowledge
Holy Trinity Church
Marylebone Road
London NW1 4DU

British Library Cataloguing-in-Publication Data

A catalogue record for this book is available from
the British Library

ISBN 0-281-04849-5

Typeset by Pioneer Associates, Perthshire
Printed in Great Britain by
Biddles Ltd., Guildford and King's Lynn

Contents

Preface

What follows is one of two volumes which had their origins in a series of addresses specially written to commemorate the nine hundredth anniversary of the laying of the foundation stone of Durham Cathedral on the 11 August 1093. However, all allusions to the original spoken context have been removed, and the material grouped and edited in a way in which it can now be read as a completely integrated discussion of a limited range of sacramental themes – in this case the extent to which movement and transformation provides the clue to understanding sacramentality in space, time, art and music. To aid further the reader's comprehension, the editors have not only provided a general introduction but also short summaries of the argument before each section and piece. The fact that these are placed in italics is intended to warn the reader that they do not necessarily represent the views of the authors of the various essays.

The editors wish warmly to thank all their contributors, Rachel Boulding at SPCK, and a number of individuals at Durham who have also helped in a number of ways, including Michael Fraser, Tim Perry, and Elizabeth Danna in the Theology Department, two members of Durham University Library staff, Elizabeth Rainey and Roger Norris, and Derek Craig of the Archaeology Department. Our gratitude is also due to those who gave financial support for the original series of addresses, in particular the Dean and Chapter of Durham Cathedral, the University of Durham and its Theology Department, and the Bethune Baker Fund, University of Cambridge.

The Contributors

JANET BACKHOUSE Curator of Illuminated Manuscripts, British Library

DAVID BROWN Van Mildert Professor of Divinity, University of Durham, and Canon of Durham Cathedral

ROSEMARY CRAMP Emeritus Professor of Archaeology, University of Durham

JOHN HABGOOD Archbishop of York

DAVID HUNT Lecturer in Classics, University of Durham

THOMAS HUMMEL American Episcopalian priest and historian

JAMES LANCELOT Organist of Durham Cathedral

ANN LOADES Reader in Theology at the University of Durham and editor of *Theology*

TERENCE McCAUGHEY Lecturer in the School of Irish, Trinity College, Dublin

ELIZABETH MANNING Senior Counsellor in the North Region of the Open University

J. T. RHODES Librarian, Ushaw College, Durham

CHRISTOPHER ROWLAND Dean Ireland's Professor of Exegesis of Holy Scripture, University of Oxford

DAVID STANCLIFFE Bishop of Salisbury and Chairman of the Church of England's Liturgical Commission

JOHN TAVENER Composer

TERENCE THOMAS Head of Department and Staff Tutor in Religious Studies, Open University

SUSAN WHITE Assistant Professor of Worship and Spirituality, Brite Divinity School, Texas

Introduction:
the Dance of Grace

DAVID BROWN and ANN LOADES

The sacraments as movement

It is very easy to think of the sacramental in essentially static, instantaneous terms: in baptism we are declared children of God, in sacramental absolution the past is blotted out, and in the Eucharist Christ is met and received. It is then but a short step to think of God also in such static terms, and so conceive of the link between his world and ours as episodic: as our fluctuating, constantly changing, temporary world just for an instant encountering the changelessness of his timeless eternity. Not surprisingly, that can create difficulties for belief: instead of seeing God's involvement with our world as the norm, it becomes the exception, the highlighted moments for which we need to search.

But, even if we confine ourselves to what are technically called sacraments, this is surely to misconceive the relationship. Take the case of baptism. To suppose that everything is done in that one act belies all the facts of human experience. The image of adoption that is employed both in Scripture and in the baptismal service surely provides a more reliable guide. As one recent Anglican report puts it:

> At one level adoption is something immediate. It comes into effect as soon as the legal process is complete. But, as all parents of adopted children realize, the reality is rather different. In terms of relationship between parent and child, gradual process rather than instantaneous act best characterizes what occurs. For, while the declarative legal act removes any possible insecurity from the relation, the subsequent bonding

1

can take as long as several years to complete. So likewise with baptism.[1]

Baptism is thus the beginning of a movement of the Spirit, a dynamic process whereby, should we continue to respond to that divine initiative, then all our lives will be a matter of continued growth into closer conformity with Christ, whose inheritance as sons and daughters we now share through adoption.

Much the same could be said about other sacramental acts. For instance, sacramental absolution is surely misconceived if it is solely identified with blotting out the past. Not only is this not always possible (the consequences of our sin can continue into the present and sometimes for years to come), more fundamentally grace is equally necessary to avoid repetition of such conduct in the future. This is why spiritual directors or counsellors can so often constitute a crucial role in the complete mediation of such forgiveness. For we need the help of others to perceive ourselves as we really are, and it is only then that we can identify what steps are most likely to generate a new future that has truly turned its back on the past. There is thus here too a dynamic of movement, the initiating of a process which carries a forgiven past into the promise of a transformed future.

It would be possible to multiply examples with other ecclesiastical acts, but the point and its implication is, we hope, now clear. As we have seen, a divinely initiated movement lies at the very heart of those acts commonly identified as sacramental. That being so, it must be right to expect a similar pattern of movement in any wider application of the notion. Indeed, wherever such movement occurs, so far from undermining a claim to the presence of the sacramental, it is surely now more likely to enhance it. The sacraments are about development and growth ('movement') within certain specified parameters or boundaries ('measure'); so wherever such movement and measure occur elsewhere in the wider field of God's creation, it becomes plausible to view such a dynamic as enabling us to participate in grace, and so share sacramentally in the life of the Creator from whom this dynamic takes its origin.

Even so, to extend this argument to space and time and claim both as potentially sacramental may still sound like the height of folly. For how can a God who has traditionally been held to be outside both be seen as particularly present in and through them? Are these not precisely the points at which we stand at greatest distance from our Creator? Clearly in some senses this must be so: time speaks of the inevitable decay of the world, space of our finitude, that we are bound to one place rather than another. Yet more can be said on the matter.

Space and time: moving to new co-ordinates

We have already seen how those rites commonly called sacramental function. It is not a matter of instantaneous divine action, as though we could be just there and then be pulled out of our specific context in space and time; rather God works through redefining who we are (giving us a new 'measure'), and thereby initiates a process of movement towards transformation. In a similar way, then, one may argue that this is how time and space themselves operate sacramentally: not by endorsing the present universe's temporal and spatial co-ordinates nor by pulling us out into a world without either, but rather through faith generating its own distinctive medium, its own set of spatial and temporal co-ordinates. Space and time are thus given a new definition (a new 'measure'), and as a result they can now help advance us on the sacramental process towards our life's transformation. The co-ordinates we adopt are no longer our own, but those given by God, and so make it possible for us to share more deeply in a God-centred perception of our world. How this might work out in detail is the theme which is pursued to varying degrees in Parts One and Four of this book.

But what comes first? Is it the quality of current faith and prayer that hallows a particular place or time as sacramental, or does the priority lie with God's actions, whether as Creator or Redeemer? Thus, has the world been so made that certain places (for example, mountains or running water) naturally evoke a sense of the divine presence? Or, again, does the fact that the incarnation took place at a specific point within time impose upon the Christian a particular way of reading the progress of history prior and subsequent to that event? Or might the truth lie in some mediating position, with a role both for the divine initiative and for human constructions?

Of all the contributors on the subject of sacred space, Susan White is the most suspicious of any suggestion of a sacramentality that is given (and can be retained), irrespective of how Christians currently behave in a particular place: it is the present devotion and love which Christians display in a particular place which legitimates treating it as sacred, not the place itself. As might be expected from someone writing on the environment, John Habgood is willing to concede a stronger role to the priority of place, insisting, as he does, that our placedness derives from our Creator, but to that is added the same strong moral emphasis that is to be found in Susan White's essay. Certainly, morality must play its part in any adequate understanding of the sacramental, but readers, as they peruse the other three contributions to the section on sacred space, might like to reflect whether the role of ethics should not be seen as properly subordinate to, and derivative from, something else: an alternative geography.

The points these other contributors make can be illustrated by some examples of our own. This book had its origin in lectures and seminars organized to celebrate the nine hundredth anniversary of the Norman cathedral at Durham, which owes its very existence to the arrival of St Cuthbert's bones on the site a century earlier in AD 995. Even today for many in the northeast of England their presence gives a different, an alternative geography to the secular one. The latter's focus is clearly the large, financial and industrial conurbation of Newcastle, whereas Cuthbert speaks of a different, more caring relation to one's environment, as more generally of a different value system altogether. The close identification of the saint with nature on the island of Lindisfarne has for many been recapitulated in his new setting on the tree lined banks of the River Wear.

Of course, the Norman cathedral was also intended as a symbol of power, and so the Christian's alternative geography could also have its negative points, as well as its positive ones. Indeed, in some cases this was to have dire consequences. To give a rather different example, the world might have escaped the carnage of the Crusades, had not medieval Europe so focused on just such an alternative geography, with Jerusalem as the centre of its world. For the resultant maps conveyed a threatening message: Christendom lying on the world's fringes with all that was most valued, most dear to God, at the world's heart in the possession of Islam.

In the face of such difficulties it is tempting to reject all such sacred geography and to follow the Epistle to the Hebrews and Paul in projecting all such longings elsewhere: 'here we have no continuing city'; instead our citizenship is in heaven.[2] But the New Testament writers were still living in a world that was as yet unable to provide them with the appropriate spatial coordinates. The sacred geography of both Rome and Israel was hostile; no alternative had yet emerged; and in any case the end of all things was expected soon.[3]

So there seems no reason, in this case at least, why we should follow suit. Where, as in the New Testament, another world is believed to be about to dawn, then perhaps our natural placedness needs no further sustaining. Otherwise, however, the everyday secular co-ordinates are likely to assert themselves, with all the problems that implies for the life of faith. It is surely for this reason that the Old Testament, unlike the New, took the question of sacred geography with the utmost seriousness. The uninteresting side is its stress on the land itself.[4] Much more intriguing is the way in which Jerusalem is treated; in part no doubt, as with the land, purely secular motives also played a role; for instance, it would be hard to discount the desire to enhance the authority of the monarchy, as also the wish to demote the status of the rival northern capital at Samaria. Yet the way in which Jerusalem came to be identified not only with the sacrifice of Isaac but also with the creation of the world and the world's end demonstrates the true power of sacred geography.[5] The fact that within Islam the Kaba or black stone at Mecca is called 'the navel of the earth' and is associated not only with Muhammad but also with events in the lives of Adam, Noah and Ishmael illustrates a similar process at work.[6] We need these alternative co-ordinates to give us an appropriate focus, and that is no doubt why to this day Jerusalem plays such a central role in the theology of Judaism.

From the subsequent history of Christianity another instance we may perhaps take is the early Irish notion of 'white martyrdom'.[7] Irish monks believed themselves called to abandon their familiar homeland and seek a new identity in a unfamiliar place. Such sacrifice was not of course intended to be purely negative, it was also supposed to induce a new sense of identity, and that is surely what all sacred geography is about. It enables one to grow – to move – in the faith by changing the measures, the familiar landmarks by which one identifies one's place within the surrounding environment. The pilgrim, by moving within secular space, thus also moves into a new and sacred geography.

A similar experience takes place within the church building itself, though here it is almost impossible to disentangle sacred space from sacred time. The traditional position of the baptismal font at the entrance already warns that one is entering a temporal zone which tells a different story from that which begins with one's birth. Then the fact that one has to move through the church to reach the altar speaks of a time which culminates in something other than one's own death, with the promise of sharing in Christ's resurrection through participation in his death. The sacred space is thus being used to initiate one into a new time. Those of more Catholic persuasion might also think of how the altar generates a new sense of space, with Christ's resurrected body now seen as occupying in the Eucharist place or position but no definite space (the claim being that the whole of Christ is present in every part of the eucharistic host, however small).[8] But it is upon the transformed under-standing of time that we wish to focus at this point.

Commentaries on the liturgy, particularly from an Orthodox perspective, make much of the worshipper being caught up into the worship of heaven. This has traditionally been taken to imply a timeless reality, and to reinforce that image it has often been claimed (falsely) that the worship of the Eastern Church, unlike the Western, has over the centuries undergone no significant change.[9] Nonetheless, what can certainly be claimed by all the major traditions is that the liturgy brings with it a new sense of time, one in which its beat or measure is determined simultan-eously by both a past and future reality being brought into the present. For the remembrance of Christ's past is also a making present of his current significance for us, just as the looking forward to the consummation of all things in his Kingdom is also an anticipation of it.

In common with the main emphasis of much contemporary theology and biblical scholarship Christopher Rowland in his contribution to Part Four focuses on the impact of that future, eschatological dimension. This rightly deserves a place, but in considering the sacramental role of time its importance can all too easily be exaggerated. Certainly it can give an alternative measure to time. But it is hard to live on the assumption that the end is only round the corner, and not thousands, perhaps millions, of years hence. That is why we need also to take into account other forms of sacred time. So, for instance, if we once more turn to the Old Testament, there we find the sabbath increasingly functioning as the measure of all else. To us the seriousness with which even a great prophet like Ezekiel takes violations of the sabbath seems quite extraordinary,[10] but there is no doubt that such patterned observance of an alternative time as God's time played a major role in preserving the iden-tity of the Jewish people over more than two thousand years of dispersion. Though the Christian Sunday never acquired quite the same status, the patterned following of the Christian year did, as the life of Christian communities determined themselves by the cycle of where they were in the story of Christ's life or that of his Church.

Art as imitation or as transcendent movement?

Probably nowhere has the ritual observance of sacred time had greater impact than in the kind of monastic community which produced the first work of sacred art discussed in Part Two, the

Lindisfarne Gospels. Almost all the examples in that section are pre-Reformation; so let our focus here be mostly later, and in particular ask what connection there is between art and sacred space and time. Perhaps surprisingly, it is possible to draw some strong connections. Superficially, art must seem at the opposite extreme, a purely human production unlike space and time, so firmly embedded as these are in the natural order. But in fact, as we have seen, in their impact upon human beings space and time are equally artefacts, whether such perceptions are consciously produced or otherwise. The secular measures of how the process of our lives and their placing in the environment are viewed are much affected by the culture in which we happen to live; the alternative, sacramental perception by the conscious adoption of alternative measures, but no less firmly removed from the purely natural.

Admittedly, to counter this accusation of being merely an artefact, art has sometimes hit back with the claim that not only is its principal aim imitation of the natural world but it gives a heightened, more profound perception of it; so, for example, as Rosemary Cramp observes in her contribution, a major concern in Anglo-Saxon iconography seems to have been to express a natural world at unity with itself and its Creator. Yet, if we consider the history of Western art as a whole, naturalism has had a very much smaller role than might have been anticipated. Indeed, one of the major themes of the Renaissance in its critique of the long history of Christian art which had preceded it was its lack of naturalism. Thus, whether we take a Renaissance theorist like Alberti (1404–72) or a practitioner like Leonardo da Vinci (1452–1519), this is something that both stress. For Leonardo painting is 'the only imitator of all visible works of nature' and on these grounds rightly called 'the grandchild of nature and so related to God'.[11] He therefore insists that the form of painting which deserves most praise is that which agrees most exactly with the thing imitated. In adopting such an attitude he stands in marked contrast to earlier views of art which had seen its role as pulling the spectator out of his world into a perception of heavenly realities. It is a contrast which is well brought out in Robert Browning's poem 'Fra Lippo Lippi', where the artist (1457–1504) is made to argue against the tradition of art in which he has been brought up, on the grounds that it simply bypassed the material world.[12]

In the long history of Christian opposition to art, naturalism has in fact been one of the major grounds of complaint. The biblical prohibition of images was used to argue that it turned one towards worship of the natural world (e.g. Tertullian[13]), or at the very least distracted one in that direction and away from more important concerns (e.g. Bernard[14]). Other arguments as well of course played their part. Jerome's moral objections, that the money was better spent elsewhere, recur frequently,[15] and formed a major plank in the Cistercian opposition, of which Bernard was part. Ironically, however, criticism came not only from those who complained of too much realism in copying the natural world, but also from those who objected to there being too little. Thus, for example, Augustine argued that art necessarily involves falsehood and so is at odds with a higher truth: as in acting it has to pretend to be what it is not, in order to succeed.[16]

The positive justifications which were offered were rather weak. Repeated reference was made to Pope Gregory the Great's image of art as the Bible for the ignorant,[17] and it is equally that educational focus which provides the rationale at the Counter-Reformation Council of Trent. But in our view to rely on this justification alone would be to ignore the way in which sacred art can, like sacred space and time, act in itself sacramentally: pointing beyond itself to another order of reality, without that other order constantly needing to be mediated through appeal to Scripture or the teaching office of the Church.

This is something which that great Christian artist Michelangelo (1475–1564) clearly perceived. In his long life his views underwent development, but even in his earliest period he is insistent that his task is not to imitate nature, though he loves and admires it. Rather, the artist's role is to draw us to a beauty that is above nature. A late poem expresses it well:

What my eyes saw was nothing that is mortal
When in your beautiful ones I found my peace
. . .
And if the creature were not made God's equal
It would not wish more than the eyes' gladness,
The outward beauty; but since it is false,
Its form moves up into the Universal.[18]

For Michelangelo this meant that the representation of physical beauty was not always appropriate, and so this justified the gross figures of his *Last Judgement*; indeed, at other times he seems to have sought even to deny physicality altogether, as has been suggested by some art critics when comparing the ethereal quality of his late *Rondanini Pietà* with its more famous namesake in St Peter's.[19] The occasional desire of Michelangelo to use physical distortion or ugliness to point to a higher beauty also finds its echo in a Christian artist of the twentieth century, in George

Rouault's decision to paint clowns, prostitutes and outcasts: their distorted figures speak of an alternative order of beauty that lies beyond their present condition.[20]

It would, of course, be absurd to suppose that we could in a few short paragraphs produce a universally applicable theory of sacred art. Two very different painters from the century following Michelangelo may be used to illustrate the difficulty. Of the two, Rubens (1577–1640) is the one who today is most subject to misunderstanding, and the accusations of pagan art have been frequent.[21] But his daily attendance at Mass suggests otherwise. What in fact has gone wrong in contemporary perception is our own ignorance; we see only clutter or pagan mythology, whereas an age more familiar with symbolism would have been drawn, as he intended, into an alternative, spiritual world. So, for instance, in his *Adoration of the Magi* one needs to know that the liturgy for the Feast of the Epiphany referred to 'the multitude of camels' (Isa. 60.6), or again with his *Ganymede and the Eagle* that the story of the young boy's abduction by Jupiter was commonly read as an allegory of the soul's ascent to heaven. Even violent action is transformed as in *The Rape of the Daughters of Leucippus*; to the casual eye it speaks of male aggression, but more detailed attention reveals heavenward gazes and a helping Cupid; and the message resolves into the very opposite of the painting's title: the triumph of love over force.[22]

Only occasionally does Rembrandt (1606–69) resort to such symbolism, as in *The Meeting of Mary and Elizabeth* of 1640 with its antique pillar, peacock and vine tendril. Instead, we are overwhelmed by the humanity of Christ, so much so in fact that some historians have argued that his views were Socinian rather than incarnational. But equally the explanation could be a stronger focus upon that very fact, with the incarnation seen as the point of the divine reaching into the human. Even so, he achieves his message without the same idealization or exaggeration of the natural that we found in Michelangelo and Rubens. Admittedly, some qualification to this is necessary since even Rembrandt did sometimes exaggerate in order to achieve an effect, as in his use of multiple lines in his etchings or his extensive use of *chiaroscuro* (light and shade) in both etchings and paintings. Even so, there is no equivalent to Turner's major alterations of the landscape to suit his purposes,[23] or, to give a more explicitly religious example, Caspar David Friedrich's heightening of the transcendent in his dramatic images of human beings dwarfed by the trees and mountains about them.[24] So either Rembrandt's art is not sacramental or it functions in a very different sort of way – perhaps more indirectly through enabling us to perceive our human world in a new kind of way, in much the same way as the artist concerned with the imitation of nature helps us to perceive a beauty in God's creation that might otherwise have passed us by.

Music and heaven's dance

Throughout history there has been friendly (and not so friend-ly) competition between the various art forms as to which was the most superior. Leonardo, for instance, argued that painting was necessarily superior to poetry because it better represented nature.[25] But, if the general direction here is followed, with art like space and time functioning sacramentally through ideal-ization and exaggeration, then a rather different answer might be expected. This is precisely what happens with the painter Kandinsky in his famous essay *Concerning the Spiritual in Art*. For him music is the highest form of art, since it escapes all the distractions of the imitation of nature. Art must become abstract, with colour its primary medium; indeed these are its notes, as can be seen by the inappropriateness of expressing yellow by a base note or a very dark blue in the treble clef.[26] Only that way will art function spiritually: as a 'movement for-wards and upwards'.[27]

In Part Three, the section on music, we are fortunate to have contributions from practising musicians, John Tavener the com-poser and James Lancelot, the cathedral organist at Durham. More than once in that section a comparison is drawn with the work of the icon painter, the introductory piece by Terence Thomas and Elizabeth Manning in fact defining the role of sacred music as 'iconographic'. However, there is one point over which we find ourselves in disagreement with its joint authors. They see what functions in this way as entirely a matter of 'cultural determination', though towards the end of their piece they do concede one small qualification, that congruence with the words may also have a bearing.

But are they entirely right? Admittedly, almost all sacred music has had secular origins in 'the devil's best tunes'. Nowadays, for instance, we tend to think of the organ as an essentially religious instrument, but for several centuries its greatest popularity lay in accompanying dance music. Similarly, despite nineteenth-century claims about the purity of Gregorian chant, there seems little doubt that many of its melodies had their origin in secular song. Nonetheless, to push the case too far would be to ignore, in our view, two important factors on the other side. First, in any credible vocal composition the music should not function separately from the words; so there is nothing in the least surprising in the fact that different words could generate a different overall effect. Second, the fact that a particular piece of music is performed regularly in church cannot of itself mean that it now acts iconographically or sacramentally, any more than that another piece should be denied that status solely on the grounds that its performance is always elsewhere in the concert hall. Thus music in church can also be used for a number of purely human purposes, such as the strengthening of communal identity or as a spur to action.

Equally, 'secular' music can act sacramentally, in giving one a sense of the divine and its attributes. To give what is probably now a rather overworked example, Mozart's secular music can speak of heavenly joy and of a divine triumph of good over evil. As is well known, both Barth and Balthasar made much of such music.[28] More recently, Hans Küng has added his voice; though he gives an extended treatment of Mozart's *Coronation Mass*, it is surely not without significance that he confesses that it was repeated playing of a secular piece that has had the most marked religious influence upon his life: the *Clarinet Concerto* which Mozart completed just two months before his death.[29] Or, to give an example of our own, Beethoven's *Missa Solemnis* may be impractical liturgically and come from the pen of a far from devout Roman Catholic. Yet, unlike his *Christ on the Mount of Olives* where purely human concerns seem to be to the fore, or even his *C Major Mass* in which perhaps consequent upon his deafness the *incarnatus* of the creed seems to revel more in pity for the condition of humanity than in wonder at the generosity of God, the focus now seems to be in a sacramental transformation, with even the *incarnatus* speaking of a mystical joy. The fact that the Hindu *Upanishads* played their part in Beethoven's religious formation no less than Christianity does not lessen the point. God can still act through him, as Beethoven himself acknowledged: 'Every real creation of art is independent, more powerful than the artist himself, and returns to the divine through its manifestation. It is one with man only in this, that it bears testimony to the mediation of the divine in him.'[30]

Of all forms of music not only is dance commonly thought to be the oldest, it is also believed to have been the earliest form taken by religious ritual.[31] In dance of course there is movement and measure to a higher degree than in any of the other four areas hitherto discussed. So it is fitting that we should draw these introductory thoughts to a conclusion by observing how it functions sacramentally. Writing in 1884, Stewart Headlam once observed: 'The art of dancing, perhaps . . . more than all other arts, is an outward and visible sign of an inward and spiritual grace'.[32] However astonishing such an application of the Prayer Book definition of a sacrament may initially seem, it seems to us to contain an important truth that will also help illuminate what we have said earlier about other forms of movement and measure.

Pythagoras' discovery in the sixth century BC that the chief concordant musical intervals (*symphoniai*) could be expressed by simple numerical ratios was to have a profound impact on the history of European thought. For it led to his conviction that number is the clue to understanding everything in the universe, and in particular that proportion and balance (*harmonia*) between its constituent parts is what holds it in existence. From that came not only the search for the One that generates plurality but also the doctrine of the harmony of the spheres. The result is that in contrast to his negative views on art quoted earlier, Augustine can write that through music 'the mind is raised from the consideration of changeable numbers in inferior things to unchangeable numbers in unchangeable truth itself',[33] while the book that was to become the standard treatise on music for the Middle Ages does not hesitate to include a discussion of the music of the spheres, the notion of the world held in perfect balance as though it were itself singing.[34] It is a way of thought now almost forgotten, though perhaps appropriately there is at least one twentieth-century public reference – in the very Cathedral in whose honour all these essays were written. For at Durham we find a window dedicated to Gregory Nazianzen which portrays him offering the music of the spheres to God, and in large letters below, his own words quoted: 'Thy attuning teacheth the choir of the worlds to adore thee in musical silence.'[35]

Unfortunately, Christianity's attitude to dance has been, if anything, even more a history of suspicion than was the case with art. More 'primitive' religion took a different view, and for very understandable reasons. The movement of the dance speaks of a heightening of our powers and energies, of freedom and exhilaration, all of which mean that we seem to come closer to the creative power and joyful freedom that characterize the divine. It is no doubt for some such reason as this that dancing played its part in Old Testament worship.[36] Again, the fact that the dance has a measure or pattern implies that the dancers can be seen as participating in the pattern or harmony which marks the undivided will of the world's Source:

Lo, this is Dancing's true nobility:

. . .
Where all agree, and all in order move;
Dancing, the art that all arts do approve;
The fair character of the world's consent,
The heav'n's true figure, and th' earth's ornament.

That is part of a long seventeenth-century poem entirely
devoted to that theme.[37] But better known is the way in which
the most famous poem of the Middle Ages, Dante's *Divine
Comedy*, ends: also in a sort of dance. The poet sees the three
persons of the Trinity as three moving 'circles' or 'spheres' in a
single orbit. Unable to comprehend how he can perceive our
own human image in one of them, he is suddenly smitten by
light and his 'desire and will, like a wheel that spins with even
motion, were revolved by the Love that moves the sun and the
other stars'.[38] Though the allusion is Aristotelian, not only has
Dante made the context fully Christian, he points the way for us
to comprehend how movement and measure can finally take us
within divinity itself. For unlike Aristotle's God who remains
inactive while the world is attracted in motion towards him, the
Christian God is a Trinity of love that is active both towards the
world and within itself in its internal relations between Father,
Son and Holy Spirit.

The notion of their *perichoresis* (co-inherence) developed
slowly,[39] but it speaks of a love that 'interpenetrates' or flows in
constant motion from one to the other. The Greek verb *choreo*
literally means 'to move' or 'to contain'. By a happy accident the
Greek for 'to dance' is *choreuo*. Hinduism is the only contemporary religion which retains in a major way the 'primitive'
image of the divine dancer, in Shiva and his consort Parvati.
Might Christianity not gain, rather than lose, if it thought of
perichōresis as a dance of divine love, even granted all the quali-
fications which must then be made for a God who exists outside
human space and time? Our movements, our dances, would
then be aimed at sharing in that divine dance. Sidney Carter's
'Lord of the Dance' is now a very familiar hymn. The imagery
of one medieval Cornwall carol is very similar, but it ends in this
way:

Then up to heaven I did ascend,
Where now I dwell in sure substance
On the right hand of God, that man
May come unto the general dance.[40]

The freedom and exhilaration of the divine dance can be sacramentally experienced by us all.

Conclusion

We began by rejecting any notion of sacraments that defined them statically as though they functioned as instantaneous moments. In each of the five cases we subsequently considered, we then observed how movement also acts in these cases as a sacrament of transformation. Place and time are redefined, and thereby we are given the true measure of a God who is beyond both. Again, the sort of art we considered did not imitate the natural world but rather strove through exaggeration and idealization to suggest a different, non-material reality. Music carries the process still further by most closely resembling the work of an abstract artist like Kandinsky. Finally, we saw how sacred dance, by hastening all our natural movements, can evoke the trinitarian God whose movements are so unhindered, so free, that they are all done with effortless ease. How all this relates to the downward sacramental movement of God in the incarnation and the sacraments of the Church is discussed in the other volume to emerge from the Durham celebrations. But in the meantime let the reader's focus in what follows be upon this 'dance of grace' that draws us beyond our worldly perceptions, as movement in space, time, art and music all experience their transformation and so enable our own.

Notes

1. Doctrine Commission of the Church of England, *We Believe in the Holy Spirit* (London: Church House Publishing, 1991), p. 77.
2. Hebrews 13.14 (AV) cf. Phil. 3.20.
3. e.g. 1 Cor. 7.29 'the time is short' (AV).
4. But for a helpful attempt to apply Old Testament insights, cf. G. R. Lilburne, *A Sense of Place: A Christian Theology of the Land* (Nashville: Abingdon, 1989).
5. 2 Chron. 3.1 identifies the hill on which Solomon built the Temple with the Mount Moriah of Gen. 22 on which Abraham had been about to sacrifice Isaac. The Temple itself seems to have been conceived as the centre of the created order, built in accordance with a heavenly plan as the garden of God (cf. M. Barker, *The Gate of Heaven: The History and Symbolism of the Temple of Jerusalem*, London: SPCK, 1991, pp. 57–103). The association of the destruction of Jerusalem with the end of the world continues into the New Testament, as in Mark 13.
6. In the case of Adam the tradition seems to be building on the *Koran* itself, which at 3.96 calls the Kaba 'the first sanctuary

appointed for mankind'. For a useful comparative study of sacred place across the various religions, cf. J. Holm and J. Bowker (eds.), *Sacred Place* (London: Pinter, 1994).

7. Though initially 'white martyrdom' seems to have meant merely the daily martyrdom of the ascetic life. So C. Stancliffe, 'Red, white and blue martyrdom' in D. Whitelock, R. McKitterick and D. Dumville, *Ireland in Early Medieval Europe* (Cambridge: CUP, 1982), pp. 21–46.

8. As in Aquinas, *Summa Theologiae* 3a, Q. 76, art. 4. Cf. also D. Brown, *Continental Philosophy & Modern Theology* (Oxford: Blackwell, 1987), pp. 174–9.

9. For an excellent discussion of development within the Orthodox liturgy, cf. H. Wybrew, *The Orthodox Liturgy* (London: SPCK, 1989).

10. As in Ezek. 20.12–13; 22.7–9; examples are of course not wanting elsewhere, as in the case of the man stoned to death for gathering sticks on the sabbath (Num. 15.32–6).

11. J. P. Richter (ed.), *The Literary Works of Leonardo da Vinci* (London: Rivington, 1883), pp. 326–7.

12. Esp. lines 282ff.

13. Tertullian, 'On Idolatry' 4; e.g. in *Early Latin Theology*, Library of Christian Classics, S. L. Greenslade (ed.) (London: SCM Press, 1956), p. 85ff.

14. Bernard, 'Apologia' 12.28–30; text in *Opera*, J. Leclercq and H. M. Rochais (eds.) (Éditions Cisterciennes, 1963), vol. 3, pp. 104–7; translation in G. C. Coulton, *Life in the Middle Ages* (Cambridge: CUP, 1930), vol. 4, pp. 172–4.

15. *Saint Jérôme: Lettres*, J. Labourt (ed.) (Paris: Société d'Éditions, 1953) vol. 3, no. 58, pp. 81–2.

16. Augustine, 'The Soliloquies' 10.18; in *Augustine: Earlier Writings* (ed.), J. H. S. Burleigh (London: SCM Press, 1953), p. 51.

17. Gregory the Great, Letter 13; in *Patrologia Latina*, vol. 77; cols. 1128–30.

18. Sonnet 103; trans. G. Gilbert, *Complete Poems and Selected Letters of Michelangelo* (Princeton: Princeton University Press, 1980), pp. 75–6.

19. For interpretations of the Rondanini Pietà cf. H. von Einem, *Michelangelo* (London: Methuen, 1959), pp. 248–50; A. Blunt, *Artistic Theory in Italy 1450–1600* (Oxford: OUP, 1962), p. 77.

20. cf. W. A. Dyrness, *Rouault: A Vision of Suffering and Salvation* (Grand Rapids, Michigan: Eerdmans, 1971), pp. 126–57.

21. For a catena of such accusations cf. E. Baudouin, *P. P. Rubens* (London: Brocken, 1977), p. 346.

22. For an excellent exposition of Rubens' use of pagan mythology in these two paintings, cf. C. Scribner III, *Peter Paul Rubens* (New York: Abrams, 1989), pp. 60, 70.

23. e.g. in his 1812 painting of Falmouth Harbour he switched the town and Mawes Castle to opposite sides of the river; for a

discussion of his aims, cf. A. Wilton, *Turner and the Sublime* (London: British Museum Publications, 1980).

24. cf. J. L. Koerner, *Caspar David Friedrich and the Subject of Landscape* (London: Reaktion Books, 1990).

25. cf. M. Kemp, *Leonardo da Vinci: The Marvellous Works of Nature and Man* (London: Dent, 1981), pp. 209–11.

26. W. Kandinsky, *Concerning the Spiritual in Art* (New York: Dover, 1977), p. 25.

27. ibid., p. 4.

28. K. Barth, *Church Dogmatics* (Edinburgh: T. & T. Clark, 1960), 3:3, pp. 297–9; H. U. von Balthasar, *Theodramatik* (Einsideln: Johannes Verlag, 1976), 2:1, pp. 244–5; cf. also C. Gunton, 'Mozart the Theologian' in *Theology* 94 (1991), pp. 346–9. Others continue to challenge his religious perceptivity, e.g. W. Hildesheimer, *Mozart* (London, Dent, 1982), esp. pp. 361–5.

29. H. Küng, *Mozart: Traces of Transcendence* (London: SCM Press, 1992), p. 27.

30. At least according to Bettina von Arnim (Brentano) in a letter to Goethe; quoted in M. M. Scott, *Beethoven* (London: Dent, 1934), p. 125.

31. So e.g. G. van der Leeuw, *Sacred and Profane Beauty* (New York: Holt, Rinehart and Winston, 1963).

32. J. R. Orens, *The Mass, the Masses, and the Music Hall: Stewart Headlam's Radical Anglicanism* (Croydon: Jubilee, 1979), p. 13.

33. Augustine, 'On Music' 6; in *The Fathers of the Church* (Washington: Catholic University of America Press, 1947), 4, pp. 324ff. The intellectualist character of his appreciation is well brought out in C. Harrison, *Beauty and Revelation in the Thought of St. Augustine* (Oxford: Clarendon, 1992), pp. 28–31.

34. Boethius, *Fundamentals of Music*, trans. C. M. Bower and C. V. Palisca (New Haven: Yale University Press, 1989), p. 9.

35. Gregory Nazianzen, *Carminum Liber*, I, 29: 'Hymnus ad Deum'.

36. cf., e.g. Exod. 15.20; 2 Sam. 6.14; Ps. 149.3; Ps. 150.4.

37. Sir John Davies, *Orchestra*, lines 666–72. Cf. also N. Frye, *Words with Power* (London: Harcourt, Brace, Jovanovich, 1994), pp. 176–7.

38. Dante, *The Divine Comedy*, trans. J. D. Sinclair (Oxford: OUP, 1971), 3, 33; p. 485.

39. H. A. Wolfson, *The Philosophy of the Church Fathers* (Cambridge, Mass.: Harvard University Press, 1956), pp. 418–28; G. L. Prestige, *God in Patristic Thought* (London: SPCK, 1952), pp. 282–301. The latter (p. 291) identifies the earliest use of the noun with Maximus the Confessor (d. 662).

40. 'My Dancing Day' in *The Oxford Book of Carols*, ed. P. Dearmer, R. Vaughan Williams and M. Shaw (Oxford: OUP, 1928), pp. 154–5.

PART ONE:
SACRED SPACE

Place has clearly something to do with measure: its placedness is a matter of its measured relation to other places, its co-ordinates on one kind of map or another. It is from this notion of place as given that John Habgood starts in his opening contribution, with the idea of our earthly home or environment as a divine 'given'. But he soon finds himself arguing beyond this point: that movement is also required on our part, since we are charged with realizing the world's full potential, though he admits it is not always easy to determine when movement has brought our placedness to its full significance and when what we have done constitutes its very denial. Susan White, in her extended examination of the various types of approach which have been adopted to the question of sacred space and the issues they raise, starts from the opposite end from the Archbishop of York. For her, our movements, what we do, is what is significant, and place can only acquire holiness in that light. Against that view some may wish to set the persistence of certain natural sites as holy, even for successive, very different and mutually incompatible religions, or the desire to re-establish Christian worship even on sites where great evil has been done. In whatever direction one's sympathies lie, the two essays clearly establish the need for further reflection on the appropriate balance between measured given and dynamic movement.

This is also an issue taken up by the chairman of the Church of England's Liturgical Commission. David Stancliffe finds a tension reflected in Church architecture and liturgy between two very different models of the Church, a static view of place with

God given in our midst and a dynamic one in which both liturgy and building move in such a way that we are pulled out from beyond them into the divine transcendence. His preference for the latter chimes in well with the essay by David Hunt which follows. Pilgrimage of its very essence requires movement, but it is often misunderstood as then coming to a halt at its destination, whereas David Hunt argues that it is precisely at this point that further movement then takes place, in a sought transcendence of both time and place. Not only do the years separating the original divine disclosure dissolve, but a new placedness, a new geography, is identified. Thomas Hummel observes the way in which such ideas continued into the minds of nineteenth-century Russian peasants. More contentiously, he presents a plausible case for maintaining that, despite their protestations to the contrary, sophisticated English travellers to the Holy Land were not far behind. Is there a dynamic of movement and place which we ignore at our peril?

The relevance of all this to the sacramental is surely obvious. It raises the question of how much God's sacramental involvement in our world is through 'givens', through a measure such as place, and how much through movement, through creative transformations, and with that how the balance between them may be most appropriately expressed.

The Sacramentality of the Natural World

JOHN HABGOOD

Taking Schmemann and Teilhard de Chardin as his starting points, John Habgood explores the notion of the world as a 'cosmic sacrament' which human beings are charged as 'priests' to offer back responsibly to God. This will mean reverencing the potential given to it by its Creator, while at the same time not always decrying the human power to transform that potential in a very different direction (e.g. forests as fuel). Nevertheless, our primary attitude should be one of 'co-operation' rather than 'co-creation', and this means that we cannot avoid facing acute moral issues, such as the conditions of life of battery hens.

Humanity as the world's priest

In explaining their request to me that I write something for this book, the editors alluded to the work of the Russian Orthodox theologian, Alexander Schmemann. Given, then, the title of my contribution, and my own indebtedness to Schmemann in the past, his book *The World as Sacrament* would seem a good place to begin.

Schmemann wanted to relate the sacraments to the life of the whole world. The first, the basic definition of *Homo sapiens*, he wrote, is that he is the priest.

He stands in the centre of the world and unifies it in his act of blessing God, of both receiving the world from God and offering it to God . . . The world was created as the 'matter', the material of one all-embracing Eucharist, and man was created as the priest of this cosmic sacrament.[1]

19

Human beings, he went on to say, are hungry for God and, cut off from God, can only eat dead food. 'Man is what he eats.' But what does he eat and why?[2] Within the Christian mystery, life is given back to us in Christ, dead food is transformed into living presence. Indeed the world itself only has meaning and value when seen as the sacrament of God's living presence. The secular vision of the world is a lie. It tells of emptiness and meaninglessness. Christianity declares precisely the opposite, the possibility of living in the world – 'seeing everything in it as the revelation of God, a sign of his presence, the joy of his coming, the call to communion with him, the hope of fulfilment in him.'[3]

Thus far Schmemann, writing in 1965. One can recognize the same vision set out a few years earlier by Teilhard de Chardin in his *Mass on the World*. It comes from a different scientific perspective and is rooted in a different theological tradition, but has the same sacramental focus.

> Like a pagan I worship a God who can be touched; and I do indeed touch him – this God – over the whole surface and in the depths of that world of matter which confines me: but to take hold of him as I would wish . . . I must go always on and on, through and beyond each undertaking, unable to rest in anything, borne onwards at each moment by creatures and at each moment going beyond them, in a continuing welcoming of them and a continuing detachment from them . . .[4]

Here Teilhard is not just contemplating a world but wrestling with it, acting in it, constructing a new united vision of it, conscious that it is no mere passive object. Implicit in his approach are questions about what we actually mean by such a simple phrase as 'the natural world'. Is it simply 'there', or is it in some sense a human construct? But more of that later. For the present, see how Teilhard deals with the idea of the world being given back to us sacramentally in Christ:

> Do you now, therefore, speaking through my lips, pronounce over this earthly travail your two-fold efficacious word: the word without which all that our wisdom and our experience have built up must totter and crumble – the word through which all our most far-reaching speculations and our encounter with the universe are come together into a unity. Over every living thing which is to spring up, to grow, to flower, to ripen during this day, say again the words: This is my Body. And over every death-force which waits in readiness to corrode, to wither, to cut down, speak again your

commanding words which express the supreme mystery of faith: This is my Blood.[5]

The sacramentality of the natural world lies in its possibility of being thus transformed. Writing at about the same time, but in a much more prosaic style, I myself tried to express something of the same sacramental vision in terms of making sense of the world by relating it to God. In a book published in 1993 I quote a passage I originally wrote thirty years earlier, and I intend to quote it again. I am sorry if this sounds a bit like theological environmentalism, a continuous recycling of old material, but at least I can claim a certain consistency:

> The characteristic method of Christian worship is to take bits of the ordinary stuff of life, bread and wine and water, and raise them to a new level of significance. The action is not arbitrary; the sacraments are what they are because they stem from Christ; they are 'given'. But once given, the sacramental principle can be extended to the whole of nature. Natural things can be clothed with new meaning by relating them to Christ. The world which would be meaningless by itself, becomes a purposeful place as men make it so; and they are enabled to do this because they themselves find a purpose for their lives in the man whose life was wholly one with God. A Christian who thinks like this can then see his vocation as an active process of 'making sense' of the world. This is different from the passive attempt to make sense of things, i.e. to understand them. The Christian attitude is to ask what sense we ought to make of them, what their possibilities are in a world responsible to God, and how far they can be made the grounds of worship and thanksgiving.[6]

By exploiting the passive and active meanings of the phrase 'making sense', I was trying to embrace the dual thrust of sacramental action – as a change in our perceptions, and a change in actuality. Sacramentalism is about perceiving a deeper meaning in things through the transforming presence of Christ. But it is also about the conveyance of grace, about the active work of God in enabling human beings to become what we truly are in him. And this duality runs through much of our experience.

I referred earlier to the difficulty of knowing precisely what we mean by the simple phrase 'natural world'. One part of the difficulty is that what we now call the natural world is to a large extent our own creation. The very fact that we now tend to use the word 'environment' in preference to 'nature' underlines the way in which we have come to regard what is 'out there' as in a close sense related to us. It is what is around us, environs us. Moreover this is an astonishingly recent concept. Don Cupitt has pointed out that the gap between the first unmistakably modern use of the word and the first Minister for the Environment was only fourteen years. Certainly in a country like Britain it is hard to find anything which has not to a greater or lesser extent been dependent on or influenced by human contrivance. We have shaped the landscape, the soil, the vegetation, much of the animal life. In a recent book called *The End of Nature* its American author lamented that the real tragedy of the greenhouse effect is that we have now irreversibly changed the earth's atmosphere, and with it every other aspect of nature which used to be its own wild self – even the weather.[7]

The idea of the natural world also gives rise to much deeper philosophical difficulties, questions about knowledge itself, and the degree to which it is conditioned by culture and language. It is a platitude nowadays that we cannot wholly escape from the business of creating a world even in the process of studying it as objectively as we can. My main point, though, is that for good or ill in trying to understand the world of nature we are never merely detached observers. Inevitably we activate some of its potential, and maybe also destroy some of its potential. To know something is also to change it, and what we now know is conditioned by what previous generations have bequeathed to us through their very thoughts and language, as well as through their more explicit actions in shaping the world. Our task in making sense of the world is thus inextricably bound up with this history and this potential for further change.

If our culture and our history convey to us a purely secular vision of the world, emptied of divine meaning, the likelihood is that we shall think of it as mere material, available for manipulation and exploitation. If, on the other hand, in trying to make sense of it, we begin with the presupposition that material things are capable of bearing the image of the divine, then we are likely to be more respectful. And we are more likely too to be receptive to the energy and grace released through encounter with God, whether through church-based sacraments or through those aspects of nature which most readily lend themselves to a sacramental interpretation.

I am conscious that this is all rather abstract. It may help if I earth it in terms of a familiar offertory prayer. It is a prayer which ought to have been in the Alternative Service Book. But it is not there because some members of General Synod felt that it was too dangerously Catholic. So it hovers on the fringes of the Book as a kind of ghost with only the response to it, 'Blessed be God for ever', actually printed in the text. As was said at the time, the responses are there, like the smile of the Cheshire cat, to remind those who know about these things of what is missing. 'Blessed are you, Lord God of all creation. Through your goodness we have this bread to offer which earth has given and human hands have made. It will become for us the bread of life.' And there is a similar prayer over the wine.

I find it a profound and satisfying prayer. It contains a subtle balance between recognizing God's gift, acknowledging our human role in developing and using it rightly, and accepting its potential as a conveyer of God's own reality. Bread, at once the most basic and ancient of foods, is also the human product that perhaps more than anything else made possible the civilized world. The development of civilization in Egypt depended on corn. So all the ambiguities I have been talking about are contained in bread. It is a product of nature and culture, and a prime former of culture. This fundamental support of life, says the prayer, will reveal a new level of meaning, made possible and actual by God's own involvement in material reality through Christ. It will become for us the bread of life, echoing the words of John 6 with all their overtones of manna in the wilderness, bread for the hungry, and eternal life in Christ himself.

What is true of bread can be true of anything else. Bread as used in the Eucharist locates us in the given historical actuality of revelation in and through the life of Jesus. But just as all the books in the world are not sufficient to contain the things which might be written about him, so all the splendour and variety of the material world is available to disclose him. Nature in all its abundance can be clothed with the divine, as in Thomas Traherne's vision of 'orient and immortal wheat which never should be reaped nor was ever sown'.[8] Perhaps it is no coincidence that these are the opening words of his description of a glorified world. In another passage he describes waking up in the world as if in our Father's palace:

> You never enjoy the world aright until the sea itself floweth in your veins, until you are clothed with the heavens and crowned with the stars and perceive yourself to be sole heir of the whole world and more than so because men are in it who are every one sole heirs as well as you. Until you can sing and rejoice and delight in God as misers do in gold and kings in sceptres you never enjoy the world.[9]

That may seem a bit too heady. At a much lower level of awareness, a sense of the goodness or meaningfulness or value of the world can form part of many people's basic religious awareness, even if it is only glimpsed in fleeting moments. Sadly such experiences are frequently never integrated into any coherent pattern of thought or symbolism, and therefore can remain isolated, unproductive, or even rejected. Again and again one hears of frustrated spiritual awareness or longings, which may have arisen through some kind of nature mysticism and remain stuck there. There is no language for them in a secularized culture. They lack the complex interplay between what is given, and what human beings must do, and the illumination that comes from setting individual experience within a developed and subtle religious tradition. A sacramental approach to the natural world as I have tried to describe it, seems to me to provide such a tradition.

Three moral issues

I want now to spell out in more concrete terms what such sacramentality might mean in practice. In doing this I shall draw rather heavily on an essay I wrote in 1990 for an American book on ecology, which I suspect has not been much seen in this country.[10] I shall do it under three headings: 1) The notion of the recognition and activation of potential; 2) The need for co-operation; 3) A few words in conclusion about transformation by redemption.

1. The recognition of potential

What might it mean in practice to live as if anything or everything might become a vehicle of divine grace? Perhaps it is easier to start by imagining the opposite, a universe in which anything or everything is ripe for exploitation. The essence of such a regime would be that human needs and desires are sovereign, and the stuff of the world can be bent to human purposes with no respect paid to what it is in itself, or to what it might become within the purposes of God. Numerous tragic pictures of ravaged countrysides, polluted seas and rivers, waters depleted of their fish, animals subjected to abominable treatment, squalid shanty towns, and so forth, make the point that this God-forsaken view of the natural world is no mere supposition. There is a vivid contrast with the sacramental vision of a world created by God, owned by God, and ultimately finding its fulfilment in God.

But this simple contrast, though I believe it to be valid, does not tell the whole story. Paradoxically, the practical consequences of these two opposed visions might not always be so very different. Rubbish, for example, might be seen as a resource by the sacramentalist who is concerned not to dismiss anything as mere waste, and may equally well be seen as a resource by the commercially-minded entrepreneur who dreams up a way of making money from it. Deep motivation may be one thing, but seeing a problem as an opportunity is not confined to those who share a particular philosophy of life; and this needs to be acknowledged if a sacramental approach is to engage with political realities.

Equally, there may be different motives for wishing to preserve, say, a forest or an animal species. Long-term prudential considerations can provide reasons for holding back, even within a general philosophy of exploitation. The destruction of forests, or of biological diversity, could be seen as foolish even on purely selfish grounds. To recognize and respect divine potential might provide a less selfish, and therefore less vulnerable, motive. It might base itself, for instance, on respect for the evolutionary process, recognizing this as the means whereby in practice most of the potential within the living matter of the universe has so far been released. To let a forest be, or to protect a species, is to acknowledge that they still have within them a greater potential for life, growth, and development, and that their development may therefore form part of the larger purposes of God in using evolution as a means of creation. But the recognition of divine potential does not provide an unambiguous answer to the question, what should be done?

The philosophy of giving things the respect due to them for what they can reveal of God through being themselves, is difficult to carry through into practical programmes. To let everything be, to respect its right to be itself, to allow it to develop in its own way, would, if carried to extremes, make human life impossible, and negate our own creativeness. Forests also have a potential to become fuel, or furniture, or agricultural land, and some of the greatest human achievements have resulted from seeing a potential in things that was decidedly not a consequence of letting them be. Human beings have interfered decisively and irreversibly in many kinds of animal breeding, often bringing out latent potentials that have been hugely to our benefit. We are now well into a genetic revolution which greatly enhances these creative powers, and we face enormously difficult decisions now, and even more so in the future, about how far this process can rightly be taken, while holding on to a proper respect for the wisdom of nature as it has evolved under the guidance of God.

There are no easy answers. The key religious insight would seem to be that whether things are let be or whether they are developed by human ingenuity for human purposes, they belong to God and not to ourselves. There is a respect due to them, an awareness of human limitations, a fine balance to be struck between penitence for what we have done to God's world in the past and hopeful creativeness for the future.

Sacramentally, such an attitude would seem appropriate also towards inanimate things, at least towards things of a certain complexity. A flowing stream, a clear sea teeming with life, a mountain landscape, surely deserve respect and care despite the large subjective element that enters into our appreciation of them. They can be treated in specific ways that still further reveal their potential. The great eighteenth-century creator of English landscapes, Capability Brown, earned his nickname for his skill, not in imposing his will on a recalcitrant nature, but in drawing out its aesthetic capabilities. A sculptor carving a particular stone or lump of wood may describe his work in similar ways: the finished object is somehow seen as being already there in the natural formation of the raw material, waiting only to be revealed. An engineer may see a valley as waiting to be dammed, a chasm as waiting to be bridged, an ugly and unhealthy swamp as potentially a place of beauty and usefulness. Such actions may become in their own way secular sacraments, an enhancement, a liberation of what is already there, a transformation which does not violate a thing's essential nature.

I fully admit that such a way of speaking creates acute difficulties for those who are more used to seeing the universe as a torrent of change. 'Essential natures' do not have much place in evolution. Clearly by itself the recognition of potential is not enough. It is too vague a concept and can lead us in too many different directions. Sacramentalism is also about God's work in complementing and giving substance to our human work in a world still in process of creation.

2. The need for co-operation

The offertory prayer speaks of bread 'which earth has given and human hands have made'. Co-operation with natural processes, working with the grain of nature rather than against it, is now part of the conventional wisdom among conservationists. Can the sacramental context add anything significant to this already familiar idea?

The Eucharist is a complex act of giving and receiving, in which the worshippers as well as God are both givers and receivers. At its highest it is a mutual exchange of love. But all this is set within the context of what God has already done.

Despite the mutuality, therefore, the key word is *response*. In the exchange of love, 'we love because he first loved us'. Sacramental action is thus essentially a matter of responsive co-operation rather than co-creation. As human beings we share a role with God in drawing out the divine potential of the world, but only because God himself has already taken the decisive steps.

The theme of co-operation receives further emphasis in communion. There can be no true giving and receiving with God unless others form part of it. As those who are themselves loved by God, worshippers caught up in the eucharistic action are commanded and enabled to love their fellow human beings. And the action spreads outward to include 'angels and archangels and all the company of heaven'. Heaven and earth praise God in mutual embrace.

But how far should this mutuality spread? Should it, for instance, include battery hens? There is an evolutionary case for including battery hens in some kind of relationship with human beings as very distant cousins, and this common membership of the community of life constitutes some kind of moral claim, even if not a very strong one. If the sense of community goes further than this, and if it is possible to hold that at a very rudimentary level there can and should be a co-operative relationship between human beings and hens, then the moral claim is strengthened. If, to put the point more strongly, God gives hens a being of their own, and values them prior to their usefulness as a cheap source of food, then the hen's point of view as a partner in this larger communion begins to assume some importance.

Admittedly it is not easy to know what a hen's point of view is, but in the case of battery hens there would seem to be a fairly simple test. In a battery the human element in the relationship with hens so dominates the conditions of life that the possibility of co-operation virtually disappears altogether. The hen is reduced as far as possible to a machine-like operation. And that would seem to me to fly in the face of morality, of good animal husbandry, as well as of communion.

Even when a relationship ends in death, it can be marked by respect for the life taken. The ritual surrounding animal sacrifice, in cultures where sacrifice was the almost inevitable preliminary to eating meat, witnessed to the seriousness of taking life, unpleasant though some of the rituals were. I recall a vivid picture of an African bushman apologizing to an impala he was about to kill. Here again, the theme of communion with the life sacrificed can perhaps help modern Westernized consciousness to develop a different feel for the products of industrialized scientific agriculture. One doesn't see anybody apologizing in a twentieth-century abattoir. Organic farming, to take another example, almost certainly does not fulfil the quasi-scientific claims made for it, but it may have moral and spiritual benefits for societies that see the need to develop a more sensitive relationship with the natural world.

The limits of co-operation become all too evident, however, when there is a mosquito in the bedroom. I am reminded of the story of the mosquito in the nudist camp which complained, 'So much to do that it is impossible to know where to begin'. One could echo the same thought in trying to make sense of the multitude of natural evils. Letting things be themselves, discerning their point of view and looking for their divine potentiality, cannot be allowed to become a recipe for the passive acceptance of whatever befalls us. Our human place in God's purposes is to co-operate with him in the process of creative change. Sacramental thinking points to a world which has to be redeemed before it can truly reveal the face of God. There is an inescapable element of struggle, discrimination, suffering, tragedy, in the process and any theological approach to the natural world that belittles or ignores these is hopelessly unrealistic. Hence my third and final heading.

3. Transformation by redemption

The sacraments are sacraments of Christ's death and resurrection. Suffering, and the transformation of suffering, belong to their very essence. Sacramental theology, therefore, has no excuse for underrating the extent to which the divine potential of the world is denied, frustrated, distorted, defaced and ignored. Nor need we shrink from accepting that the very means of creation through evolution entails conflict and suffering. Sacramental awareness is not at all the same as sentimentality. The perceptions of divine glory in a world capable of bearing God's image have to be matched by the belief that God bears the weight of the suffering of his own creation on the cross.

All this is basic Christianity. To interpret the cross in the light of a sacramental understanding of the natural world can help to strengthen the bridge between the redemption of human sin and suffering, and the redemption of the rest of creation. St Paul's language about creation groaning and suffering and waiting for the redemption of the Son of God expresses the same link. To allow the doctrines of creation and redemption to exist, as it were, in separate compartments is to fall into ways of thinking about the natural world which make any sensible containment of its ambivalences impossible. It seems to me that the link is there in the Old Testament, too. I find myself increasingly attracted by the idea that it was Israel's consciousness of being a redeemed community, created as it were 'out of nothing', which provided the context for Isaiah's great vision of God as Creator. 'Look unto me, and be saved, all the ends of the earth: for I am God, and there is none else' (Isa. 45.22 AV). To believe in creation is to believe in an ultimate security, an ultimate order, a 'place' and a responsibility for humanity, within the saving purposes of God.

And part of that responsibility is, in fulfilling what Schmemann called our human priestly role, to offer back to God in penitence and thanksgiving our broken and ambivalent world, shot through with so much good and evil, that it may by his grace be consecrated and transformed. The evil and the ambivalences are not ignored. They may have to be located intellectually in the mystery of God's inscrutability. But a sacramental approach to nature allows us to do this, without becoming disheartened or debilitated by all that does not reflect the glory and goodness of God. We can still say, in the sacramental experience, 'He is here,' and accept it as a foretaste of what is yet to come.

As we ourselves are part of the natural world which is to be offered and transformed, there is no room for arrogance, or for the exploitative mentality which assumes that creation is 'ours'. But as those called by God to our priestly role, and who dare to describe ourselves as made in the image of God, we have a responsibility not simply to accept the world as it is, but to recognize and pursue its possibilities for revealing more fully God's glory. Christian thinking has to move between these two poles of acceptance and transformation, humility and creative power. And one of the great strengths of sacramentalism is that it provides a sufficient richness and diversity of imagery for this movement to take place.

Notes

1. A. Schmemann, *The World as Sacrament* (London: Darton Longman and Todd, 1965), p. 16. For a brief account of Schmemann's career and the influences on him see J. Meyendorff, 'Postscript: a life worth living' in Fisch, T. (ed.), *Liturgy and Tradition: Theological Reflections of Alexander Schmemann* (Crestwood, New York: St. Vladimir's Seminary Press, 1990), pp. 45–184.
2. ibid., p. 13.

3. ibid., pp. 140–1.
4. P. Teilhard de Chardin, *The Mass of the World* (London: Fontana, 1970), p. 26.
5. ibid., pp. 22–3.
6. J. Habgood, *Making Sense* (London: SPCK, 1993), p. 22.
7. B. McKibben, *The End of Nature* (London: Viking), 1990.
8. T. Traherne, *Centuries of Meditation*, Third Century, paragraph 3.
9. ibid., First Century, paragraph 29.
10. J. Habgood, 'A sacramental approach to environmental issues' in C. Birch, W. Eakin and J. B. McDaniel (eds), *Liberating Life: Contemporary Approaches to Ecological Theology* (Maryknoll, New York: Orbis 1990), pp. 46–53.

The Theology of Sacred Space

SUSAN WHITE

Susan White opens by observing that, while there are a number of reasons (such as the rise of creation theology) why her topic is particularly pertinent today, nevertheless at least five factors make discussion difficult. However, the attempt is made, and a biblical (and Barthian) approach offered. Though interest in place within both Old and New Testaments is acknowledged, this is seen as properly subordinate to the actions which made (and continue to make) any particular place holy, an attitude which was also eventually encapsulated in the ritual for consecrating churches. Competing theologies of space are illustrated by, among other examples, arguments over the convent built at Auschwitz.

An important and difficult question

My title may sound pretty rarefied. But I think anyone who reads the newspapers on a regular basis will begin to realize that the way we think about sacred places is of the profoundest human, social, political and religious import. A mosque located on a Hindu pilgrimage site in North India is demolished, and there is bloodshed, hundreds and hundreds killed, nine hundred according to the last count. Aboriginal peoples in Australia and Canada take up arms in order to protect their ancestral sacred places, while synagogues are bombed in the former East Germany and Serbs deface mosques and so on.

So if there is going to be a renewed interest in the theology of sacred space in the late twentieth century, this will provide fuel for that interest: because from the sense of the sacredness of spaces arises profound challenges to the contemporary Christian quest for peace, justice, religious toleration, and holiness of

31

life. That is the first reason why we need to begin to be serious about a theology of space: it confronts us every day from the outside. But there are other 'internal' factors, trends within contemporary Christian theology itself, which make a theological conversation about sacred space particularly timely just now.

One such factor is the rise of creation-based theologies and spiritualities. This renewed sense of the whole earth as somehow imbued with holiness from its inception is going to force us to ask some pretty hard questions about what we mean when we talk about holy places in the more particular sense. In addition, this so-called Green Theology has led us to some serious rethinking of certain fundamental theological issues: what do we mean when we talk about the 'fall' and particularly the 'fall of nature'? What about the dichotomy between nature and grace? How were pagan understandings of space appropriated by Christianity? This questioning feels like a breath of fresh air, especially for those of us within mainline post-Enlightenment Protestantism where the impact of the material-spiritual divide has probably been most keenly felt.

The third reason that this should be a fruitful time for thinking about a theology of sacred space is intimately related to the rise of Christian theology, namely that there has been a recovery of the biblical roots of a theology of place. So we have not only begun to think seriously about the creation narratives in this regard, but also the importance of things like land, Temple, and pilgrimage in the Hebrew Bible as a whole, and the degree to which those concepts were spiritualized in later Judaism.[1] Then we have had to ask about the relationship between the 'locatedness' of God's saving activity as revealed in the Hebrew Scriptures on the one hand, and on the other hand, where the holiness of places fits into the economy of salvation in the New Testament. We shall return to this theme later.

The fourth way in which the contemporary mood in Christian theology provides nourishment for thinking about the nature of sacred places has to do with the beginnings of a renewal in sacramental theology among Roman Catholics and Protestants alike. The reasons for this revived interest are several, but one thing that I think has been overlooked is the influence of Christian poets, who began asking questions in their poetry about how, in a modern industrial-technological age, God was communicating through the material. Some readers will know the poem 'A, a, a, Domine Deus' by the person who has been called the Welsh William Blake – David Jones. Consider the following pertinent lines:

I have watched the wheels go round in case I might see the living creatures like the appearance of lamps, in case I might see the Living God projected from the Machine. I have said to the perfected steel be my sister and for the glossy towers I thought I felt some beginnings of His creature, but *A, a, a, Domine Deus*, my hands found the glazed work unrefined and the terrible crystal a stage/paste . . . *Eia, Domine Deus*.[2]

Finally, the new discussion about sacred space today is fertilized by a new seriousness about religious plurality. We have actually been talking to one another about our respective theological worlds and theological models, for whenever we come into contact with someone else's vision it gives us the opportunity to re-evaluate our own theological position. This involves not only Christian inter- and intra-denominational conversations, but also attention to the major world religions as well as to tribal religions. Take, for example, the testimony of Palikapu Dedman of Hawaii, to the way in which sacred space is envisioned in his own spirituality and that of his people:

My mother and my grandmother raised me in Pele religion. We would go to the volcano to pray, and many people still do that. Go to the volcano's edge and you will see a hundred people saying prayers and leaving offerings for the Goddess. The white people can't get it, that for us Pele is all the land. She's the volcano and everything that grows there is her. The steam and vapor and lava are all parts of her body, and her family is all the forest plants and the life in the sea. You can't go shoving drills into her body like that. The old people say it will injure Pele to drill into her and to cap the steam for power, the old people say it will stop her creative force. And it will cause spiritual and psychological damage for people who worship and live with her.[3]

That kind of vision of sacred space challenges us to define and articulate how we stand within our own theological framework; how we stand in relationship to the physical world and its contents, as well as to those places which we specifically designate as 'holy'. How are we to talk about a specifically Christian idea of the sacredness of place?

But fertile as the ground is just now, there are real difficulties, stones in the furrows (to keep the metaphor going), for those of us who as theologians want to think about the theological status of place. Most of those difficulties have to do with the way theology of sacred space has been done in the past. There seem to me to be five categories of difficulty here.

The first is that the whole subject has not had much rigorous treatment from systematic theologians. I took five òr six recently published books off my shelf (books by such people as David Tracy, Hans Küng, David Ford, John MacQuarrie, and Keith Ward), all of which were attempting integrated treatments of Christian theology; not one made any reference to sacred space at all. Even those with more particular interest in sacramental theology seem to have had other priorities. One recent book by the French Dominican Jean Corbon is unusual in that it devotes four and one half pages (out of two hundred) to the subject of sacred space. But then you wonder about its ultimate value when you find statements like: 'The church of stone or wood that we enter to share in the eternal liturgy is . . . set apart because it is a space which the resurrection has burst open'.[4] Most theologians today, I suspect, would want to challenge that sort of statement on systematic grounds. How does the resurrection 'burst open' a space? And is there a kind of space which the resurrection has not 'burst open'? So the first problem is that there is little sustained systematic reflection.

Second, this has meant that the discussion of sacred space has by default passed to others than theologians. Mostly the work has been done by liturgists (like Ronald Grimes from Wilfred Laurier University in Canada and J. G. Davies formerly of Birmingham), or by people whose primary interest is the architectural history of church buildings (like Peter Hammond and Frederick Etchells) and by a few historians of religion – Mircea Eliade is the one who comes to mind. This has given the discussion about sacred space a certain direction and a certain character in that the interpretations of sacred space that have been proposed have tended to rely very heavily on aesthetics, on the inherent religiosity or lack of religiosity embedded within various architectural forms and styles and proportions. 'Worship the Lord in the beauty of holiness' has most often been turned into 'worship the Lord in the holiness of beauty'. This has meant that most talk about sacred space has been derived from a more general theology of visual arts;[5] so the whole thing has been something of a translation exercise. One important result of this attention to aesthetics has been an almost-exclusive concentration on the 'great' examples of sacred space – like Durham – but this has ignored the very real sense of the holiness of place that people may experience in, for example, the 1961 purpose-built Methodist church on the growing fringes of Telford.

The other trend in discussions of sacred space has been guided more by liturgists and historians of religion. Generally the interpretation of sacred space they propose is taken over almost wholesale from studies of how sacred spaces function in tribal religions or Eastern religions, sometimes (but not always) with Christian terms interpolated here and there. Eliade is a good example.[6] In general, there has been a lot of talk about ley-lines and mandalas, and poles of the universe and aboriginal dreaming-places and such. Some of this is intertwined with depth-psychology and semiotics, which no doubt is interesting to be sure, but it should not be mistaken for Christian theology. So the first problem is that up to now a Christian theology of sacred space has not been very theological; and the second problem is that the Christian theology of sacred space has not been very Christian.

The third problem is that when we do encounter those concerned with the more specific questions of Christian theology in relation to sacred space, we find they have confined the discussion almost completely to explications of the influence of theology on church architecture. How have the theological principles of a given time and place translated themselves into ecclesiastical buildings? Erwin Panofsky's *Gothic Architecture and Scholastic Thought* is one very good example of studies which have related shifts in ecclesiology over the centuries to changing architectural plans.[7]

This has been important work, and it is rooted in something very good that has been happening to theology at large, and that is an attention to and a growing respect for non-discursive forms of theology, the sense that theology can be articulated in various modes, and in various languages. We have also begun to talk about how theology might be articulated ritually/liturgically or visually or affectively; so we find people thinking about sacred space, in this case church architecture, as a non-discursive way of doing theology. But it has meant that more fundamental theological issues have been pushed aside. So questions like 'in what way and for what purpose does God communicate through place?' and 'how is self-consciously "sacred" space different from ordinary space?' are rarely asked in the current climate.

A fourth difficulty is a lack of historical perspective. While we have had brilliant histories of church architecture,[8] we have had very little work in historical theology to rely on. What sort of theologies of sacred space have been operative in the Christian past? It is very difficult to build a contemporary systematic theology of sacred space on sand. It is groundwork that must be done if a Christian theology of sacred space is to have any depth to it.

Finally, the theological discussions of sacred space that have taken place have generally failed to take seriously issues of justice, mission and evangelism, and social ethics. I think that there is no way of doing Christian theology of any kind any more as if there is not a world out there. In the specific case of a theology of sacred space, this was brought home to me forcibly by discussions surrounding the building of the new Roman Catholic basilica in the Ivory Coast. Millions and millions of pounds were spent on this lavish, triumphalistic ecclesiastical space in the middle of a people who are for the most part trapped in cycles of poverty and disease, unemployment and exploitation. Can this building ever be 'consecrated'? On what does the 'sacredness' of this space rest? The social and political context of contemporary theology demands an edge to this discussion that has simply not been there.

Actions make places sacred

But I must try to make a beginning at saying what a theology of sacred space might look like, one that takes advantage of the fertile ground and avoids the stones in the furrows as far as possible. I think we need to start by asking of what sorts of things an adequate Christian theology of sacred space would have to take account. What are the boundaries of such a discussion? There are, of course, the same boundaries that we would use in attempting a systematic theology of anything: Bible, Christology, ecclesiology and so forth. It is rather like an interactive computer game since the choices, the moves we want to make within those boundaries, will determine where we end up. So in a sense this is an exercise in methodology, because we might want to make other (and equally valid) choices and then we will come out at a different place. That is to say that the title of this essay may infringe the Trade Description Act a little, since there is not just one single Christian theology of sacred space possible within the boundaries, but a whole range of responsible Christian theologies. Personally, I am inclined to begin with the Bible. And you can see already the implications of my choice of where to begin. Like Karl Barth, I am suspicious of allowing the natural world to speak for itself; it must always be read in the light of revelation. But even if you disagree with me, you will still have to come to terms with Scripture and its teaching; so we might as well do it now.

There are all sorts of pitfalls when you get into the biblical material and begin to ask questions about 'place', and about how the knowledge of God as Creator and Redeemer is related to place. This is because what you have in the Hebrew Scriptures is a theological dialogue between landedness on the one hand, and landlessness on the other; between being a people of a place and a people of no place. Theology is done out of both experiences. The God of the promised land is also the God of the exile; God can be encountered in Jerusalem and in Babylon; there are historical, local visions of 'the holy place' and there are apocalyptic, a-historical visions of it; all of which are woven together into an intricate pattern of prayer, covenant, pilgrimage, belief, and promise – a spirituality in which 'place' may have different meanings but is never incidental. Hanging over all of this, of course, is the sword of idolatry. It is possible for the people of God to be as idolatrous about place as about the worship of graven images.

When we move into the New Testament material, other problems are added to those we have already, because we have to come to terms with the words and actions of Jesus of Nazareth. This is the Jesus who has nowhere to lay his head; who said that he would destroy the sacred place, the Temple, and build it again in three days; who said to the Samaritan woman that there was coming a time when God would not be worshipped at the shrine on Mount Gerizim or in Jerusalem but rather in spirit and in truth; and this is also the Jesus who said that wherever two or three were gathered in together, he would be in the midst of them. So there is an overwhelming amount of anti-placedness about the message of Jesus. Certainly, the Kingdom of God which was the central message of his preaching was clearly not to be identified with a place, but was describing that encounter with the living God, the fruit of which is peace and love and reconciliation.

Yet, on the other hand, we get a profound impression, especially from the gospels, of a deep concern with spatial particularity. Jesus went here; he taught in that place; as he was going from here to there he healed someone; he was born in Bethlehem, preached in Galilee, prayed in the Garden of Gethsemane, died on Mount Calvary, and was seen on the road to Emmaus. And it was important for the gospel writers to have remembered these places by name. But the thing to recognize is that these places are of importance not for their own intrinsic holiness; they are memorable, important rather because Jesus was there. Even when Jesus goes to the traditional Jewish holy places, he transforms and reinterprets their meaning by his actions. (That seems to me to be what the turning over of the tables of the money-changers is all about.)

So the spatial particularity we see in the New Testament is

not so much a statement about the holiness of certain Palestinian locales as a statement about the nature of the incarnation. Tom Torrance says that the incarnation 'asserts the reality of space and time for God in the actuality of relations with us, and at the same time binds us to space and time in our relations with God.'[9] Place, then, has a different status in the new economy. You might even go so far as to say that whereas the revelation of God in the Old Testament is tied to *places*, in the New Testament it is tied to a person and his actions, and that all of the promises tied to land in the Old Testament become fulfilled in Jesus of Nazareth. The Australian theologian Geoffrey Lilburne puts it this way:

> No longer can the community of faith hope for God to give them a special land, exclusively for their use. No longer can they expect God will unite all God's blessings of peace, security, and plenty in one physical locality. For God has concretely located those in the person and work of Jesus Christ . . . By dwelling with the human community in and through Jesus Christ, God has demonstrated that God wills to dwell in the environment of each community.[10]

This in no way undercuts the notion that all created space is a potential locus for divine revelation by virtue of its divine origins. In fact it is dependent upon it; all places partake of the christological centre of creation. But when we talk about Christian sacred places in the narrower sense, as loci of explicitly Christian revelation, then the form and content of that revelation is shaped by the explicit identification of that space with the saving work of Jesus Christ.

Of course this sense of the centrality of Jesus' particular actions in particular places making God's love visible for the sanctification and reconciliation of the world will be important when we turn to talk about ecclesiology. Whatever model of the Church we choose, all of them are rooted in what is seen to be a carrying forward of and embodiment of, the work of Christ by a community of believers for the sake of the world.[11] So just as we say that there was a necessary locatedness to the ministry of Jesus, that his life of healing, teaching, preaching and forgiving was identified and attached to certain particular places and that those places derived their sacred significance from the action performed there, the same is true with the Church. There is a necessary locatedness about its ministry as well. There are places attached to its life of healing, teaching, preaching, forgiving, and the sacred significance of those places is wholly dependent on the dominical authenticity of that ministry.

What the Church has understood about its sacred places you see clearly if you look at the history of the liturgical consecration of church buildings, which is really the practical outworking of this idea. From the early sixth century (when we find the first extant rites for the consecration of church buildings), up to the present day, we see rites that revolve around and liturgically elaborate the use to which that building will be put. The whole liturgy of consecration presupposes that, wherever the people of God gather faithfully for prayer, to hear the word, for teaching, healing, and preaching, that will be a holy place by virtue of those things.

So to 'consecrate' a church building, then, two kinds of things happen. One set of liturgical elements focuses on the ways in which the building will actually function in the future. And so the officiant travels around the building and in the appropriate places a sermon is preached, a Eucharist celebrated, and a baptism, wedding or funeral performed if suitable candidates can be found, and so forth. The other ritual complex revolves around the translation and the deposition of relics. But even in this case it is clear that the relics' principal function is to link the present and future use of the building to the ministry of Christ. The relics serve, so to speak, as the witness and guarantor of the apostolicity of the ministry that the building will encase. Certainly as the history of church dedications and consecrations progresses, more and more elements are added. But any time ritual words and actions of consecration veer away from the idea that sanctification of sacred space is rooted in the holy use of that space, you will find a lot of debate in which words like 'idolatry' are frequently thrown around.

Rival theologies and their consequences

All of this has a profoundly ethical dimension, because to call a church building a sacred space in this sense is to demand that in its use it be an authentic sign and a witness to the love of God in a particular place; a sign and a witness that the people of God in that place are striving to be a holy people for the sake of a broken world. And as soon as we begin talking about 'authentic signs' we are into the realm of sacramental theology. How do we talk about the sacramental sign-value of sacred space? And what makes the sacramentality of a sacred space in any sense 'valid' or 'efficacious', to use older categories?

Though this is worthy of extended discussion, suffice it to say that we cannot any longer talk about the sacramentality of things in the way we used to thirty years ago. That is, we cannot

)ut sacramentality as an isolated intrusion of divine grace
at is basically a profane world; or say that somehow grace
flows through an ecclesiastical plumbing system and emerges out
of the sacramental taps. The work of people like Schillebeeckx,
Rahner, and Lonergan has shifted our thinking. Sacramentality
now has to be talked about as part of the ongoing, mutual
encounter between free, transcendent persons (divine and
human) in which the physical, the material, becomes a mode of
self-disclosure for both.

As an issue, it is all bound up with the nature of symbols and
signs, and here we can include the sign value of sacred space.
What is the relationship between the symbolic significance of
sacred space and the use to which that space is put? Sacramental theologian Ralph Keiffer is very clear about this. He says
that sacramental signs 'do not actually "speak for themselves"
. . . their ability to "speak" is derived from what people are
willing or able to attribute to them . . . [for] there is a peculiar
obliqueness to symbols such that they are unintelligible without
reference to the community that uses them. The Church's sacramental signs do not float free, but are intimately bound up
with its *kerygma*, *koinonia*, and *diakonia* – [in other words] with
its behaviour.'[12] So if we are going to talk about sacred space in
terms of sacramentality, then in the same breath we must talk
about the social ethics and also about the spirituality which is
the thread which runs throughout this whole book.

There are certainly missiological and ecumenical implications to all this. What happens when our theology of sacred space
comes up against an entirely different vision? What happens
when my idea, that sacredness of space is somehow related to
its holy use, comes face to face with, for example, Palikapu
Dedman's sense that all places are of the essence of the Goddess,
and are to be regarded as such? Or the idea that some places are
positively profane? You can see the very real ecumenical consequences of this kind of clash in paradigms in a recent dispute
in Poland. Early in 1984, a group of Discalced Carmelite nuns
was given permission to establish a convent in a vacant theatre
building on the perimeter of Auschwitz. This was done at the
suggestion of a charitable organization whose work involved
helping churches behind the Iron Curtain and after conversations with the Polish Roman Catholic community and the
Vatican. Several nuns took possession of the building in the
autumn of 1984, and a search for sources of funding for its reno-
vation began. In the various appeals for money, it was said that
the convent was to be a 'manifestation of a desire to pray and
repent' in the face of the outrage done at Auschwitz to Jews and

to others; it was to serve as a witness to the memory of the Roman Catholic martyrs who died there, and was established so that 'the presence of God might be brought to a place of sacrifice and terror'. A wave of protest ensued. The Jewish community all over the world was quite simply outraged. Mass-actions and demonstrations and inflammatory rhetoric on both sides reached a climax when a group of United States Jews attempted to enter the building by force. Finally in 1989, the Pope was persuaded to agree to the convent being moved.

What happened was a veritable catalogue of misunderstand-ings, ably chronicled by Wladislaw Bartoszewski.[13] Polish anti-Semitism, Jewish anti-Polonism, the real rhetorical and political ineptitude of officials on both sides of the debate, and two utterly divergent readings of the history of the place, all con-tributed to the situation. But there was something else as well which Bartoszewski did not pick up on. And that is that the Jews and the Christians involved in this controversy were operating out of two entirely different theologies of sacred space.

Clearly, for the Jewish community, Auschwitz by its very existence and by the fact that it intersected with Jewish history, and that sacrificial blood was spilled there, was a place of special status as a locus of divine revelation. (This is even true of Jews to whom Auschwitz had revealed simply that God is dead.) The Carmelites, on the other hand, coming from a tradition of the sanctification of a place by its use, thought that they could reconsecrate the ground by putting it to holy use, in this case by a ministry of continuing intercessory prayer and confession. That difference in theology was never really dealt with in the bilateral discussions; instead both sides have been left with profound feelings of resentment and bitterness. So that is just one small example of the consequences of not taking theologies of sacred space seriously.

Undeniably, there are lots of threads left to be picked up here. We have not talked about the human sciences (semiotics, depth-psychology, ritual studies),[14] nor about religious geography; we have not returned to aesthetics. There is also much work to be done on shifts in theology and spirituality which have helped shape the understanding of sacred space; fortunately David Stancliffe will be tackling that issue in the essay that follows mine. But it seems to me that all of these are second-order issues, for anything we say about such matters must be checked out against, must be in conversation with, a core of a *Christian theology* (and I deliberately put emphasis on both words) of sacred space.

So what does it mean, then, to call a particular place a

Christian sacred space? Is Durham Cathedral a sacred space? Well, I think it is, but its sacredness is not self-evident, nor is it self-perpetuating. It is not a Christian sacred space because the land it sits upon called out to the friends of St Cuthbert and said 'here I am, I'm a holy place!', nor because it sits on some ancient ley-line or place of natural spiritual energy, not even because of its great beauty, or the dim religious light that filters through it, nor even because people have been known to have had religious experiences there.

If Durham Cathedral is a holy place, a sacred space, it is so because it has been, is now, and (God willing) will continue to be used by faithful Christian people who are striving to live according to the gospel, who gather to hear the Word of God and to learn what it means to act upon it, who seek a ministry of reconciliation and who seek to draw the Cathedral into that ministry in the name of Jesus Christ. It is a sacred space because it has aligned itself to the powerless by giving sanctuary to those in trouble. It is sacred space because all of these things together make it a valid sign, an authentic witness to the sacrificial, self-giving love of God for the world. And if ever it stops being that, if it ever becomes associated with violence, greed, injustice, pride, division, it will stop being a holy place until those things are repudiated. This is what talk about desecration is all about, it seems to me; that a place can become materially associated with values, actions, and attitudes that are contrary to the gospel.

This also means that the Durham Christian community, like each and every Christian community, bears a terrible responsibility for the sacredness of its space, and that every Christian community needs to be involved in the continual work of remembrance or anamnesis, and keep in mind the richness of that concept. Anamnesis is not simply a pious memory exercise, but it is the threefold enterprise of remembering, embodying, and handing on (repeating) the sacred use of the space it inhabits. This seems to me (as I have already noted) to be fully in line with modern sacramental theology which says that sacramentality is not only about God using the material to communicate self to us, to give self to us, but also about human beings using the material to give themselves to God. It is about a relationship, a mutuality of encounter, with the arrows going both ways, and the material as a medium of communication.

All of this is why I think that the consecration of the basilica in the Ivory Coast is perhaps open to question; all of this is why I can say that the ugly concrete block worship-space in Telford can be a holy place, because it is occupied by and associated with a community of Christian people who are known, publicly known, for their acts of charity and peacemaking and who have drawn their building into the struggle for a radical openness to the will of God. And I would argue that to root the holiness of Christian sacred space in anything else is to be involved either in idolatry or in magic.[15]

Notes

1. W. Brueggemann, *The Land: Place as Gift, Promise and Challenge in Biblical Faith* (Philadelphia: Fortress, 1977).
2. D. Jones, 'A, a, a, Domine Deus' in *The Sleeping Lord* (London: Faber and Faber Ltd, 1974), p. 9.
3. J. Mander, *In the Absence of the Sacred* (San Francisco: Sierra Club, 1991), p. 333.
4. J. Corbon, *The Wellspring of Worship* (New York: Paulist, 1988), p. 130.
5. J. Dillenberger, *A Theology of Artistic Sensibilities* (London: SCM Press, 1987).
6. M. Eliade, *Symbolism, the Sacred and the Arts* (New York: Crossroad, 1986), pp. 105–29.
7. E. Panofsky, *Gothic Architecture and Scholasticism* (Cleveland, Ohio: Meridian, 1957).
8. N. Yates, *Buildings, Faith, and Worship* (Oxford: Clarendon, 1991).
9. T. F. Torrance, *Space, Time and Incarnation* (London: Oxford University Press, 1969), p. 107.
10. G. R. Lilburne, *A Sense of Place* (Nashville: Abingdon, 1989), p. 103.
11. A. Dulles, *Models of the Church* (Dublin: Gill and Macmillan, 1976).
12. R. Keiffer, 'The RCIA and sacramental efficacy' in *Worship* 56:4 (July 1982), p. 333.
13. W. T. Bartoszewski, *The Convent at Auschwitz* (London: Bowerdean, 1990).
14. A. Bultimer and D. Seamon, *The Human Experience of Place* (London: Croom Helm, 1980).
15. See further S. J. White, *Art, Architecture, and Liturgical Reform* (New York: Pueblo Press, 1990).

Creating Sacred Space:
Liturgy and Architecture Interacting

DAVID STANCLIFFE

As the historical part of this essay observes, it is not always easy to determine the dynamic of the relation between developments in architecture, theology and the wider cultural setting, in determining the precise use to which liturgical space is put. However, one basic tension has always been between a single, gathered space, suggesting the immanence of God, and a progression of rooms or divisions, pointing towards divine transcendence. The latter with its traditional division between nave, choir and sanctuary can very easily degenerate into an all too human hierarchy. David Stancliffe reflects on the way in which the reordering of Portsmouth Cathedral attempted to combine the best aspects of both approaches, and what it was hoped this would convey about the significance of baptism, Eucharist and eucharistic presence.

Identifying the issues:

In the summer of 1982, I began to draft a brief for the development and reordering of Portsmouth Cathedral. It was a substantial undertaking, and although the brief listed our basic needs and added a number of desiderata, it was substantially occupied with charting the development of the life and ministry of English cathedrals, and Portsmouth in particular, describing how we did the liturgy, and reflecting on what we wished the cathedral to say. From that exercise, I began to work out in a rather pragmatic, Anglican way a methodology for understanding the rationale for church building.

The traditional way of chronicling the development of church

44

buildings has been to chart the layers of change apparent in the architecture, providing us with an essentially archaeological understanding of the church's development. But the changes that have taken place over the centuries cannot be explained solely, or even primarily, with reference to developments in building techniques or materials. As well as this historical approach, which reflects the architectural historians' interest in how the pierced walls of Romanesque developed into Gothic arcades of pillars and arches, or how 'the language' of Early English became Decorated and eventually Perpendicular, for example, there is also the question of why.

This is an area in which theology is, or should be, concerned. And three branches of theological discipline are concerned: ecclesiology, liturgy, and spirituality. The concern of ecclesiology is to see how different models of the church – none of them claiming an exclusive rightness – shape a community of faith's consciousness, which is then expressed in the way they worship. The particular concern of the liturgist will be to map the major developments in liturgical practice, and relate these to shifts in the way the spaces are ordered, and liturgical furnishings given more or less prominence. The concern of spirituality is that less defined area, summed up in the question: 'What does or should this space say about the nature of God, and of our incorporation within the divine life of the Trinity?'

But which is cart and which is horse in all this? Was it, for example, a new emphasis on the physical sufferings of Christ, and a shift in the way in which eucharistic theology and practice concentrated on the sacrificial aspects of the Mass which led to the way in which the crucifix was set on the rood beam above the nave altar in a medieval church building? Or was it that developments in building techniques – the height that could be gained with the skeletal vaulted structure of late gothic – led to an emphasis on the skeletal figure of Christ on the cross as the means of our salvation? Or was it that the cumulative effect of the Black Death and the Hundred Years War led to a loss of confidence in any kind of earthly paradise, and renewed an emphasis on the distance between the Father and his creation, for which only the innocent suffering of Christ could atone? Any of these starting points has a degree of plausibility, but beneath them all lie changes in the doctrinal agenda, in the sociological context and in the Church's understanding of itself – what we would now call 'explicit ecclesiology'. In mapping out these interlocking developments, we can learn to read the church building as an index in built form of the history and development of the Christian tradition, a palimpsest of its past as well as a centre for celebration today.

When I visit a church to help a congregation think through how to express their worship in the particular church building that they have inherited, they frequently need help in sorting out why their worship seems unconvincing. They may use Rite A imaginatively, and preach in terms which would make a Liberation theologian look like Cardinal Ratzinger, but often the coded message of the worship will be powerfully contradicted by the way in which the building is ordered. The result is a muddle, and they cannot easily put their finger on why. The difficulty lies, I suspect, in trying to remain clear-headed about these overlapping disciplines. No one starts with a clean sheet: either there is an existing building with its own story to tell; or there are inherited liturgical practices; or there are meanly utilitarian constraints; or an assumed ecclesiology; or simply ignorance of the fact that the weekly eucharistic assembly is the most powerful statement of, and means of forming, Christian doctrine and practice for nine-tenths of the church community.

There are three tasks in which any worshipping community needs to engage if it is to look at its worship in relation to its building. They need to understand the history of their community and locality as expressed in the historical development of their church building – to be in touch with their roots; they need to see how their understanding of themselves as a worshipping community is related to tradition and models of the Church – to articulate a conscious ecclesiology; and they need to work out the patterns in which they want to offer their worship – what liturgies will both express and form who they are becoming, as, conscious of the particular context in which they live and work, they respond to the gospel. Conscious decisions that result from this process will not only determine whether the worship will be a coherent offering, but will also shape what the church 'says' to those who enter it: about the relationship of members of the community to one another – corporate worship and the Eucharist; about proclamation of, and reflection on, the Word of God; about initiation into and commitment in the life of the baptized; about personal growth in the spiritual life; and about the Church's ministry in the community. As a result of this, a programme can be devised which will help the parish make decisions about the relationship of the altar to the assembly which celebrates: the position, size, and proclamatory function of the font; the function of the ministers (and choir) in relation to the total assembly; the place of and space for personal prayer.

How I can best illustrate the interrelation of these ecclesio-
logical, liturgical and spiritual planes is to describe the process
of reflection and planning on which I was engaged over a ten-
year period in the completion and reordering of the Cathedral
at Portsmouth. But before we plunge into this worked example,
let me first offer a theological tool which attempts to relate
space and function to different emphases in our relationship
with God.

In simple terms, we describe the encounter between ourselves and God in two ways: sometimes we discover God in what
we are doing, in the events and experiences of our jobs, our
work, our leisure, our moments of creative fulfilment, or experience of joy or pain. At other times we experience God beyond
us, calling us out on a new stage in our journey. We can experience God among us in his creation, in the act of incarnation; or
we experience God as one who saves us, who takes us out of the
mess we are in, and offers us a new start. For Christians, these
two ways of experiencing God are focused on our celebrations
at Christmas, celebrating the incarnation, God's coming among
us to share our life; and Easter, the celebration of Christ's resurrection from the dead, the victory of life over death, of love over
evil. Of course, all Christian worship contains both elements,
but in different acts of worship, as at different times of the
Church's year, different patterns predominate. Christmas, the
celebration of the incarnation, is primarily a celebration of God
among us, sharing our life; and Easter, the festival of the resurrection, is primarily a proclamation of our passage from death
to life.

Then there is the difference in the experience between those
who sit in a circle waiting on the word of God in their Bible
study and those who begin the journey of Lent at Ash Wednesday and are baptized into the death of Christ, going down with
him into the waters of darkness, to rise into the light and joy of
Easter morning. The discovery of God in our midst is something that the twentieth century has emphasized in common
with the years of the Reformation and the experience of the
early Church. It was the reformer Martin Bucer who urged a
circular room with the minister in its midst, something which,
though hinted at in circular martyriums of the early Church,
and the centrally-planned churches of the Italian Renaissance,
had to wait until the Roman Catholic Cathedral of Liverpool by
Gibbard for its clearest expression.[1] A community which wor-
ships in this way emphasizes the equality of its members under
God, their unity in the Body of Christ, and their fellowship with

each other, as God is discovered in their midst in the breaking of the bread. But such circles are hard to break into, and tend to look inwards.

The other tradition in the Church has always expressed its sense of imperfection, of not yet having arrived, but of being the pilgrim people on the way to the promised land, by more linear architectural form. Christ, the Risen Saviour, who is also our judge, calls us to follow him, and trusting that 'Christ leads me through no darker room than he went through before',[2] church buildings for much of the Church's history have been either a succession of rooms – an atrium, a narthex, a baptistery, a eucharistic room – or else a long church of the Gothic period, divided by one or more crossings and screens, with a sanctuary or shrine, the goal of the pilgrimage, at the far end. And while a simplistic polarization of these two approaches can be enshrined in the distinction between longitudinal or centrally planned buildings, reflecting the pilgrim people or body models of the Church, mature Christian experience needs to embody both strands, and so do the best buildings. With this in mind, we can chart the shift from early basilica to the golden mosaic throne-room, from the skeletal ribs of high Gothic to the churches of renaissance Italy, from the auditory churches of Wren to the carefully calculated perspectives of the opera-sets of continental catholicism.

Have there been any serious architectural or theological statements since? We will probably have to answer 'Yes, but only by reinventing the wheel'. However, Tractarian gothic is where most 'lay' perceptions of a proper church come to a halt, with their desire for shrines, for the pastness of the past (no interfering relevance!), and for peace and quiet, witness the comments in the Visitors' Books. I recall in earlier years in Portsmouth objections to the audible and significant fraction of a number of priests' hosts, on the grounds that it was distracting for people who were trying to pray! It is easier to think of churches divorced from the world, and therefore the immanent/incarnational model (as in the Cathedral of Christ the King at Liverpool, with its enforced community celebration model) poses a threat: it provides us with a model of God's presence among his people which we cannot ignore. Yet this model is often cruelly misinterpreted by people who make their church like any middle-class drawing room, with its fitted carpets and potted palms, and firescreen frontals and tapestry kneelers, not to mention the kitch art – the equivalent of the china ducks and cuckoo clocks.

There are two hazards with this immanent/transcendent

divide. First, the immanentist position is often highly uncom-promising. There is no escape from the charmed circle at Liverpool, and no possible point of entry for the outsiders: you are either within the circle or wholly excluded. For all the warmth of the Body of Christ model, nothing is so exclusive as the inward look of the closed ring. Second, it is possible for the church to capitulate to transcendence alone, by sinking itself exclusively in the pastness of the past: is it not one death, once only, once for all? It is possible that there is no meeting with present reality, only a wistful longing associated with childhood memories.

Let me give an example: when the Liverpool Congress gathered together Roman Catholic lay people from all over the country in the early eighties, they emerged with a sense of for-ward movement and a slogan: 'We are the Easter people, and our song is Alleluia.' One can't help thinking that if the Church of England were ever to manage such a significant conference of its lay people, they will be more likely to come out, looking back over their shoulders at the past, saying wistfully, 'We are the Christmas people, and our song is "Once in Royal David's City"'! There is not only a division between the immanent and the transcendent; there is also a divide between whether you think the true glory is yet to dawn, or is still just visible, glowing dimly in the past.

The question I raised earlier needs taking seriously: if you do not understand how the building has come to be, how the grain works, how the worshipping life has been formed, you cannot evolve: there can only be revolution, and revolution is bad for buildings, bad for congregations' sense of continuity and identity, and bad for popular perception with charges of sectarianism.

Key historical shifts

Using a somewhat crude division, we can begin to evaluate the way in which the series of rooms in a house church of the early centuries – originally defined by function and each with their own focus (e.g. table) – were juxtaposed with large-scale impe-rial public buildings after the conversion of Constantine to form a new complex, where the circular form of a shrine sanctuary was combined with aisled basilica-hall, and a baptistery added or built nearby. As the emphasis in eucharistic worship moves from celebrating the presence of the risen Christ in the Breaking of the Bread to the anticipation of the fullness of the Kingdom in the foretaste of the heavenly banquet, the vision of the Lamb enthroned in Revelation takes over from the Lukan Emmaus supper. The assembly is no longer an extended family at domestic table, but a division of the holy empire of Christ the King triumphant. These imperial overtones influence not only the subject-matter of the mosaic decoration, but the use of the building: the place of the Procurator and his assessors is taken by the bishop and his clergy; the table with the depositions and the bust of the emperor (before whom a pinch of incense was required as a sign of allegiance) became the altar, and the ambos (reading desks) for the public addresses became the places from which the Word was proclaimed. And this imperial confidence did not fade with the collapse of the old empire: Charlemagne overlooked the throne-room of the court of heaven from his marble chair in the west-work of his great chapel in Aachen.

A key feature in the development of church buildings was their early association with the tombs of the martyrs. Simple shelters over the shrines of the saints may have been the origin of the ciboria over altars in which a relic of a saint was enclosed. Rotundas compete on equal terms with basilical forms. And baptisteries, still separate buildings in which the different sexes could have decent privacy, were normally circular or regularly polygonal in form. Fonts were no birdbaths, and cruciform baptismal sheepdips symbolic of death and resurrection or octagonal basins to suggest the perfection of a paradise garden were a normal expression of a serious baptismal faith, which embraced the promise of the new creation as well as death and resurrection; and a sense of empowering for service as well as being clothed with Christ. Pulpits for the paschal proclamation, with mosaics representing Jonah being expelled from the great fish, were set opposite enormous candelabra; ambos, and the books of the gospels carried into the assembly as an icon of the Word made flesh, bore the beasts of the apocalypse in jewelled metalwork. The primeval conflict of light and dark, the twining sea-serpents against the ark of faith, the crusading warrior monks against worldliness, lent a robustness to the conflict between the darkness of this present world and the glory of the Kingdom of Christ.

Development came to the buildings with a change in emphasis. As Christianity moved north, and became settled practice, infant baptism became the norm, and the fonts shrank to tubs set within the main building. In a shrine church, the translated saint in his or her gilded reliquary became the focus of the building, and in a sense a more tangible president of the rite than the Lord made momentarily present in the eucharistic action. The screen that kept him from vulgar gaze, and induced the pilgrim to go right up to the east end, and not merely gawp from afar, became the backdrop to the altar, now placed against it like a sideboard.

In the Middle Ages, following the Black Death and the Hundred Years War, the skeletal rib-vaults of late gothic, like the carcass of some beached whale, expressed a preoccupation with death; the Office of the Dead, the growth of Chantry Chapels, a theology of redemption heavily dependent on a doctrine of penal substitution, brought a wholly different climate to worship, whose symbol was the agonized death of Jesus on the cross rather than the Christ enthroned in majesty of a previous generation. In the darkened interiors of these spiky and pinnacled exteriors, the distant and vengeful God, apparently seeking his pound of flesh, seemed remote, hidden behind a series of screens. They felt they knew 'but the outskirts of his ways'.

By contrast, the jelly-mould churches of the early Italian renaissance with their mathematically perfect forms derived from the Platonic rules of harmony attempted to convey in buildings what Michelangelo's Sistine Chapel roof did in painting, where God the Father reaches out and touches Adam finger to finger. Here, in the light and sunshine of the Mediterranean world, the new creation seems a possibility again. Leonardo's sketchbooks are bursting with such designs, but north of the Alps in the Protestant world, sober clarity and severe reason banish not only exuberant excess but all suspicion of emotion in their appeal to the intellect. And when Palladio begins (again, echoes of the fourth century) to link a nave – an auditorium – to a circular form, introducing the proscenium arch and perspective tricks of the opera house, we realize that the liturgy is grand opera, a performance into which – though as spectators – we are skilfully drawn.

In England, the conservative Laudian reorderings of the early seventeenth century were followed by the auditory churches of the Restoration period, and the amazing opportunity offered to Christopher Wren in the wake of the great Fire of London.[3] I can do no more than allude to the South German Baroque – more of a ballroom than an opera house – and Neapolitan Rococo, where a *fête champètre* as the contemporary image of the heavenly banquet seems to have invaded the church; or the Lutheran merchants' opulence in Hamburg with polished wood, brass chandeliers and Schnitger organs; and the New Englanders' clapboard simplicities in Boston. We could analyse the romantic gothicism of Pugin and the Victorian probity of Scott and Street; we could follow the quest for man-made space to Gaudi, or Comper's 'unity by inclusion'.

In spite of this great historical backdrop, many English

churchgoers are wholly unaware of any sense of development in the architectural and liturgical setting of worship. They imagine that their church is how things have always been. The key reason is that the majority of our parish churches in England received their last major reordering in the wake of the Tractarian ideals, and are suitable for little other than Victorian worship. Pitch-pine pewing throughout, kneelers, a raised sanctuary, a chancel crowded with a surpliced choir (or now more frequently cluttered with the empty stalls which once held a surpliced choir), a birdbath font (sometimes euphemistically excused as being 'portable'), scraped walls, dark stained glass windows, a side chapel crammed with a huge organ, a curtained-off vestry: all these were the hall-marks of one particular period, and designed to foster a particular strand of piety, which set great store on order and obedience – 'facing the commanding officer in neat rows'. Much of its shape was derived from an individualistic, non-eucharistic piety fostered by a didactic style of worship, where the congregation do not expect to meet God, and might not recognize him – or her – if they did. They are looking for a substantive presence mediated through the stained glass in the East window, or the unchanging word on the page of the Authorized Version or in the authoritatively performed sacraments of the Church, rather than an encounter in the common life of the community at prayer.

In passing it is worth contrasting Basil Spence's Coventry Cathedral (the last of the gothic cathedrals), still built on Tractarian principles and heavily dependent on Sutherland's great tapestry as its dominant 'altarpiece', with 'Paddy's Wigwam', Gibbard's Liverpool Cathedral of Christ the King, the most thoroughgoing of the circular/Body-of-Christ type buildings. But more instructive are the reorderings of the post-war churches in Germany, particularly those carried out by Rudolph Schwartz and Domenikus Bohm in the Cologne area. Here we can evaluate what the architects made of the fine directive of the German Liturgical Commission, published in 1947 and largely the work of Dr Theodor Klausser.[4]

The worked example: Portsmouth Cathedral:

If that is the theory and the background, what of the practice? In the final section of this essay, I propose to introduce you to some of the aims we set out for the reordering and development of Portsmouth Cathedral, with the thinking as it was some ten years ago, and to illustrate it with some reference to what we did during my time as Provost there (1982–93).

How did we arrive at the brief? By considering first what the cathedral should say, and only secondarily by looking at ways in which the functional aspects – what various liturgical assemblies demanded – could be accommodated. It began with the salvation/incarnational model I have already described in general terms, and then reflected on how this and a key liturgical model – the celebration of the Paschal Vigil – applied to Portsmouth as a building with a remarkably disjointed architectural history, but a carefully thought-out liturgical style.

Any church building needs to give expression to both these patterns, to both these ways of experiencing God. A single-room building often fails in its proclamation if it manages to suggest that God's being can be found exhaustively and exclusively in the here and now, and that there is nowhere to be led, no beyond, no perfection to which he will take us. Conversely, linear churches, or those conceived as a series of rooms leading from one another, can be restless and unsatisfying unless each section or room has a strong focus, speaking of a particular way in which God's being is discovered, while at the same time pointing us to the next stage.

One simple progression is that of the early Church, where an atrium, an open forecourt, allowed people to gather and hear the Faith, a baptistry provided the gateway through which those who accepted Christ would pass, to enter into the eucharistic room, the earthly image of the heavenly messianic banquet. Another is the two-roomed structure of a medieval English church as rearranged after the Reformation: a nave, with a reading-desk and pulpit where the Word of God could be celebrated and proclaimed, and a chancel, where those who wished to draw near with faith could kneel and receive the sacraments. In both these patterns there is a dynamic sense of movement, of growth in and through the worship: each room has a *distinctive function* through which the worshipper is led in a journey towards God. This contrasts with the late medieval picture, which most cathedrals in England today still echo, of a church divided not by function but by hierarchy: in the choir or sanctuary, the clergy or monastic foundation, and in the nave the ordinary people, often separated by a substantial screen. In an arrangement like this, the people are eavesdroppers or more distant observers of a liturgy performed within the enclosure by the holy people on their behalf. This pattern of worship reflects the more inward-looking, the quasi-monastic, collegiate life of the Cathedral Foundation rather than the picture of the bishop as the father in God of his diocesan family gathered with him to offer worship, and has its roots in the divergence between the bishop's diocesan ministry and his cathedral's collegiate life.

Of these two patterns, Portsmouth inclines towards the former. Portsmouth is not, and never has been, a monastic foundation, and that building, though linear in form, is a succession of nearly square spaces, whose use is determined by function rather than hierarchy or allocation: in other words, the nave does not belong to the people, the choir to the choral foundation, and the sanctuary to the clergy; but rather the whole worshipping body makes the most appropriate use of each space, frequently moving from one to the other as in the early Christian festival complex or a Laudian reordering of a two-room church.

The distinctive cathedral liturgies reinforce this point. Unlike a parish church, where the distinctive liturgy is the parish communion with the parish priest as celebrant assisted by a number of lay people, the distinctive cathedral liturgy will be a celebration of the Eucharist at which the bishop presides, assisted by his Chapter, as the culmination of a rite of passage either of baptism and confirmation as at the Easter Vigil, or of an ordination. In such services, the discovery of God's power and presence among us, whether in the proclamation of the gospel, the act of ordination or the celebration of the Eucharist, is balanced by the experience of God leading us and changing us 'from one degree of glory to another'.

At the Easter Vigil, the archetypal episcopal rite of initiation, the church meets in the Nicholson (d. 1949) nave around a flaming fire to keep Vigil and hear the Old Testament stories of rescue and redemption. This nave is a square, with a raised cloister-like walk-way around it giving more than a feel of the atrium before an early basilica, like San Clemente in Rome, for example. As the Paschal Candle is lit and the bishop challenges candidates to turn to Christ and renounce evil, the whole congregation moves from the flickering darkness of the nave under the tower and into the 1690 choir which becomes a blaze of candlelight drawn from the Light of Christ while the Proclamation is sung. All, that is, except the candidates for baptism, who remain in the darkened nave until they have declared their faith in the risen Christ, and passed through the waters of baptism, through the font placed under the cross-pierced central tower. They pass through this to experience the warmth and support of the Church, coming before the bishop for the laying on of hands, joining the company of the redeemed who will celebrate the risen Christ in the breaking of bread at the dawning of the new day. In this way – and this pattern is true of such diverse services as the Advent Procession, the Epiphany carol service, the regular diocesan baptisms and confirmations, as

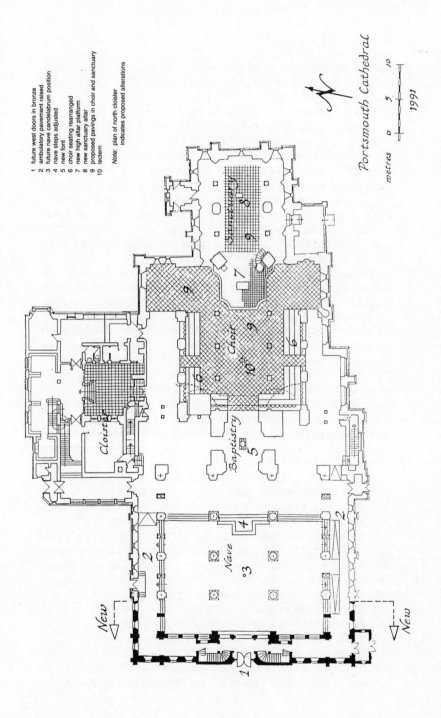

1 future west doors in bronze
2 ambulatory pavement raised
3 future nave candelabrum position
4 nave steps adjusted
5 new font
6 choir seating rearranged
7 new high altar platform
8 new sanctuary altar
9 proposed pavings in choir and sanctuary
10 lectern

Note: plan of north cloister
indicates proposed alterations

Portsmouth Cathedral

metres 0   5   10

1991

Sanctuary

Choir

Baptistry

Nave

Cloister

New

New

well as the Easter Vigil – the experience we hope worshippers and visitors will both receive from a visit to the building is of the nave as the place where people gather and meet to hear the stories of the faith, where we wait for the word of Christ, revealed in Scripture or disclosed in the teaching of the bishop to bring people to Christ. Going into the dark tunnel under the tower crossing, we pass from death to life, as we enter the old church. 'With Thee is the well of life, and in Thy light do we see light'.[5] Here we enter 'the glorious liberty of the sons of God' (Rom. 8.21 AV), where once the jumbled collection of cut-down box pews tended to give the impression that life in Christ is a boxed-up muddle! The graceful 1690 classical architecture has been freed to give us a sense of order and spaciousness: we move through the dark tunnel into a patterned and ordered temple which gives us a foretaste of the clarity of heaven: 'Thou hast set my feet in a large room' (Ps. 38.8 AV).

Though the culmination of our earthly worship is the celebration of the Eucharist, where we make the memorial of Christ and find our unity as 'we who are many become one body, for we all partake of one bread', we need to remember that we still have not arrived. God's Kingdom lies ahead and beyond the best of our human endeavours. Christ, whose life we enjoy, has gone on before us and 'ever lives to make intercession for us'. Beyond the classical choir lies the twelfth-century sanctuary, given access by the aisles. Here, in the fourth and last room of the building, is the place beyond, the still space whose focus is a hanging pyx (containing the eucharistic elements). Here is the sign that God is both with, and yet not contained by, his Church. Here is the reminder that when we have done all we can, the journey still continues and that 'here we have no abiding city'. In practical terms, this is the weekday chapel; the place for private prayer and meditation, set apart.

The crossing in the old church is the site of our high altar, and the regular place for eucharistic celebration on Sunday. There is space enough round the altar for the bishop to be surrounded by his Chapter, eighteen priests, and for the Foundation, especially the choir, to have a distinctive, though not exclusive place. Is it the right place to sing the daily offering of Morning and Evening Prayer? The eighteenth-century classical character makes us want to say 'Yes', though we need to remember that the nave may not only be an ante-chapel, a narthex where all sorts of experience and teaching is offered, an 'Old Testament Church' which implicitly reveals Christ, but is also a place for Ministry of the Word, where the bishop preaches on such occasions as an ordination or a baptism and confirmation.

Is the centre of the Nicholson nave the right place for some fairly permanent sign that here Christ is revealed, the mysteries of
God laid open, like a great seven-branched candelabrum?

The square under the tower, pierced on all four sides, is not
large: some feared that the font would get in the way of processions. But it has proved to be a good and constant reminder that
it is 'through the grave, and gate of death' that we 'pass to our
joyful resurrection' as the collect for Easter Eve puts it. Entering
the church should be a constant reminder of our baptism into
the death and resurrection of Christ, a daily reminder to die to
sin that we may rise in him as a rehearsal for our own death.
With the new font placed under the central tower, few people
can enter the Cathedral without being confronted with the
claims for their baptismal faith.

The new font is carved out of Purbeck stone, rich in fossils,
and echoes the design of a ninth century Greek font standing in
Sandringham churchyard. The inscription round the rim comes
from the *Mystagogical Catecheses* of Cyril of Jerusalem.

> When you went down into the waters it was like night and
> you could see nothing: but when you came up again, it was
> like finding yourself in the day. That one moment was your
> death and your birth; that saving water was both your grave
> and your mother.[6]

As fewer children are brought to baptism in infancy, a greater
proportion of those who come to 'conscious and intelligent
faith' in teenage or adulthood are unbaptized. In this font it is
possible to baptize infants, toddlers, teenagers and adults with
equal ease, and with varying degrees of immersion. The solid
tomb-like quality, combined with its cruciform shape, make a
clear statement of our going down into the deep waters of death
in order that we may be raised to new life in Christ.

The new nave, of course, offers the most flexible space
imaginable. Among its many uses for revealing God to us,
whether in music or art, drama or display, creative work or craft,
teaching or dance, or in conversation and social intercourse, the
nave will sometimes be the right place, because its space is so
flexible, for the whole of the celebration of the Eucharist. While
it feels something of an agora or market-place, the church will
sometimes want to be in the market-place, too. We do not wish
this nave, this atrium, to have so distinctive or narrowly ecclesial
a feel as to set limits on our activities there. We need to draw
people into it, but then to challenge them.

Portsmouth is a worked example, far from perfect, but illus-
trating the opportunities of working within an existing tradition,

getting to understand the grain of the building, clarifying what are the principal liturgies, and how they should be expressed, and allowing a development of the building to take place by leisurely interaction, with a clear aim that the building should communicate a sense of journeying into faith. It is a pragmatist's apologia for sacred space.

Notes

1. See 'Martin Bucer on the Position of the Minister' in G. W. O. Addleshaw and F. Etchells, *The Architectural Setting of Anglican Worship* (London: Faber, 1948).
2. A line from R. Baxter's hymn, 'Lord it belongs not to my care'.
3. See Addleshaw and Etchells as in note 1 above. And for a recent appreciative analysis of the eighteenth-century contribution, and the way it was misunderstood, see N. Yates, *Buildings, Faith and Worship* (Oxford: Clarendon Press, 1991).
4. They are printed as an appendix to an important collection of essays ed. by P. Hammond, *Towards a Church Architecture* (London: Architectural Press, 1962). Nothing of comparable quality has emerged in the last thirty years, save a slender volume by F. Debuyst, *Modern Architecture and Christian Celebration* (Ecumenical Studies in Worship, London: Lutterworth, 1968).
5. Psalm 36.9, Book of Common Prayer.
6. Cyril of Jerusalem, *Catechetical Lectures* 20 *Library of Nicene and Post-Nicene Fathers*, Second series vol. vii. (Grand Rapids, Michigan: Eerdmans, 1974), p. 148 (author's translation).

Space and Time Transcended: the Beginnings of Christian Pilgrimage

DAVID HUNT

*Though pagan attitudes to holy sites no doubt gave impetus to
the practice, Christian pilgrimage seems as old as the New
Testament itself and, as David Hunt demonstrates, it is widely
attested long before the more spectacular developments which
took place under the Emperor Constantine. Though historical
motives and the desire for proofs of the faith played their part,
the primary motive seems to have been the conviction that,
through recreating the time liturgically and recreating the space
by retreading the place, both time and space could be tran-
scended and more effective contact thus made with the original
divine disclosure in that time and place. Such participation,
mediated sacramentally through present space and time, also
generated a new geography, first with the tombs of the martyrs
on the outskirts of cities and then with Jerusalem itself becoming the real centre of the Christian empire.*

The early roots of pilgrimage

'One who journeys to some sacred place, as an act of religious
devotion'; this is how the *Shorter Oxford Dictionary* defines the
'prevailing sense' of the word 'pilgrim'. To speak, however, of
Christian pilgrimage in this sense is, on the face of it, to
encounter a contradiction in terms: for the Christians' devotion
is of a kind which is in essence indifferent to sacred places. The
founder of Christianity enjoined the worship of the Father 'in
spirit and in truth', not in particular locations, and the life of
each Christian individual is its own pilgrimage, each God's

59

temple in which the Spirit dwells. Emphasis on the sanctity of
people rather than places has charged the debate about the
rights and wrongs of Christians going on pilgrimages, all the way
from antiquity through the Protestant reformation to the present day: God's revelation, we are reminded, is one universal to
mankind, which cannot be confined within specific earthly
locations. St Paul's words to the people of Athens could not be
clearer: 'The God who created the world and everything in it,
and who is Lord of heaven and earth, does not live in shrines
made by men' (Acts 17.24 NEB).[1] Yet such spiritual high-
mindedness is overshadowed by the facts of Christian history,
throughout which the faithful have undertaken journeys with
the object of sacred encounters in holy places – as here in
England to St Cuthbert's shrine at Durham or that of St Thomas
à Becket at Canterbury. It is overshadowed, too, by the realities
of the world into which Christianity was born, a land dotted
with memorials of its Jewish forefathers, places visited and
honoured by Jesus' contemporaries; and a wider Mediterranean
Greco-Roman culture with a lively sense of the presence of its
gods, be they on top of sacred mountains or in the depths of
sacred caves, or enshrined in great cult-sites which attracted
devotees to wonder and to worship, to see divine visions and hear
divine voices. St Paul's Athenian audience would have found
his strictures utterly contrary to their perceptions of their contemporary world. In a universe so littered with holy places and
people on the move to reach them, it can hardly be a surprise
that Christianity caught the pilgrimage habit.

Is there a date when Christian pilgrimage 'began'? As with
all aspects of the history of the Christian church, many have
pointed to the era of Constantine as the pivotal moment, particularly when it comes to considering the evolution of the
Christian Holy Land: one recent account, for example, sees
Holy Land pilgrimage as 'essentially a new phenomenon that
first flourished during the age of Constantine'.[2] Constantine's
mother Helena, who made a celebrated journey to Jerusalem
in the later 320s, is frequently presented as the prototype of
the Christian pilgrim. I propose to return later to a consideration of the real contribution of Constantine to my theme;
for the moment suffice it to say that confident statements of
the Constantinian origins of Christian pilgrimage are, I believe,
misplaced. I shall try to show that, individually and collectively,
Christians can be demonstrated visiting places deemed to have
a sacred significance for their faith long before the advent of
the first Christian emperor. Even if such journeys had not
yet acquired some of the associations of more fully-developed

pilgrimage – there is no evidence that they were undertaken for ascetic, penitential, or therapeutic purposes – none the less it would be unduly pedantic to deny these travellers the label of 'pilgrims'. In any case we have to go much *later* than Constantine – and much later than I shall reach in this essay – to discover the phenomenon in such fully-fledged guise. As for Helena, her status as number one pilgrim owes more to the elaboration of subsequent legend than to the historical facts of her eastern journey, which was less that of Christian pilgrim than of imperial traveller on a 'state visit' to provinces which had only recently come under her son's rule.[3]

My point is that the followers of Christ could not be immune to the pious mobility which was endemic to the Jewish and Gentile worlds in which their new religion took root. Christian pilgrimage evolved naturally out of its environment; it did not spring into existence in some definitive form or at some decisive moment in history. We might even detect it surfacing in the New Testament itself. Luke's two disciples recounting the death of Jesus of Nazareth to the unknown stranger on the road to Emmaus are already speaking of him as a powerful prophet whose tomb was being visited by his followers, and said to be the scene of a miraculous vision of angels; while John's Gospel of course furnishes a description of the tomb's topography – set in a garden, and near to the place of the crucifixion on Golgotha (Luke 24.18–24; John 19.41 NEB). Is John hinting at a place preserved from the beginning in the memory of Jerusalem's first Christians, a rock-tomb already being sought out by the faithful? It would not be until Constantine, of course, that the Lord's Tomb was unearthed from beneath the then Roman city of Aelia Capitolina, and turned into an object of universal Christian pilgrimage; yet a tradition about its location seems to have gone back through the changing physical appearance of Jerusalem to the early community of Jesus' followers. Another New Testament tomb may also have generated some devotional interest among contemporaries. 'Devout men buried Stephen,' so runs the narrative of Acts, 'and made great lamentation over him (8.2 NEB). In contrast, though, to the tomb of Jesus, Stephen's burial finds no location in the Bible, and it was to be nearly four centuries – in 415 – before the 'invention' or 'discovery' of the protomartyr's tomb in a village twenty miles distant from Jerusalem.[4] There is no trace of any local tradition about the place of Stephen's burial prior to this fifth-century discovery; but we may be justified in concluding from the language of Acts that his resting-place was not forgotten by the first Christians.

Dislocation of space and time

Nor, of course, were the tombs of those who were to follow Stephen's example of martyrdom forgotten. In mid-second-century Asia Minor, Polycarp's congregation at Smyrna determined on an annual commemoration at his tomb of his 'birth' as a martyr (i.e. the day of his execution), in a manner which suggests that this was not a novel procedure.[5] A century later, in Cyprian's day in north Africa, such martyr commemorations were a recognized and important feature of church life; and in the meantime we first hear of Roman Christians marking out the places associated with the deaths of Peter and Paul, on the Vatican hill and beside the Ostian Way.[6] That these Christian gatherings at the tombs of their first saints were perceived as more than just private acts of respect for the dead (which is what their pagan equivalent might be) seems to be confirmed by the well-documented attempts of the secular authorities to obstruct the recovery and burial of martyrs' remains. As the Christian faithful assembled in burial grounds or at the roadsides on the outskirts of their towns, they asserted a communal identity which turned the cities of the Roman empire 'inside out'. The focus of their gatherings was at the margins, outside the walls, of their contemporary secular world: not much of a journey, maybe, in spatial terms (although, as the fame of martyrs spread abroad, some of the devotees may have travelled some distance), but a far more substantial cultural displacement, a real dislocation to a centre of gravity beyond the bounds of the society in which they lived. Such annual martyr commemorations were local acts of pilgrimage. From the fourth century modest shrines sprouted grand architectural complexes, with basilicas, courtyards, colonnades and fountains, to house and envelop the assembled crowds of worshippers – and from the martyr sermons of church fathers, or from the poetic depictions of a Prudentius or a Paulinus of Nola, we are able to visualize the buildings swirling with their pilgrims. They were locations which their Christian devotees envisaged as separate worlds, set apart from the communities which they bordered: thus Paulinus' buildings around the tomb of St Felix outside Nola amounted to a new town in themselves; and Jerome memorably pictured the city of Rome uprooted from its foundations, as its Christian people forsook the faded glories of the 'gilded Capitol' for their own martyr shrines beyond its walls.[7]

In addition to their prevailing sense of detachment and displacement from contemporary surroundings, these early martyr commemorations display another feature which was to prove

influential in the fashioning of Christian pilgrimage. They w\
fired by an acute awareness of historical particularities of pla\
and time. As is clear as early as the case of Polycarp, the date
was all-important – it was the annual celebration of the martyr's
'birthday', the day which saw the beginning of his immortal life
with God. Cyprian urged on his clergy the necessity of record-
ing the date when 'confessors' died in prison 'so that we are
able to celebrate their memory among the memorials of the
martyrs';[8] and in Cyprian's own case, although his burial was
delayed in order to avoid attracting the attention of pagan
opponents, it was, of course, the day of his death which was to
be kept as his festival. The first ecclesiastical calendars com-
prised such lists of martyr dates. Also crucial for the collective
memory were the martyr's *Acta*, the literary record of his glorious confrontation with the world which would be read as the
public centrepiece of the annual commemoration, and through
which the martyr's faith would be relived year by year. Thus at
the specific place where his body rested (often distinct from the
actual site of martyrdom, which might well be one of the major
public arenas in the heart of the city), and on the specific date
when he had entered into eternity, the Christian community
congregated to honour their local saint.

It was an assertion of identity which transplanted them not
only spatially outwards from the centres of secular life, but also
temporally backwards into the history of their community –
actually, so it was firmly held, into the presence of the sainted
martyr and on the very day when he had been glorified.
Sermons of the fathers in honour of saints and martyrs abound
with the notion of their presence in their tombs and through
their remains. The holy place was the spot which bridged the
gulf between past and present, between living and dead – as
in a sermon of Gregory of Nyssa, honouring the relics of the
martyr Theodore: 'those who behold them (i.e. the remains)
embrace them as though the actual body, applying all their
senses, eyes, mouth and ears; then they pour forth tears for his
piety and suffering, and bring forward their supplications to the
martyr as though he were present.'[9] Although he belongs after
the age of martyrs, the inscription on St Martin's tomb at Tours
is often cited: 'here is buried bishop Martin of sacred memory,
whose soul is in the hand of God; but he is wholly present here,
made manifest to everyone by the goodwill of his miracles.'[10]

I have sought to identify among the early Christian generations a lively sense of going out from their contemporary world
to come face to face with a martyr saint at the specific place and
time sanctified by his or her glorious exploits. Such notions are

capable of being extended beyond the context of local martyr festivals. In that same mid-second century era which saw bishop Polycarp put to the flames in the stadium at Smyrna, another Christian bishop from Asia Minor, Melito of Sardis, made a journey eastwards to find out more about the books of the Old Testament and the extracts of the Law and the Prophets which related to Christianity. He described himself as travelling as far as 'the place where it [or 'things'] were proclaimed and enacted'.[11] I (and others) have been taken to task for reading into Melito's meagre statement of the object of his journey the conclusion that he travelled to the Holy Land as a pilgrim, that he was indeed the first identifiable such pilgrim. Admittedly the recorded results of his journey – an authoritative list of the books of the Old Testament, from which Melito was able to compile his own extracts – sound more like the outcome of a visit to a good library than the benefits of a devotional pilgrimage (at least as we might now understand it). Yet Melito's encounter with sacred history in the places 'where it was proclaimed and enacted' is surely a longer-distance version of the motives which led Christian congregations outside their walls to the graves of their martyrs. The locations in the Holy Land associated with the Old Testament Scriptures constituted a present recollection of biblical prophecy and its Christian fulfilment in much the same way as the saint's tomb gave present reality to a past demonstration of (or witness to) the faith. In the next century Pionius, who was to follow Polycarp to a martyr's death before the crowds in Smyrna, told of his travels in the Holy Land around the Dead Sea. It was the land which 'to this day bears witness (*marturousan*) to God's anger against it' because of the sins of its inhabitants: the smoke which continues to rise from it, its burnt-up ground which sustains neither food nor water, and the sea unable to support life, refusing to accept human bodies (i.e. leaving them to float) lest it be punished a second time.[12] Pionius came up against a more threatening face of Old Testament history than had the scholarly Melito; but they both shared an experience of confronting the biblical past as a tangible reality in the contemporary Holy Land. To describe this merely as 'travel helpful for making Scripture vivid'[13] seems to me to miss its powerful impact on the practitioners, for whom it was surely a journey which would come within the *Oxford Dictionary* definition of 'pilgrimage': the place was rendered sacred by its history, and the traveller's response was not casual, but one which sprang from religious devotion.

It is around the time of Melito's journey from Asia Minor to the Holy Land that we begin to hear not just of the Old

Testament heritage attracting the interest of travellers, but also of New Testament locations entering the picture. The silence which has descended on the topography of the Gospels is gradually lifted. Perhaps as early as the middle of the second century a cave in Bethlehem was being pointed out as the place of Christ's nativity, seemingly a Christian attempt at appropriating some frequented local pagan cult-site.[14] At the same time it may be that the Christians of Jerusalem were already laying claim to a rocky outcrop in the Forum area of Hadrian's recently completed city – and another focus of pagan cult, to Aphrodite – as the hill of Golgotha, the place of the crucifixion. This much at least has been read into Melito's own insistence, in his surviving Paschal sermon, that Jesus was crucified in the *centre* of the city. If this is to be taken literally, then it is a departure from the gospel account, which may owe its explanation to Melito's awareness of the actual layout of second-century Jerusalem and of the claims of its contemporary Christian inhabitants.[15] These Christians of Jerusalem also came to find their uses for another sacred cave, near the summit of the Mount of Olives, where they located Christ's teaching to the disciples about the mysteries of the end of time, and nearby his own ascension into heaven.

This sprouting of gospel locations, and the identification of holy caves which are likely to have been preserves of earlier pagan cult, may suggest a degree of competition for the possession of religious sites in Palestine, as the Christians sought to capitalize the potential of bringing home the present reality of their sacred past in the contemporary landscape. To show forth 'where it was proclaimed and enacted', to advertize places which 'bore witness' to biblical history, was not only to respond to the arrival of pilgrims bent on some devotional identity with holy places; it was as much an extension of apologetic arguments about the truth of Christianity. So a passage of Origen's *Contra Celsum* (aimed particularly at the Jews):

> If anyone wants further proof to convince him that Jesus was born in Bethlehem besides the prophecy of Micah and the story recorded in the Gospels by Jesus' disciples, he may observe that, in agreement with the story in the Gospel about his birth, the cave at Bethlehem *is shown* where he was born and the manger in the cave where he was wrapped in swaddling clothes. What is shown there is famous *even among people alien to the faith*, since it was in this cave that the Jesus who is worshipped and admired by Christians was born.[16]

As I have argued elsewhere, Origen's, and later Eusebius', emphasis on the holy places 'showing forth' the truth of the gospel adds yet another significant dimension to the kind of witness which they were seen to represent – not merely for the edification of those in the faith, but also a proclamation of truth to those outside it.[17] For Eusebius such arguments reached their climax with the Constantinian discovery of the Holy Sepulchre itself: this had brought into the light the 'witness' (*marturion*) of the Saviour's resurrection, providing 'for those who came to see it a clear record of the marvels which had occurred there, testifying (*marturomenon*) to the Saviour's resurrection with actions speaking louder than all words.'[18]

Pagan parallels

Eusebius' term translated here as 'record' is *historia*, a Greek word which since the age of Herodotus had signified a species of erudite tourism, a process of investigative travelling, coupled with the end-product of 'historical' knowledge which resulted from such enquiry. At the height of Rome's golden age of peace in the second century AD, the time when we first begin to encounter isolated mentions of Christians like Melito travelling to the Holy Land, such journeys of *historia* were in full swing around the Mediterranean world. From emperors and their retinues to individual explorers, the vogue was to visit and marvel at places of antiquity, and come face to face with past worlds.[19] Specially favoured destinations, of course, were Egypt and Greece, both rich in the physical reminders of a glorious history. On the tombs and monuments of the Nile valley an abundance of inscriptions testifies to the frequency and diversity of the travellers who visited them, be they elegant Greek verses or 'Kilroy was here'-type graffiti; while for the antiquarian tourism which enveloped the classical sites of Greece our most telling evidence remains Pausanias' guide, composed towards the end of the second century to accompany visits to the Greek fatherland. It is a work which (as many have noted) portrays contemporary topography only in so far as it is a framework for reawakening and reviving the past. Pausanias' travellers were conducted around the bygone Greece of myth and history, not the Roman province of the second century AD.

This wider context of 'historical' tourism, set largely in the lands of the eastern Mediterranean, can hardly fail to impinge on our understanding of those first Christian journeys to the Holy Land. If Melito's encounter with his Bible in second-century Palestine was akin, as I argued earlier, to the experience of worshippers confronting the presence of their martyrs, it was also closely analogous to this prevailing vogue of secular *historia*.

For the Christian learned in the Scriptures, the Holy Land offered the same prospect of following on the ground the physical topography of his heritage as Pausanias' Greece held out to contemporary Hellenes. *Historia*, for the biblical scholar, led naturally to Palestine. So Origen, famously, was induced to correct the text of John's Gospel on the location where John was baptizing, as a result of his own *historia* in search of the 'traces of Jesus and his disciples and the prophets'[20] – and there are other occasions in the course of Origen's biblical commentaries (the relocation of the 'Gadarene swine', for example) where he betrays a similar personal investigation of the topography of both Old and New Testaments. It was with such biblical *historia* in mind that Eusebius came to compose his so-called *Onomastikon*, a gazeteer of some 1000 place-names listed alphabetically from the books of the Bible, complete with their contemporary location if one was available. I used to think that Eusebius was writing a pilgrim guide, matching the travellers' contemporary Palestine with the biblical record; but I now see that the principle of its organization – according to the biblical books rather than as an itinerary to be followed 'on the ground' – points to an essentially scholarly, and not devotional, intent.[21]

Yet is such a distinction tenable? One of these early visitors to the Holy Land was a bishop in Cappadocia named Alexander (in fact he never got back home, for the Christians in Jerusalem claimed him as their own bishop). Eusebius tells of his journeying to Jerusalem in the time of the emperor Caracalla (early third century) 'for the purpose of prayer and investigation of the places'.[22] The stress on the combination of prayer and *historia* is the motivation ascribed by Eusebius writing a century later, and not necessarily Alexander's own – but it would surely be hard to deny that the Christian traveller setting foot in the land of the Bible on an expedition of *historia* also had some onrush of religious devotion when confronted by places sanctified by Christian history, certainly if contemporary secular travellers are any guide.[23] For those tourists of the pagan world (already mentioned) were readily inclined to turn into pilgrims when faced, for instance, by the monuments of Egypt. Journeys of *historia* would become acts of worship, as travellers inscribed on the stone a prayer to the gods for themselves, their companions, or those they had left behind. The onset of such piety seems especially prevalent in remote regions of the upper Nile, at the island of Philae sacred to Isis, or even further afield in the temple to the god Mandulis at the frontier post of Talmis – where one traveller at least, Maximus by name, felt himself powerfully amid a divine presence, and inscribed on the temple wall his vision of Mandulis and Isis at this holy spot.[24] Egypt's visitors evidently encompassed, often in the same person, both devotional pilgrim and explorer investigating the past.

A recent study has come to similar conclusions about the Greece of Pausanias.[25] His guide to the sites of Greece, it is argued, is in fact a manual of pilgrimage, guiding contemporary Hellenes on a journey of self-identity back to their cultural roots (and in defiance of their present subservience to the Roman empire). A major element in Pausanias' text are the sacred precincts which lay outside the political centres of Greece: to these his readers are carefully led, and their special religious aura is only enhanced by his calculated silence about the mysteries and ritual which they housed. The Christian travelling to the biblical lands was engaged (as we have seen) on a similar journey back to the origins of his faith and the basis of his religious identity – it is impossible to disentangle the 'prayer' from the *historia*. Eusebius was to find elements of them both, as he did with bishop Alexander, in the throngs of pilgrims 'from all over the world' gathered by the summit of the Mount of Olives, following in Christ's footsteps to behold from there the evidence of the destruction of the Jewish Temple, and the desolate temple rock of Hadrian's Aelia Capitolina.[26] To stand 'where Christ's feet had stood', and contemplate the fulfilment of his gospel prediction, was an objective which answered every bit as much to religious devotion as it did to any spirit of 'historical' investigation.

Constantine and the empire's new geography

It was in the years prior to Constantine's victorious arrival as Christian ruler of the eastern empire in 324 that Eusebius portrayed this worldwide assemblage of pilgrims in Jerusalem. His apologetic enthusiasm has probably got the better of his command of the facts, for the sketchy evidence we possess of Holy Land travellers in the period before the Constantinian development of the holy places suggests that they were a relatively local bunch from elsewhere round the eastern Mediterranean, Egypt and Asia Minor (and perhaps from further east in the region of Mesopotamia). It goes without saying that with Constantine many more pilgrims, and from further afield, found the way open to the holy places. Not that, as has recently been claimed, the first Christian Roman emperor made pilgrimage 'legal', for it would be hard to document that it had ever been specifically *il*legal;[27] but of course the public demonstration of Christian allegiance – in a whole variety of forms – could now take place in a new climate of imperial protection and privilege: quite literally in a new world. Constantine changed the map of the Roman empire, moving its centre of gravity eastwards when, on 8 November 324, the refoundation of the ancient Greek city of Byzantium as Constantinople was formally inaugurated; but Constantinople's subsequent illustrious history should not blind us to another city 'refoundation' which was high on Constantine's agenda after his arrival in the East, that of Christian Jerusalem. The emperor may even have planned a visit to the Holy Land himself, for in the winter of 324/5 an imperial progress certainly took him as far as Antioch, and he was expected in – though never reached – Egypt. He did not, it seems, get beyond Syria. Our only lingering glimpse of the emperor Constantine as pilgrim *manqué* is to be found in Eusebius' portrayal of the death-bed scene of his baptism, when he reportedly told the assembled bishops that he had once intended to follow the example of Christ and be baptized in the river Jordan.[28] We can only speculate what might have been the impact of the sight of the ruler of the Roman world receiving Christian baptism in the waters where Christ had gone before him.

As it was, Constantine had to content himself with demonstrating the new-found imperial interest in the holy places from a distance. It was probably in the context of the council of Nicaea in the summer of 325 (which included a delegation from Palestine led by the bishop of Jerusalem) that the emperor initiated the demolition of part of the Forum area of Aelia Capitolina, near the exposed rock held to be the biblical Golgotha, which led to the discovery of a tomb hailed as the Holy Sepulchre itself, and the creation over the site of a new sacred precinct, dominated by a basilica which in the emperor's own words was to 'surpass all the beautiful buildings in every city' – and again, 'it is appropriate that the most wondrous place in the world should be worthily beautified'.[29] For Eusebius closely observing the building work, this was the creation before his eyes of the 'new Jerusalem' of the Apocalypse, confronting the destruction of the Old still visible in the shape of the desolate temple rock. Other holy places in and around Jerusalem also now received the *imprimatur* of imperial munificence, as Constantinian churches sprouted on the Mount of Olives, in Bethlehem, and at Abraham's oak at Mamre near Hebron. The new buildings were adorned to imperial specifications, and at public expense, and the emperor's interest was personified by the presence in the Holy Land – if not of himself – then of members of his family: not just the celebrated sojourn of Helena

Augusta, but also the less publicized visit of Constantine's
mother-in-law Eutropia (who it was who instigated the imperial interest in Mamre).[30] This is not the place to rehearse the
details of the central significance of Jerusalem for the political
and ecclesiastical history of Constantine's later years; but it was
clear for all to see by September of 335, when the dedication of
the Golgotha basilica was the occasion for a gathering of
Eastern bishops in Jerusalem, in the presence of a high-ranking
official from the imperial court, which not only celebrated the
thirtieth anniversary of Constantine's rule and the dynastic
prospects for the future, but which was also aimed at setting the
seal on the process of unifying the divided Church of the Greek
East.[31] Jerusalem was intended as the setting for a double triumph for the Constantinian empire: one of imperial longevity
and the future survival of the dynasty, and the other of the
Christian ruler's mission to bring before his God a united
Christendom.

The 'new Jerusalem' thus lay at the heart of a transformed
topography of empire, in some ways displacing even the newly-
founded Constantinople (which had to wait for a 'second instal-
ment' of Constantine's thirtieth anniversary celebrations the
following year). That 'turning inside out' locally reflected by
Christian processions going out to the cemeteries for their martyr commemorations could now be seen writ large on the map
of the Roman empire, as traditional urban centres were passed
by *en route* to a new focus in the Holy Land and Jerusalem.
Within Constantine's lifetime this new perspective of the
Mediterranean world is supplied by the surviving document
known as the *Bordeaux Itinerary*, the record of a journey to
Jerusalem from the Atlantic seaboard of Gaul undertaken in
333. Most of this text is a Roman itinerary (comparable to other
similar survivals) documenting staging posts, overnight stops,
and the distances between them, on the long land journey from
Bordeaux to Constantinople, then on through Asia Minor and
Syria to Palestine; the return journey is similarly catalogued,
from Jerusalem to Constantinople, and back to the west this
time via the Adriatic crossing and northwards through the
length of Italy. The detailed list of places and distances makes
this text an unrivalled dossier of evidence about the organization
of routes and transport in the Roman empire. Yet its roads do
not lead to Rome, as they would have done in earlier times – for
the Bordeaux traveller the former capital is no more than an
unremarked-on stage on the return through Italy. It was
Constantinople which provided the principal break in his journey in both directions, and which he presents as the real start

and finish of his enterprise; but the *goal* of the enterprise was Jerusalem and its surrounding holy places. Here lay the centre of his world, and it is with our traveller's arrival in Palestine that the Roman itinerary becomes the narrative of a Christian pilgrimage.[32]

At this point a bureaucratic list of places and mileages is transformed into the description of a journey into the biblical past, where every location visited and named in Jerusalem and its environs is identified by a scriptural label – it is biblical *historia* run riot. There is more of the Old Testament than the New, hardly remarkable given that most of Palestine's sacred topography – as indeed the habit of visiting biblical monuments – was inherited and appropriated from the Jewish past. The pilgrim beholds all before him – places, monuments, buildings, natural features – as the stage where biblical events had unfolded: even, as I can never resist noting, Zacchaeus' sycamore tree on the way down from the Mount of Olives towards Jericho, or on the Jerusalem side of the Mount the palm-tree whose branches were strewn before Jesus on the first Palm Sunday, or still visible on the temple rock the psalmist's 'stone which the builders rejected', and so on; down to streaks in the rock on the site of the Temple as the remains of the blood of Zechariah. To accuse the Bordeaux traveller of unthinking credulousness in soaking up the tall stories of his guides would be to miss the point of the pilgrim's total immersion in the world of his Bible: even a sceptical Jerome would later concede the genuine piety of 'simple brothers' who believed tales like the bloodstains of Zechariah.[33] In the Holy Land the pilgrim had eyes only for the pages of the Bible brought to reality before him, much as Pausanias' Greek pilgrims were transported back to their roots in myth and history. When he left the contemporary environment of the Roman empire which brought him to the borders of Palestine, he was plunged into a quite different 'time-frame' which all but excluded the present day.

But not completely. There are a few significant post-scriptural intrusions into his field of vision. The site of the Temple, for example, replete as we have seen with biblical associations, also displayed to the pilgrim 'two statues of Hadrian' (actually the second was perhaps an image of his successor Antoninus), and close to these the pierced stone 'which the Jews come once a year to anoint, and they lament with mourning and tear their clothes, and then go away again'.[34] These contemporary reminders of the Roman destruction of Jerusalem and the Jews' annual commemoration of the loss of the Temple were in fact all of a piece for the Christian pilgrim with his biblical world,

confirming before his eyes the fulfilment of Jesus' prophetic
utterances about the fate of Jerusalem: they only added to the
scriptural totality of what confronted him. The same might also
be said of the other (very) contemporary additions to the biblical landscape, the four new basilicas built 'on the orders of
Constantine' which he observed around the holy places; in the
case of two of them, at the Holy Sepulchre and at Mamre, he
added the qualification that the buildings were 'of wonderful
beauty' – just as we have seen Constantine had intended they
should be. To behold, in the year 333, these brand-new imperial edifices embellishing the biblical horizon was surely only to
reinforce the elision of time between scriptural past and Constantinian present. The contemporary triumph of Christianity made
visible by such imperial munificence could be taken to represent
the culmination of the Bible's history: the destruction of the
Temple, the fate of the Jews, and in marked contrast the Roman
emperor building Christian churches to adorn now Christian
holy places, all this was the fulfilment of God's purpose set out
in the Bible – the 'new Jerusalem' come down to earth.

Textual placedness and liturgical time

Some fifty years after the Bordeaux traveller accomplished the
long journey to Jerusalem, another pilgrim from the far west of
the empire arrived in Jerusalem, in the spring of 381. Egeria was
to spend three years based in the holy city, touring the rest of
the Holy Land and going on expeditions to Egypt and Sinai.[35]
Her unquenchable *desiderium* (or longing) to reach holy places,
however inaccessible, permeates the surviving portion of the
travel journal which she composed for her companions back
home in the west, a longing which was for ever overcoming the
drudgery of trudging on foot to mountain summits or embark-
ing on lengthy detours to sacred destinations. Hers is a travelogue
much more personally revealing than the formal detachment of
the Bordeaux traveller's gazeteer. As she herself admits (16.3),
Egeria had an insatiable 'curiosity' about all that she saw – the
details of the mountainous terrain of Sinai, for example, which
open the surviving part of her text – and an urge to miss no
opportunity of visiting places both on and off her route: thus her
return journey was marked by a long diversion from Antioch
into Mesopotamia to be shown the Christian shrines of Edessa
and neighbouring cities, and a shorter detour from Tarsus to
visit the martyr Thecla's shrine at Seleucia. At the time of
writing, having arrived back in Constantinople she is proposing

to set off again into Asia to visit Ephesus and the shrine of the apostle John. Journeying after the Christian past, we are reminded, was never the exclusive preserve of Jerusalem and the Holy Land.

By contrast with the Bordeaux traveller's impersonal record, Egeria's world is crowded with other people. By the 380s her impression of Jerusalem is one full of other pilgrims like herself, come to see and worship at its holy places: the throngs, for example, 'from far afield' (49.1) who assembled every September for the Dedication festival of the Golgotha basilica. Monks, in particular, populate her canvas, which is as much given to holy *men* as it is to holy places: everywhere they are her guides and companions, who offer hospitality and gifts, and who earn her gratitude second only to God for enabling her to complete her *desiderium*. The proliferation of monasticism, in the years between the Bordeaux traveller and Egeria, will have contributed substantially to the expanding map of pilgrim sites in the Holy Land, as local monks took it into their hands to identify and interpret the biblical landscape, and to promote their favoured claims where disputed traditions pointed to alternative sites.[36] For Egeria it was, repeatedly, the monks who 'showed' her the spot where a biblical event was located. Yet they are more than merely intermediaries between the pilgrim and her biblical objective, facilitating the accomplishment of *desiderium* – for the monks are themselves a goal of pilgrimage. By Egeria's day the monastic heartland of Egypt was joining the holy places of Palestine as an essential component of the Christian pilgrim's 'grand tour', as in the other direction Egyptian monks joined the assemblage of those who came to worship in Jerusalem; in the lost section of her itinerary Egeria had described her own visit to the Egyptian Thebaid in search of the monks – prompted again, according to a later source, by her familiarly insatiable *desiderium*.[37] Part of the attraction of the detour to Mesopotamia on her return to Constantinople was the possibility it offered of encounters with monks, 'who are said to be very numerous there and of such admirable life that it can scarcely be told' (17.1); and she counted it a great bonus of her arrival in Carrhae on the occasion of a local martyr festival that it provided an opportunity to meet monks from the surrounding region whom she would not otherwise have seen. For Egeria, the monks and their doings were an extension of the scriptural panorama which she beheld all around her: she longed to see, converse with them and learn of their deeds, just as to look upon the places of the Bible. In the neighbourhood of Carrhae at the

eastern edge of the Roman world Egeria saw in the monks the
successors of Abraham and his family, of whose biblical homeland they were now the present occupants.

As in the Bordeaux text, Egeria's Bible was, quite literally, the
very ground of her travels. It is a happy accident of manuscript
transmission that the surviving portion of her narrative opens,
as she approaches Mount Sinai, with the broken sentence '[the
places] were being indicated to me in accordance with the
Scriptures': such places had become the text of her Bible, in this
case the movements of Moses and his people recorded in the
books of Exodus and Numbers, not least the very bush from
which the Lord had spoken to Moses in the fire, 'which is still
to this day alive and sprouting branches' (4.6). Even Egeria's
enthusiasm could tire of the crowded catalogue of biblical
observation – and the repetition of the verb *ostenderunt* (they
showed):

> and so we were shown *everything* written in the holy books of
> Moses that was done there in that valley which stretches
> before the mount of God, holy Sinai. To write down all these
> one by one is too much, since it is impossible to retain so
> much – but when you [*sc.* her correspondents] read the holy
> books of Moses, you may picture more clearly all that hap-
> pened there. (5.8)

So Egeria's experience, the object of her much-vaunted *desiderium*, was the visual realization of what she read in her Bible, and
like the Bordeaux traveller, but much more expressively, she had
eyes only for the biblical past.

It was a perspective more sharply focused in her case by the
practice of accompanying each stop with a simple act of worship, of which the centrepiece was the reading of the appropriate
extract from the Bible. The appropriateness is reinforced in her
Latin, with the word *locus* serving both for geographical location
and the passage of Scripture. The 'place' on the ground and the
'place' in the Bible amounted to one and the same, and to be
able to unite the two was the devotional climax of Egeria's pilgrimage. Amid, for example, the biblical panorama to be viewed
from the summit of Mount Nebo was the 'locus' of the pillar
which had been Lot's wife, 'a "place" which is also read in the
Bible'.[38] The force of this conjunction between geography and
Scripture seems not to have been weakened in Egeria's eyes by
the fact that the salt-column itself was not visible to her, alleg-
edly covered by the waters of the Dead Sea: it was the *place*
which mattered. When Egeria extended her pilgrimage to non-
biblical destinations, to Thomas' shrine at Edessa, or Thecla's

at Seleucia, the same conjunction of geographical and textual location is preserved in the reading of the relevant *acta* on the spot.

In Jerusalem and its immediate environs, the places which marked Christ's last days on earth and their glorious sequel, the liturgical reinforcement provided by the juxtaposition of physical location and scriptural reading took on yet a further dimension – that of *time*. By Egeria's day the church of Jerusalem had evolved an annual cycle of liturgy which reproduced the gospel narrative in temporal as well as spatial terms, marked by biblical readings which were 'suited to the day and to the place', as clergy and people moved between Golgotha, the Sepulchre, the Mount of Olives, Mount Sion, even out to Bethlehem – matching biblical events not only to their locations but also to the timing of the gospel sequence.[39] It is Egeria, of course, who furnishes our classic description of Jerusalem's stational worship, the prototype of the familiar ecclesiastical year, and her reactions are those of the pilgrim whom the liturgy absorbs ever more completely into the biblical course of events, to see the places and hear the deeds *in situ*. Everything about the worship in Jerusalem struck Egeria as always 'appropriate and suitable for the time and the location' (47.5).

These particularities of place and time, and the immersion into a sacred history unfolding around her, set Egeria in a tradition of pilgrim devotion reaching back at least to Polycarp's devotees in second-century Smyrna. Yet she also stands at the threshold of a new era. On Good Friday in Jerusalem she observed the annual veneration of the wood of the cross. The fragments had to be closely guarded in their rightful place by the bishop and his clergy, to prevent – so Egeria was told – over-zealous worshippers from biting off their own portion of the sacred wood as they knelt and kissed it. The precautions, as we all know, were of little avail. Already by Egeria's time wooden fragments purporting to be those of the true cross were circulating around the Mediterranean world, and they would soon be followed by the dispersal and proliferation of numerous other sacred remains: like those of Stephen, rapidly, after his 'invention' in 415. As these flood gates opened, holy places which had once each been a fixed, unique preserve of a particular sacred history became dislocated from their roots, and were, potentially at least, portable: no longer necessarily outside walls or beyond the world of the present, but carried into the heart of it as the relics and sacred remains passed around the empire and permeated city boundaries to be deposited in churches increasingly *within* urban centres.[40] Antiquity is turning into the Middle

Ages, an appropriate transition to mark the end of 'the beginnings of Christian pilgrimage'.

Notes

1. On Christian and pagan perceptions of place, see S. MacCormack, 'Loca Sancta: the Organisation of Sacred Topography in Late Antiquity' in R. Ousterhout (ed.), *The Blessings of Pilgrimage* (Urbana: University of Illinois Press, 1990), pp. 7–40.
2. K. G. Holum, 'Hadrian and St. Helena: Imperial Travel and the Origins of Christian Holy Land Pilgrimage' in Ousterhout, op. cit., p. 70. The same point is stressed repeatedly in Joan E. Taylor, *Christians and the Holy Places* (Oxford, Clarendon Press, 1993).
3. E. D. Hunt, *Holy Land Pilgrimage in the Later Roman Empire AD 312–460* (Oxford: Clarendon Press, 1982), p. 34ff.; J. W. Drijvers, *Helena Augusta* (Leiden: E. J. Brill, 1992), ch. 5.
4. Hunt, op. cit., pp. 212ff.
5. *Martyrdom of Polycarp* 18, in H. Musurillo, *The Acts of the Christian Martyrs* (Oxford, Clarendon Press, 1972), p. 17.
6. Eusebius, *Church History* 2.25.7; for Africa, Cyprian, *Letters* 39.3.
7. Jerome, *Letters* 107.1; cf P. Brown, *The Cult of the Saints* (London, SCM Press, 1981), pp. 7–8.
8. Cyprian, *Letters* 12.2.
9. *Patrologia Graeca* 46, p. 740.
10. Trans. R. Van Dam, *Saints and their Miracles in Later Antique Gaul* (Princeton: Princeton U. P., 1993), p. 315.
11. Eusebius, *Church History* 4.26.14.
12. *Martyrdom of Pionius* 4.18–20 (Musurillo, op. cit., pp. 141–3).
13. K. G. Holum, in Ousterhout, op. cit., (n. 2), p. 69.
14. For a sceptical account, see Taylor, op. cit., (n. 2), ch. 5.
15. A. E. Harvey, 'Melito and Jerusalem', *Journal of Theological Studies*, n.s. 17 (1966), pp. 401–4, with Taylor, op. cit., pp. 116ff.
16. Origen, *Against Celsus* 1.51, trans. H. Chadwick (Cambridge: Cambridge U. P., 1953), pp. 47–8 (my italics).
17. Hunt, op. cit., (n. 3), pp. 95ff.
18. Eusebius, *Life of Constantine* 3.28.
19. E. D. Hunt, 'Travel, Tourism and Piety in the Roman Empire', *Echos du Monde Classique/Classical Views*, n.s. 3 (1984), pp. 391–417.
20. Origen, *Commentary on John* 6.40.204, ed. Blanc, *Sources Chrétiennes* 157 (Paris: Éditions du Cerf, 1970), p. 286.
21. H. S. Sivan, 'Pilgrimage, Monasticism and the Emergence of Christian Palestine in the 4th Century AD' in Ousterhout, op. cit., (n. 1), pp. 57–8.
22. Eusebius, *Church History*, 6.11.2.
23. Against Taylor, op. cit., p. 311.
24. R. Lane Fox, *Pagans and Christians* (Viking: Harmondsworth, 1986), pp. 166–7.

25. J. Elsner, 'Pausanias: a Greek pilgrim in the Roman world', *Past and Present* 135 (1992), pp. 3–29.
26. Eusebius, *Proof of the Gospel* 6.18.23.
27. J. Wilkinson, 'Jewish Holy Places and the Origins of Christian Pilgrimage' in Ousterhout, op. cit., (n. 1), p. 43.
28. Eusebius, *Life of Constantine* 4.62; for the practice of baptism in the Jordan, see his *Onomastikon*, ed. Klostermann, *GCS* 11.1 (Leipzig: J. C. Hinrichs, 1904), 58.19–20.
29. Eusebius, *Life of Constantine* 3.31. On the Constantinian development of Golgotha, see Hunt (1982), ch. 1; P. W. L. Walker, *Holy City, Holy Places?* (Oxford, Clarendon Press, 1990), ch. 8; R. L. Wilken, *The Land Called Holy* (Newhaven, Yale U. P., 1992), ch. 5.
30. Eusebius, *Life of Constantine* 3.52.
31. ibid., 4.40–7.
32. Trans. J. Wilkinson, *Egeria's Travels* (Revised edn Jerusalem: Ariel, 1981), pp. 153ff.; with Hunt, op. cit., pp. 83ff.; Wilken, op. cit., pp. 109–11.
33. Jerome, *Commentary on Matthew* 23.35, ed. Bonnard, *Sources Chrétiennes* 259 (Paris: Éditions du Cerf, 1979), p. 182.
34. *Bordeaux Itinerary* 591 (Wilkinson, op. cit., p. 157).
35. For English translation and commentary, see Wilkinson, op, cit. The most recent edition is that of P. Maraval, *Sources Chrétiennes* 296 (Paris: Éditions du Cerf, 1982). See also Hunt, op. cit., pp. 86ff.
36. For influence of monks on pilgrimage see H. S. Sivan, in Ousterhout, op. cit. (n. 1), pp. 54–65.
37. See letter of Valerius edited by Maraval, op. cit. (n. 35), p. 338.
38. *Itinerary of Egeria* 12.6; on the conjunction of place, text and worship see J. Z. Smith, *To Take Place: Toward Theory in Ritual* (Chicago: University of Chicago Press, 1987), pp. 88ff.
39. Hunt, op. cit., ch. 5; with J. F. Baldovin, *The Urban Character of Christian Worship* (Rome: Pont. Institutum Studiorum Orientalium, 1987), chs. 1–2.
40. R. A. Markus, *The End of Ancient Christianity* (Cambridge: Cambridge U. P., 1990), ch. 10.

The Sacramentality of the Holy Land: Two Contrasting Approaches

THOMAS HUMMEL

In this essay the practices and attitudes of nineteenth-century English and Russian pilgrims are compared and contrasted. Initially it might seem that the Protestant approach of the typical English visitor had nothing to do with sacramentality, but though the search for reassurance in the face of biblical criticism seems to have played its part, the principal motive appears to have been the desire to have the land of Jesus re-presented or called to mind (both traditional Protestant ways of conceptualizing the Eucharist) as a 'fifth gospel'. By contrast, for the Russian pilgrim what mattered was entering more fully before death into the truths of the liturgy, where the focus was not on the past humanity of Jesus but his divinity and humanity united in an eternal present. The inevitable mutual misunderstandings are fully explored.

In his book *Orientalism* Edward Said explores the extent to which the West has projected upon the Orient its own interpretation rather than discovered the Orient in its own right. If this is true of the Orientalist scholars who strived for a real, objective understanding, how much more so is it true of the pilgrims who come to visit the Holy Land not to discover the real Jerusalem but the Jerusalem of their faith. I propose to look at two sets of these pilgrims – the English Protestants and the Russian Orthodox. I have selected these two because they both travelled to Jerusalem and the Holy Land primarily on a religious quest and because the Jerusalem which they found and their attitudes towards it were shaped by their respective religious perspectives and by their ideals of sacramentality in particular. The focus is narrowed to the nineteenth century because at this time the political situation brought an unprecedented number of both English and Russian pilgrims to Jerusalem. The political conditions which fostered pilgrimages were the colonial expansion of Britain into the Near East (especially Egypt) and the weakening of the Ottoman Empire, thereby encouraging both Britain and Russia to seek a 'presence' in the Holy Land. The technological developments were the deployment of steamships on the Mediterranean routes and the creation of railroads and supporting infrastructure which made travel cheaper, safer and able to be done on a mass scale. These led to tour organizations such as Thomas Cook Tours for the British or the pilgrimage tours organized by the Russian Orthodox Palestine Society.

I intend to pose to each of these two groups – the English Protestants and the Russian Orthodox – a series of questions: 1) who were they and why did they visit the Holy Land? 2) what was their itinerary while travelling in Palestine? and finally 3) what did Jerusalem and the pilgrimage experience mean for them, what religious purpose did it serve?

English Protestants and Russian peasants: an interesting contrast

The majority of English pilgrims were clergymen and their families, as well as people of a travelling and literary bent. In either case their education inculcated in them a great appreciation of the Bible as both a religious document and a work of literature. These pilgrims tended to be of the Protestant wing of the Anglican Church or one of the Protestant dissenting denominations which centred its faith on the Bible as the authorized revealer of God's will to the world. For them salvation came through Christ but Christ was mediated through the Bible. The Holy Land was important as the setting for the Bible – by going there the Bible could be made to come alive. Besides, it had long been a tradition of the English aristocracy to finish their education with a Grand Tour of classical sites. The technological advances in transportation meant that the more religiously serious, if less socially noble, could now afford to visit safely not just the sites of pagan Greece and Rome but of Christianity itself. And if the Romantic poets could rapturously describe the salutary effects of the classical on the nobility of the mind, how much more inspiring would be the places of Jesus' salvific death and resurrection on the sensitive soul. So the English Protestant pilgrim was for the most part an educated, literate person who visited Jerusalem and the Holy Land in order to vivify the Bible as well as to have the adventure of visiting an exotic place.

The Russian Orthodox pilgrims were very different socio-economically from their English counterparts. They were predominantly peasants (eighty per cent were peasants according to the statistics of the Orthodox Society) and illiterate. Those Russians of the literary class who did go on pilgrimage so despised the peasant and his culture that they did not record the peasant pilgrim experience and so we are dependent for information on the reports of the Russian societies in Jerusalem and Western observers.[1] The vast majority of Russian peasant pilgrims were elderly because they went on pilgrimage once the responsibilities towards family, village and Tzar had been fulfilled and they were free to turn their attention towards God and death. This brings us to the major reason for the Russian pilgrims to visit the Holy Land – that is, to prepare for death. They felt that to make a pilgrimage to Jerusalem – especially at Easter when they could be present at the Life-Giving Tomb during the Holy Fire – was both a foretaste of their future home, the heavenly Jerusalem, and a means of grace that would assure their passage. It was both a preparatory visit and a ticket to the New Jerusalem where death would be conquered and peace would reign.

If the Protestants were motivated to visit the Holy Land by reading their Bibles, the Russians were motivated by the Divine Liturgy and their icons. The Divine Liturgy interested people in Jerusalem and the Holy Sites by its constant references to the altar as the Tomb of Christ and the number of interpreters of the Liturgy who understood the actions to be re-presentations of the various acts performed in Jerusalem and its environs about two thousand years previously. So if every Divine Liturgy is a re-enactment of the passion in Jerusalem and every altar the tomb of Christ and every Church a Holy Sepulchre, why not go to the archetype, that very tomb where Jesus' body was buried and from which he arose?

The icon also influenced people to visit the Holy Land because it was so frequently the backdrop to the sacred scenes portrayed. A quick survey of significant Russian icons for the various seasons shows, for example, the baptism of Jesus at the Jordan River, the nativity in the manger in Bethlehem, the transfiguration on Mt Tabor, and the crucifixion in Jerusalem. Since the theology of icons made them windows into the sacred realities they pictured and a source of divine energy, so the Holy Land must be in some way an icon of that which took place there and a valuable window into the sacred mystery of Christ's birth, life, death and resurrection. But even more importantly these places could be, like icons, a door into the realities as well:

in this case the earthly Jerusalem could serve as a door into the heavenly one.

The particular ways that imagery of the Liturgy and the icons shaped the desire to visit the Holy Land differed from person to person but they all agreed upon the efficacy of going – their lives would be transformed and the opportunity to secure eternal life more firmly within their grasp.

The pilgrims' itinerary

Before the increase in pilgrims and the advent of tours many English travelled through Egypt and the Sinai but by the mid-nineteenth century almost every one landed in the traditional pilgrim port of Jaffa. There the act of being decanted from ship to rowboats – and thrown as Mrs King suggested like a sack of potatoes into the arms of waiting Arab sailors[2] – was symbolic for the English of leaving behind the comforts and security of the West for the strange, exotic world of the Orient. Once ashore they were inundated with solicitations from all sorts of people selling everything from hotel rooms to hire camels; so the first job of any pilgrim was to find a responsible dragoman (guide, interpreter) to create a buffer against the merchants and to conduct negotiations on one's behalf. Finding the right dragoman was a difficult undertaking and it was not unheard of for a dragoman to agree to serve and then once on the road threaten to leave the pilgrim stranded unless payment was increased considerably. The usual technique for finding a trustworthy one was to rely upon letters of recommendation written by previous clients. Those on a Cook's Tour were, of course, provided with a dragoman from the organization (in the early years this would have been the American Rollo Floyd), which was one of the great selling points for Cook's.

After a brief stay in Jaffa, the pilgrims would venture to Jerusalem. Before the railroad this took two or three days and before 1846 was usually done in large groups escorted by Turkish soldiers because of the bandits of Abu Gosh. Many commentators write of the colourful spectacles of these groups accompanied by dragomen in their uniforms and the soldiers in theirs, riding a wide variety of animals as they slowly wound their way up the hills toward Jerusalem. The people on the Cook's Tour, called 'cookies' by the others, would be readily recognizable by their more sauntering pace and the tents and field kitchen which accompanied them for the whole journey.

With the advent of the railroad in 1892 the journey was reduced to a few hours but there was a spiritual component which was recognized by the Protestants in the road trip and they lamented its loss. They missed the experience of first seeing Jerusalem in the distance and knowing that a long and tiring trip lay ahead but feeling refreshed and sustained by that brief glimpse of their goal. This was seen as symbolic of faith which, once it is attained, makes the difficulties of life easier to endure because the goal of heaven has been fleetingly seen but not yet realized.

Once they reached Jerusalem these Protestants made for the most modern convents (frequently the Armenian) or the newly developed hotels. Until quite late in the century, however, the Cook's Tour set up tents outside the city walls where they stayed and ate their own imported food. With lodgings and other bodily needs provided, they undertook to see the sights of the city – the Holy Sepulchre, the Dome of the Rock (site of the Temple) once it was open to non-Muslims, the Garden of Gethsemane, the Mount of Olives, etc. They also walked the Via Dolorosa but without the Catholic programme of the stations of the Cross. Having 'done' the sites in Jerusalem they then branched out to visit Bethlehem, Hebron, the Dead Sea (both as a biblical site and a natural wonder), the Jordan River, Nazareth, Mount Tabor, and the Sea of Galilee. In all of this touring, however, it was not the Holy Sites which most excited the interest of these Protestant pilgrims but those landscapes and village scenes which made the Bible come alive. The Mount of Olives where they could 'imagine' Jesus weeping over Jerusalem, or, once it was available, the Garden Tomb where the tomb of Christ could be seen as a tomb and not as an icon-encrusted Church – these were the Jerusalem sites most beloved. The Fountain of the Virgin in Nazareth where Mary could be visualized collecting water with the baby Jesus and the Sea of Galilee where Jesus could be encountered preaching on the shore or calming its waves were among the favourite sites outside the city.

The Church of the Holy Sepulchre, on the other hand, was universally viewed by these Protestants as the most horrific desecration of the site's original purity. Their reactions ran the spectrum. Some accepted the site as possibly genuine, and were even prepared to venerate it as a place sanctified by generations upon generations of believers who worshipped at this spot. But it was not for them where Jesus was to be found. As Bartlett says in his *Walks About Jerusalem*:

For ourselves, we would rather go forth, without the walls, and seek some solitary spot, and endeavour, with the page of the New Testament before us, in silence to image forth the awful scene. But though we cannot be affected by the Holy Sepulchre, as others may, yet when we think of the thousands who have made this spot the centre of their hopes, and in a spirit of piety though not untinctured with superstitious feelings of bygone ages, have endured danger, and toil, and fever, and want to kneel with bursting hearts upon the sacred rock; then, as regards the history of humanity, we feel that it is holy ground.[3]

This is one of the more charitable observations. Others looked at the spot and rejected it outright as did the Reverend W. K. Tweedie: 'Here [in the Holy Sepulchre] superstition runs riot; here the impulses of emotion are substituted for the power of truth; and here Satan has his seat – all amid hideous caricatures of the heavenly plan by which the lost are saved.'[4] He finds it impossible to accept that this was the place of Jesus' resurrection and is confident that further study will show these places with their 'corrupt, superstitious, blasphemous practice of Christianity . . . will be regarded as mere curiosities.'[5]

Why did the Protestants find the Holy Sepulchre so disagreeable? It was approached through narrow streets of importuning merchants and insistent beggars. Once inside the senses were accosted with a virtual cacophony of sights and smells of pilgrims engaged in extravagant and ostentatious piety – kissing stones and icons, crying profusely, rubbing the stone of unction and prostrating themselves before the cross on Calvary. This demonstrative piety was very different from the more attentive piety of their own tradition where listening to sermons and reciting liturgy in well orchestrated unison was the norm; so all this seemed especially jarring to the English Protestant sensibilities. The result was that the Holy Sepulchre became viewed as a modern version of the Israelite Temple of Jerusalem. And just as Herod's temple had been taken over by money changers and robbers and had promoted ritualistic sacrifice instead of moral improvement, so these vices were what many pious Protestants saw in the temple of Jesus' resurrection. Their response was that the temple of Jesus should be cleaned out of these inappropriate elements, just as Jesus had cleaned out the temple in his own day.

Of all the aspects of the Holy Sepulchre which distressed these Protestant visitors, nothing could compare with the Holy Fire ceremony on the Saturday before Easter. Orthodox and Armenian pilgrims with tapers in their hands gathered from all over the world and packed into the church with little or no room to move. The atmosphere became increasingly excited until a bell announced the Patriarch was on his way. Singing and chanting began and local young men began shouting and swinging their bodies in a rhythmic movement. Finally into the church snaked a procession and a way would be miraculously cleared among a crowd that seemed to have no slack to be exploited in this way. The Patriarch and an Armenian Vartabed (monk) then disappeared into the sealed tomb where every light had been extinguished the day before. Shortly, from the little round opening in the tomb emerged a hand with a lighted taper. With no visible source of ignition inside, the burning light was seen as a miraculous sign from God declaring Jesus' resurrection. From person to person the light passed as the pilgrims lit their own tapers and passed it on to family, friends and strangers alike. Hymns, prayer and shouts all intermingled in a cacophony of sounds. Finally the Patriarch came out exhausted and would be carried into the Greek Church. The crowd, meanwhile, became even more excited as everyone pushed and shoved to get the light as soon as possible (for that was seen as a favourable sign). The next task was to bring the lighted taper safely home by navigating through a sea of pilgrims.

It was both the boisterous nature and the miraculous claims of the event which so upset the English. Dean Stanley called it 'probably the most offensive delusion to be found in the world'.[6] C. L. Neil's opinion was that it was 'the greatest fraud of all time'.[7] Treves says of the Holy fire: 'it is only to be equalled with those degrading religious orgies which are to be met with in the forests of savage Africa.'[8] He then quotes from Hichen's account of how 'later on, the ceremony degenerated into a kind of witches' sabbath, the church being deafened by frenzied yells and screams, while its floor becomes a boiling cauldron filled with arms and hands, with writhing shoulders, backs and knees.'[9] The Reverend W. K. Tweedie, whom we have already met, comments after a brief description of the fire ceremony: 'it seems as if Satan were doing his utmost to stamp out the Truth.'[10] The Church of the Holy Sepulchre and its blasphemous rituals were in need of a thorough cleansing as far as these visitors were concerned.

But since they had neither the influence nor the power to clean out the Holy Sepulchre, these Protestant pilgrims left the Holy Sites to their 'deluded' brothers and sought out instead those places where the spirit of Jesus could still be found. This tended to be in the landscape and small villages where the biblical stories could be visualized. Out of the city the landscape could speak with an eloquence that had been drowned out and buried by centuries of misdirected devotion. Sir Frederick Treves commented:

> It was in this plain and unassuming country that the religion of Christ was taught. It was taught in the simplest language, in words that a child could understand, and by means of illustrations drawn from the lowliest of subjects. There was in the teaching no stilted ritual, no gorgeous ceremony, no fore-shadowing of the princely prelate or the chanting priest. It was a religion associated with such sounds as the splash of a fisherman's net in the lake, the patter of the sheep, the call of the shepherd, the tramp of the sower across the fields.[11]

This was the Jesus they sought and it was on Olivet or on the shores of the Sea of Galilee that this image could best be evoked.

By contrast, the itinerary of the Russian pilgrims were much more communal than those of the independent Protestants with their personal guides (with the exception, of course, of those on a Cook's Tour) but within the structure there existed a great deal of freedom. It was a bit like an Orthodox service where there is one major event, the Liturgy, but people are milling around visiting the icons and engaged in their own devotions. And just as in the service, the spirit is communal despite the lack of orchestration and common activity. For most Russians the pil-grimage began not in Jaffa but at home where they began preparing for the trip by hoarding away old crusts of bread which they would use as their staple food on the journey. This bread, when the mould was scraped off and put in water was able to give nourishment in the form of a soup or bread pud-ding. The pilgrim also collected money from friends and fellow villagers to purchase holy souvenirs or to solicit prayers from the monks in the Holy Land for the souls of their loved ones. The pilgrimage itself began with the act of leaving home and many walked to a seaport, stopping at shrines along the way and sleep-ing rough or as the honoured guest of some peasants who felt sheltering pilgrims to be a source of blessing. For those who did not relish the more penitential walk there were inexpensive train fares available for pilgrims or one could ride as a 'hare'. This last category meant squatting rabbit-like for the journey under a seat in the train.

One of the policies of the government was to encourage a domestic steamship industry to challenge the position of the Austrian Lloyds. So most pilgrims travelled on Russian ships packed with pilgrims on deck and in empty holds. The atmos-phere on these ships was tatty and pungent but also strangely calm. Virtually everyone had decided to forgo alcohol until the Easter feast and so despite close quarters the tone was sedate and even religious with groups praying together and singing hymns. Wherever the ship put into port a collection of pilgrims set out to visit any local shrines.

Arriving at Jaffa they were met by representatives of the Society who escorted them to the Greek monastery where the floor of one wing was spread with straw pallets. Once the railroad was built the pilgrim had to decide which route to take, the more comfortable and more expensive train or the cheaper, gruelling but more appropriately penitential trip by foot. Whether by train or foot the pilgrims travelled together and were met again by a dragoman of the Russian Orthodox Society which was responsible for the pilgrims' welfare. This dragoman was usually a physically imposing Montenegrin and he escorted them to the Russian compound and the hostels.

The new arrivals at the hostel were welcomed by those already there like long lost loved ones. As one observer wrote: 'It gave me the idea that after death, when, after life's pilgrimage the Russians come to the judgement seat, there will be such a feeling of brotherhood and affection . . .'[12] Those already resident served as initiators into the customs of the place and acted as guides to the city for those newly arrived. It was also the policy of the hostel to take a deposit of money from each pilgrim as they arrived so that even if they were robbed by bandits or unscrupulous merchants there would be something left for the homeward journey. The hostel also served as a bank to protect money although few peasants seemed to trust any official with their coins.

The Society's tickets to Jerusalem were round trip and good for a year but those who came to Jerusalem for one feast were expected to leave before the next began. There were four major pilgrim feasts during the year. Easter was the most momentous with Ascension Day, the Dormition of the Virgin, and Christmas being the others. The feast around which the pilgrimage centred provided the major focus for the pilgrims' activities but other sites would be sought as well.

The Easter pilgrimage attracted three-quarters of the year's visitors partially because of the favourable weather but primarily because the celebration of Christ's victory over death was the central message of the Church and the major concern of the pilgrim. The Easter pilgrimage centred around the Holy Week events but there were also a number of other edifying excursions. There was a long and arduous journey to Nazareth and the Sea of Galilee, stopping at Mt Tabor of Transfiguration fame along the way. This trip took four days each way and tried to be in Nazareth for the feast of the Annunciation, if Easter were not too close and they could get back to Jerusalem for Holy Week. The pilgrims returning from this journey were met on the outskirts of Jerusalem and accompanied back to the Russian Compound with such joy that many Western observers felt that these were people just arriving from Russia by foot and their bedraggled appearance reinforced such a misapprehension.

There was, of course, also a mandatory trip to Bethlehem to visit the manger and a stop at the tree of Mamre where Abraham lived and gave hospitality to the three angels. In Orthodox iconography Mamre represents both the Trinity and the foretelling of the eucharistic meal; so it was popular with the Russian pilgrims and eventually bought by them as a Holy Site. The most important excursion, however, was to the Jordan River. As part of the preparation for Holy Week it was traditional for the pilgrims to walk to Jericho where they spent the night and then continued on the next day to the spot of Jesus' baptism, an oasis of trees and flowers symbolizing the spiritual fertility of the acts performed there. Before leaving Jerusalem each person would buy one or more burial shrouds to wear as they went into the river in a rite of re-baptism. Thousands lined up on the river bank wearing their white shrouds while the priest blessed the water by dipping crosses into the flowing stream. Once the preliminaries were over they jumped, slipped or slowly lowered themselves into the water, re-enacting their being entombed with Christ so that later when present at his resurrection in Jerusalem they could participate in his victory over death. It all symbolized Paul's assertion that those who are baptized into Christ's death will share his resurrection, but like all Orthodox rites it was not a mere remembrance but an effectual, sacramental symbol which conveyed what it represented.

When the people had bathed and been blessed they emerged from the water and sat in rows along the bank drying out, and filling small water bottles to bring home. Then with their shrouds hung on sticks like flags, the pilgrims meandered down to the Dead Sea to view the place which tradition marked out as the location of the Last Judgement. The priests provided commentary along the way pointing out how the river of life sank into the lake of death, symbolizing the fall of humanity. The imagery reiterated the human need to be lifted up out of the curse of death by the Life-Giving Tomb of Christ back in Jerusalem, to which the pilgrims now slowly returned, stopping at a monastery or two along the way.

For the Russian pilgrim each of these excursions represented an important divine mystery. Bethlehem was, of course, the place of the incarnation. Further to the south was Mamre where the doctrine of the mystery of the Trinity was prefigured in the angelic triumvirate who visited Abraham. At Nazareth and the Sea of Galilee the life and teachings of Jesus were especially celebrated. 'Here He pronounced great truths, here were accomplished most of His miracles, almost the whole gospel was fulfilled on the shores of the Sea of Galilee.'[13] Finally the Jordan river was the place of Christ's baptism and symbolic of the entry of the faithful into the soteriological work of Jesus, which in turn made the Dead Sea, representing death and judgement, something which could be faced without fear. By visiting each of these places in turn the pilgrim followed not only the life of Christ but meditated upon the divine mysteries embedded in each event.

The central feature of every pilgrimage, however, (especially of the Easter one) was the Holy and Life-Giving Tomb of Christ in Jerusalem. The Holy Sepulchre with its village of chapels commemorating the various elements of Christ's passion was primarily home of the two major sites of Christendom – the hill of Golgotha and the Tomb itself. Every pilgrim visited the church but during Holy Week the rites and the place coincided. Graham's description of the Russian pilgrims during that Holy Week was of a lamp before a shrine because they seemed never to sleep and always were prostrate before a holy site.

The Holy Week services began for the pilgrims on the Saturday before Palm Sunday when they gathered in Bethany to march into Jerusalem, picking flowers and waving palms bought from Arab merchants. The occasion was a festive one with stops at various churches along the way and devotions at Bithsphania where the ass's colt used by Jesus was collected by the apostles. A large number went out the night before and slept there in order to be ready for the procession. The event ended with a grand service at the Holy Sepulchre taken by the Patriarch accompanied by bishops and monks in sumptuous vestments. 'The new crystal lamps were lit, and innumerable wax candles; the black depth of the church was agleam with lights like a star-lit sky brought down from heaven. The singing was glorious.'[14]

The Palm Sunday service the next morning was equally impressive with a large olive tree decked out with flowers used in a three-fold procession around the Sepulchre. At the end of the service this tree was cut into bits and distributed to the pilgrims who would cherish it as a relic and take it home in great honour.[15] On the Monday of Holy Week those pilgrims who had not yet visited the Jordan and prepared for their Easter communion did so. On Wednesday many went to the monastery of St Constantine and St Helena to watch the consecration of Holy Oil. Holy Thursday services began an almost twenty-four hour a day regime for the dedicated pilgrim. In the morning in the courtyard of the Holy Sepulchre Church the Patriarch performed the Washing of the Feet service. This act of humility, however, came dear to those who watched because they were charged for the privilege. Later that day the Patriarch took a service at the Sepulchre commemorating Christ's sufferings and where the gospels were read in a multitude of languages. Most Russians, however, would return to the Russian Cathedral for their Communion, preferring the Russian language service.

Good Friday commenced with the service of Great Hours at 9.00 a.m. and High Vespers at 2.00 p.m. At this time most pilgrims began to take up their places in the Holy Sepulchre which they would guard tenaciously until the Holy Fire on Saturday afternoon. For this long vigil, they brought along stools and a small food supply. At 8.30 p.m. on Friday evening the procession and burial of the Holy Shroud commenced. Two by two the clerical participants appeared before the Patriarch for his blessing, and put on their robes when all was ready for the march to Golgotha. There, on a table, would be a shroud with the embroidered picture of Jesus covered with fresh flowers. Over the shroud the Patriarch read the last chapter of Matthew's Gospel. The shroud was then reverently picked up and brought down to the stone of unction where, after being processed around the stone three times, was placed on it and anointed with oils and wrapped in linen. This was accompanied by prayers, psalms and a short sermon. Having prepared the 'body' the shroud was again borne aloft, this time to the Sepulchre where it was laid to rest after processing three times around the tomb. The 'body' was then visited and kissed by dignitaries before being sealed into the tomb and finally around 3.00 a.m. the lights were extinguished. Jesus was in his tomb but the church, filled with expectant pilgrims, was still vibrantly alive.

The Sacred Fire ceremony itself began the next afternoon at 2.00 p.m. The long wait and the preparatory procession all worked together to create heightened expectations and excitement. Graham claims that the Russians did not find the Sacred Fire central to the Easter ceremony and yet they gathered there in great numbers and even had specially constructed lanterns with two chambers each containing a wick so that they could transport the light from the Holy Fire back home. As the Patriarch and the Armenian Vartabed (stripped of all robes so as not to be hiding any flame) broke the seal and entered the tomb the church became filled with a sudden and eerie silence. Would it happen, would the Fire appear, was Christ really risen? These interrelated questions seemed to hang in the air. Finally out of the tomb would come the lighted taper – all was well – the Easter celebrations could begin. At this point 'hundreds of pilgrims produced their black death-caps filled with sweet scented cotton-wool, and they extinguished the candles in them. These death-caps embroidered with bright silver crosses they proposed to keep to their death-day and wear in the grave.'[16]

Following the Sacred Fire came the vigil which ended with the Easter service at midnight in the Sepulchre; then finally the Russians would return for a service at the Cathedral in the compound at 1.00 a.m. Once the service was over the pilgrims went back to the hostel where a real break-fast was waiting for them and the lenten discipline gave way to feasting, dancing and the return of alcohol which most had given up for the duration.

Once the celebrating had subsided the pilgrims began to plan for the journey home. Last minute purchases were made and if possible, shipped. Graham recounts one woman who wanted a nearly life-sized madonna for her village. She persuaded the shopkeeper to give it to her on deposit and then sat with the 'doll' on a well-travelled route and begged for the money to make the purchase – in a few days she paid off her debt. Others picked up olive wood crosses and similar souvenirs, and packed them in sacks to carry on the long trip home. But their hearts, if not their luggage, seemed light because they had been to Jerusalem over Easter and they were the inheritors of a great promise that out of death would come life. Many brought a mark of their new found heavenly status home with them in the form of a tattoo on the arm to demonstrate to all that they were pilgrims – *hajjis*. (This Islamic term was appropriated by Christians to refer to those who had done the Jerusalem pilgrimage.) The true rewards might be heavenly but the status of a returned pilgrim in earthly Russia was not to be dismissed lightly.

Land and sacrament: two understandings

As their accounts and even the titles of their books proclaimed, the Jesus of the land rather than of the sites was of the essence to the English Protestant pilgrims. The 'land' seemed to have served for them two interconnected theological functions. First of all, it was in a very important and also very Protestant way a sacrament, and, second, it was one response to the growing apprehension among the English literary classes that the Bible might not be historically true. Let us look at each of these in turn.

The Holy Land as a sacrament is an idea mentioned by a number of pilgrims and at first glance it seems an odd expression for these Protestants to use. But it is quickly evident that this is a very Protestant, one could say Zwinglian or Calvinistic, understanding of sacrament. That is to say, the Holy Land is understood either to represent or memorialize the scriptural events (Zwingli) or to re-present them in a spiritualized form (Calvin). John Kelman writes in his book *The Holy Land*:

> A journey through the Holy Land may reasonably be in some sort a sacramental event in a man's life. Spiritual things are very near us, and we feel that we have a heritage in them; yet they constantly elude us, and need help from the senses to make them real and commanding. Such sacramental help must surely be given by anything that brings vividly to our realization those scenes and that life in the midst of which the Word was made flesh. The more clearly we can gain the impression of places and events in Syria, the more reasonable and convincing will Christian faith become.[17]

The proper understanding of the Holy Land as sacrament, therefore, is to understand its power to bring the Bible and its stories and characters alive, a dramatic way of impressing them more vividly on the memory and the imagination. In this sense the Holy Land makes Jesus and the Bible real in the same way that Jesus is real in the Lord's Supper – a memory which re-presents him to those who participate in faith.

Another phrase used to express the same idea is that the Holy Land is a fifth gospel or another Bible. J. M. P. Otts, an American with an attitude very representative of the English Protestants, says of his book:

> this is not a 'book of travels', though it never could have been written if the author had not travelled in Palestine; for it is the result of the careful reading of the Gospels in the lights and shades of the land where Jesus lived and taught. When so read it is found that the land of Jesus so harmonizes with the four written Gospels, and so unfolds and enlarges their meaning, that it forms around them a Fifth Gospel.[18]

Otts draws the term from Renan's use of it in his *Life of Jesus* but he gives it a very different meaning because whereas Renan saw the Bible as a human story mistakenly made divine, Otts sees the Bible as a divine story made human and, therefore, fundamentally sacramental. The purpose of the Bible like the Lord's supper is to make Jesus come alive in hearts and imaginations and this is what the Holy Land can do, he feels, to those who approach in faith. Tweedie reiterates this common Protestant theme when he comments: 'A visit to the Land of Promise, so long the land of grief and oppressions, furnishes a thousand proofs and confirmations of the Bible. It is indeed a second Bible, all responsive to the first.'[19]

To the extent that the Bible stands at the centre of the Protestant faith as the primary vehicle of God's communication to his people, then the Holy Land as a revealer of the Bible and its meaning is itself a form of revelation making it a channel of grace – a sacrament. Not everyone can travel to the Holy Land, of course, and it is not necessary in fact, because those who do so communicate their experiences (just as the original disciples did). Through books about the Holy Land and, eventually, photographic essays, even those who have never been pilgrims come to know the Jesus whom the Holy Land proclaims and whose true domain is in the hearts of believers. This is one explanation for the plethora of Holy Land books produced in English in the nineteenth century.

The second theological function which the Holy Land served for Protestant pilgrims was to give renewed credence to the Bible as it came under attack from the corrosive effects of historical and scientific criticism. Initially this may sound like something that has nothing to do with the sacramental, but in due course I hope to show that the reverse was very much the case, that this also has a sacramental dimension. The majority of those visiting the Holy Land as faithful pilgrims were vague about the nature of the criticism being levelled against the Bible. It was not a specific intellectual problem or set of problems that concerned them but rather an uneasiness that the old assumptions no longer stood so confidently against the powers of unbelief. Living as they did in the midst of a century where the 'Bible story' was being dissected into a whole host of different and often contending sources they felt their religious foundations shake as the *Zeitgeist* or 'spirit of the times' seemed to threaten the Bible as the Word of God. In the increasingly industrialized, secularized and science-dominated West the Bible seemed to be losing its credibility. It spoke of miracles and it drew upon exotic and quaint characters and customs. The Bible was becoming increasingly marginalized from real life. To these Protestants the Holy Land seemed to provide 'evidence' of the truth of the Bible because if 'read' properly the topography and geography and study of the customs of the area seemed to make the Bible sensible and therefore credible once again. It was not a specific response to specific attacks but a generalized feeling that because the imagery, customs and atmosphere of the Bible meshed so thoroughly with the Holy Land itself it gave renewed confidence to those who did not want to accept the new sanitized and demythologized Bible being created in Western universities.

This argument that the Holy Land is an 'evidence' for the truth of the Bible and therefore Christianity, is well framed by Otts in his *Fifth Gospel: The Land Where Jesus Lived*: 'Thus the well-informed and observant traveller in the land of the Bible will find more to confirm its truth and unfold its meaning while journeying through the land where Jesus lived, than he could ever gather from whole acres of printed evidences of Christianity.'[20] This evidence for the truth of the Bible, however, unlike the evidential theology developed by John Locke, is not based upon logical argument but upon the persuasiveness of the experience of the Holy Land in relationship to the Bible story and the resonance created by the juxtaposition of the two. In this way it is part of the shedding of the Enlightenment's search for logical evidence and a turn to the more Romantic concern with experiential persuasion.

But there were a minority of pilgrims who were aware of the intricacies surrounding discussion of the nature of the Bible and the type of truth it meant to convey. They had read Strauss' and Renan's *Life of Jesus* and they had read or read about the ideas of biblical interpretation promulgated in *Essays and Reviews*. For these people the collapse of the Jesus Christ of tradition, the Jesus of divine power (miracles) and prerogative (judge), created by historical criticism, challenged them to return to the Jesus of Galilee, the man who stood behind the myth created by nineteen hundred years of obfuscating tradition. Owen Chadwick comments on this in *The Secularization of the European Mind*:

> For some religious men of the middle of the nineteenth cen-
> tury the 'discovery' of the historical Jesus gave a marvellous
> fresh food for their faith. They had known, or had hardly
> known, a remote figure of ritual, and now perceived the
> humanity at last. They felt they could begin where the apost-
> les began – come to a man because he was such a man, and
> then slowly find conviction that more was in him than men.[21]

Well, what better place to begin this search for the 'historical' Jesus than in the Land of Jesus – this same sentiment we have already seen expressed by Kelman when he said: 'It is wiser to abandon the attempt at forcing the supernatural to reveal itself, and to turn to the human side of things as the surest way of

ultimately arriving at the divine.'²² The Holy Land was, therefore for some not only a way to get behind the Jesus of the
Church but also to get behind the Jesus of the Bible to the historical Jesus and confront him personally (as the disciples did)
and out of this personal relationship rediscover the Jesus of
faith.

For those who did not seek to reaffirm the complete iner-
rancy of the Bible nor jettison the Christ of the Gospels for the
historical Jesus there was a reasonable interaction between
geography and Bible which, in a way similar to the symbiotic
relationship between history and the Bible and science and the
Bible, could deepen faith rather than destroy it. Dean Stanley,
the famous biographer of Thomas Arnold, was such a personage. A leading figure of the Broad Church faction his preface to
Sinai and Palestine argued that although it is easy to exaggerate
the significance of the relationship of the sacred history and the
geography of the Holy Land it is, if properly used, a fruitful one.
He goes on to enumerate six specific ways that the connection
can be helpfully employed. In all cultures history is influenced
by geography; so the geography of the Holy Land helps explain
biblical culture and therefore the Bible itself. Second, the geography is bound to affect the images which a culture's poets
and philosophers will use: so knowing the land will be useful
in elucidating their thought. Third, the geography can be used
to explain specific actions such as why Jesus went to certain
towns or why battles were conducted in certain ways. Fourth,
the coincidence of biblical narrative and geography provides a
presumption or evidence of its fundamental truthfulness.

> It is impossible not to be struck by the constant agreement
> between recorded history and the natural geography both of
> the Old and New Testament. To find a marked correspon-
> dence between the scenes of the Sinaitic mountains and the
> events of the Israelite wanderings is not much perhaps, but it
> is certainly something towards a proof of the truth of the
> whole narrative. To match Gospel allusions, transient but yet
> precise, to the localities of their early origin . . . Such coinci-
> dences are not usually found in fables of eastern origin.²³

Fifth, beyond the real connection between the Bible and the
Land rests the ability of the places, especially the landscape, to
vivify the biblical story because 'the framework of life, of customs, of manners, even of dress and speech, is still substantially
as it was ages ago'.²⁴ Finally, 'the whole journey, as it is usually
taken by modern travellers, presents the course of history as a
living parable before us, to which no other journey or pilgrimage

can present any parallel'.[25] Here he means that a pilgrimage
allows the Bible to be seen as a sacred history or drama rather
than a set of proof texts: a drama or holy history where God is
not the history itself but revealed through it. This agreed with
the approach his mentor, Thomas Arnold, took to the Old Testament. For Stanley the ability of the Holy Land to re-present the
Bible stories (the sacramental) and the evidential nature of the
coincidence of land and text are combined with other factors to
underline the value of a pilgrimage for English Protestants – an
opinion which is echoed by other English authors as well.

When we return to the Russian pilgrims we find that they
present a very different picture. They expected the Holy Land to
be like the Jerusalem pictured in the Divine Liturgy and their
icons. And to the extent that Orthodox spirituality had been
shaping the Holy Sites for centuries and turning them into icons
of the spiritual mysteries they represented, these expectations
were largely met. That which most alienated the Protestants is
what the Russian Orthodox both demanded and got. The
Russians wanted the Holy Places to be encrusted with the rites
and iconography of their faith. They did not want the human
Palestine nor the human Jesus – it was the Nestorian heresy to
see the human Jesus separated or separable from the divine. The
Russian peasants, of course did not express their views in these
theological terms but the same instincts were operative.

The Palestine the Russians sought, just as the Jesus they
sought, was a salvific combination of divine and human and it
was this mystery which they came to contemplate, and the sites
were expected to reflect and proclaim that mystery. After all, the
cave within which God became man is not a cave like any other
and in order to proclaim the 'reality' of that holy spot the cave
needed to be marked out and its inherent glory symbolized. It is
extra-ordinary and needs to radiate that status to the blinded
eyes of the world. Similarly, the Life-Giving Tomb of Jesus is not
a mere geographical spot but a place of cosmic significance. The
world of divine reality broke in at this spot and the structure
of reality – its ontological nature – was altered forever. Such a
reality is not adequately represented by a tomb which looks
like a tomb because then the reality of this Life-Giving Tomb is
hidden rather than revealed. So the Tomb of Christ, like the
manger, needs to be made into an icon where the objective is
not a pedantic concern to preserve the past but rather the desire
to unmask underlying spiritual truth and thereby put the worshipper in contact with the divine energy that lies within and
behind the object.

The Protestants saw the Holy Places and were distraught at

how they had been altered from the simplicity of the biblical picture, whereas the Orthodox were uninterested in keeping the spot historically pure. It was not the spot itself that is holy but what happened there that made it holy: so it is the significance of the spot that is represented. One example of this interconnection between the icons, the holy places and the theological truths represented can be seen in a crucifixion icon of around sixteen hundred created by the Russian School.

In this icon Christ crucified stands in the centre of the composition, with the two Marys on one side and John and a soldier on the other. At the base of the hill of Calvary is a fissure below which opens up a gap containing the skull of Adam and then widening into a deep black pit. Behind Jesus is a crenellated building or wall. The informed reader of this icon immediately understands the symbolism of Jesus being crucified over the skull of Adam because it is as the New Adam that he will re-create the world. And the black pit of hell is where the power of the cross will reach when the resurrected Christ visits that spot to bring life out of death. The walled Jerusalem which is both the city of sorrow and the city of joy represents the transformation of the human community into the divine community.

When the observer of this or any one of thousands of icons like it visited Jerusalem what did they find? They discovered Calvary to be a small hill supplanted with an icon of the Crucifixion; below it they saw a fissure and would have had the skull of Adam pointed out to them. They also saw the edicule or little building of the Holy Sepulchre, shaped much like the backdrop of this icon, standing in the background. The story told in the icon and the story told at the Holy Site would connect because they both drew upon a common iconographic vocabulary and because behind both of them was the theological truth that Jesus' crucifixion had redeemed the sons of Adam from death. The icons, the Divine Liturgy and the Holy Sites were all proclaiming one essentially interconnected gospel for those with eyes to see, for those with ears to hear and for those with faith to understand.

Similarly, the Protestant search for the historical Jesus, or at least the human Jesus which motivated so many of the English pilgrims, was considered by the Orthodox as a misconceived project. In his *The Mystical Theology of the Eastern Church*, Lossky says of the Western interest in the historical Jesus:

> The 'historical Jesus Christ', 'Jesus of Nazareth', as he appears to the eyes of alien witnesses; this image of Christ, external to the Church, is always surpassed in the fullness of

the revelation given to the true witnesses, to the sons of the Church, enlightened by the Holy Spirit. The cult of the humanity of Christ is foreign to Eastern tradition; or rather this deified humanity always assumes for the Orthodox Christian that same glorious form under which it appeared to the disciples on Mt Tabor.[26]

So, whereas many Protestants, especially in the latter half of the nineteenth century, were searching for the human Jesus, the Orthodox were in quest of the equally biblical Jesus – the one of the Transfiguration and St John's Gospel – the Jesus whose divinity shone brightly through the flesh for those with the eyes of faith.

The Protestants were also acutely sensitive to the problems presented to the faith by an awareness of human historicity. David Hume's *Enquiry Concerning the Human Understanding* had questioned whether any historical testimony could be an adequate reason for believing miracles, and historical studies were beginning to alert people to the historical nature of Christian doctrine and of the Bible itself. The corrosive effects of this developing historical consciousness on confidence in the truth of the Bible was for many of crisis proportions. These Protestants realized that as residents of nineteenth-century Britain their connection to the Jesus of first-century Palestine was problematic. The traditional route to Jesus was through sacred text – the Bible – but that was becoming increasingly difficult as confidence in the historical accuracy of the text was questioned. The other route was that of religious experience where the Jesus who transcends time is available through faith. But this Jesus, disconnected from history, became a mythic Jesus who seemed to lack reality. So for these Protestants the Holy Land was a place to try and recapture the historical Jesus or at least the biblical Jesus and then, like the disciples, confront him and hopefully like them find faith.

For the Orthodox, however, there are places where the eternal and the temporal intersect and where in a partial way the human with all its faults, sins and limitations can partake in the heavenly realm. Most specifically this takes place in church during the Divine Liturgy. But if the Divine Liturgy is in its way the manifestation of the New Jerusalem it is also true that at Easter in the Holy Sepulchre the Old Jerusalem and the New Jerusalem are united in an exceptional way. What happens is not just the representation of the first Easter, although it exists and is important; nor is it that the eschatological community is gathered around the heavenly throne in an ecstasy of praise, although that is present; and it is not merely the experiencing of the presence of Christ in the Eucharist with the effects on the body and soul that it produces. In fact all of these elements are combined – past, present and future; human and divine; history and eternity – in one glorious place and time. The Russian Orthodox pilgrim did not worry about problems of historicity because God had broken through time and finitude so that we could do the same.

One way of seeing this Orthodox transcendence of time into an eternity where everything is simultaneously present is to look at the liturgical texts for the various feast days. For example the text for Good Friday is: 'Today he who is by nature unapproachable, becomes approachable for me, and suffers his Passion, thus setting me free from passion.' And the Annunciation text reads:

> Today is revealed the mystery that is from all eternity. The Son of God becomes the Son of man, that, sharing what is worse, he makes me share what is better. In times of old Adam was once deceived; he sought to become God, but received not his desire. Now God becomes man, that he might make Adam God . . . O marvel! God is come among men: he who cannot be contained is contained in a womb: the timeless enters time.

Each of these texts is in the present tense – expressing the conviction that they are not events relegated to the past and therefore inaccessible except through memory. These mysterious acts of God are in fact eternally present and available to be entered into through the Church. So the Liturgy, the icons and the Holy Places are not only windows into that eternity but doors as well, because one can pass over the threshold and what one sees can also be participated in. So that which is represented and symbolized is also, to the faithful, available because it is re-presented, made present once again.

It is this effectual nature of the Holy Places as channels of grace which distinguishes the Orthodox view of the Holy Land from the English Protestants and explains why the Russians are so determined to go there. In his article on Byzantium Henri Gregoire sums up the spirit which motivated the Russian pilgrims:

> Christians were Christians only because Christianity brought them liberation from death. If one would penetrate to the heart of Eastern Christianity one must be present on the night when the Easter liturgy is celebrated; of this liturgy all other rites are but reflections or figures. The three words of the

Easter *troparion* – the Easter hymn – repeated a thousand times in tones ever more and more triumphant, repeated to the point of ecstasy and of an overflowing mystical joy – 'By His death he has trodden death beneath his feet' – here is the great message of the Byzantine Church.[27]

And to be able to participate in the celebration and re-presentation of that victory over death on the very site where it happened so that the victory would be theirs as well, this was what the Russian pilgrims sought in Jerusalem. The importance of Jerusalem, therefore, was as a source of salvific grace and as a journey to the earthly Jerusalem in preparation for the journey to the heavenly one.

Both the English Protestants and the Russian Orthodox pilgrims of the last century were in search of Jesus. The Protestants saw the Jesus of history found in the Bible, and the Orthodox embraced the Jesus who transcends time through the liturgy. For Orthodox and Protestants, Jerusalem and the Holy Land were instrumental in vivifying the Bible or intensifying the symbolism of the liturgy and the icons. Neither community appears to have understood the piety, the iconography, the sacramentality, the theological fears or the theological paradigms of the other.

But to say that the English Protestants and the Russian Orthodox are two communities speaking different theological and iconographic languages is only part of the story. The Russian Orthodox might emphasize the sacred power, the iconic identification of the place with the event, the symbol with the archetype, but it is still the biblical story – the narrative – which makes sense of it all. And it is the biblical story which is read or liturgically represented by the sites. Similarly, as much as the Protestants attempt to trivialize the significance of the place, they are none the less enthralled by the power of the land to vivify the story. They assert every place has equal access to the divine grace but they endure hardship to travel to the Holy Land, they recommend it as part of a theological education, they make the experience available to those at home through book and picture, and they call it the 'fifth gospel'. The power of the place seizes them and they are bereft of a suitable language to express that experience adequately; their sacramentality is not expansive enough for the task.

This is not to ignore or devalue the wide gulf that separates the two communities' view of the Holy Land. But it is to claim that they are not, to use the terminology of Thomas Kuhn, operating from two incommensurate paradigms. Although they may rarely understand each other, the English Protestants and the Russian Orthodox pilgrims in the nineteenth century are not in fact speaking two languages incomprehensible to each other. They are communicating in two dialects of the same language, sharing the one underlying faith in the person whose earthly home they find so supernaturally enchanting.

Notes

1. For example, S. Graham, *With Russian Pilgrims to Jerusalem* (London: Macmillan), 1913.
2. Mrs A. King, *Dr. Liddons' Tour in Egypt and Palestine in 1886* (London: Longmans, 1891), p. 24.
3. W. H. Bartlett, *Walks About the City and Environs of Jerusalem* (London: Virtue, 1844), p. 176.
4. W. K. Tweedie, *Jerusalem and its Environs* (London: Nelson, 1859), p. 81.
5. ibid., p. 81.
6. A. P. Stanley, *Sinai and Palestine in Connection with their History* (London: Murray, 1864), p. 469.
7. C. L. Neil, *Rambles in Bible Land* (London: Kelly, 1905), p. 134.
8. F. Treves, *The Land that is Desolate* (London: Smith, Elder and Company, 1912), p. 77.
9. ibid., p. 77.
10. Tweedie, *Jerusalem*, p. 83.
11. Treves, *Land*, p. 87.
12. Graham, *With Russian Pilgrims*, p. 85.
13. Khitrof as quoted in Graham, op. cit., p. 212.
14. Graham, op. cit., pp. 242–3.
15. ibid., p. 243.
16. ibid., p. 290.
17. J. Kelman, *The Holy Land* (London: Black, 1902), p. 3.
18. J. M. P. Otts, *The Fifth Gospel: The Land Where Jesus Lived* (Edinburgh and London: Oliphant, 1893), p. 5.
19. Tweedie, *Jerusalem*, p. 102.
20. Otts, *The Fifth Gospel*, p. 31.
21. W. O. Chadwick, *The Secularization of the European Mind* (Cambridge: Cambridge University Press, 1975).
22. Kelman, *The Holy Land*, p. 3.
23. Stanley, *Sinai and Palestine*, pp. xix–xx.
24. ibid., p. xxiv.
25. ibid., p. xxvi.
26. V. Lossky, *The Mystical Theology of the Eastern Church* (London: Clarke, 1957), p. 243.
27. H. Gregoire, *Byzantium: An Introduction to East Roman Civilization*, ed. N. H. Baynes and H. St L. B. Moss (London: Oxford University Press, 1948), pp. 134–5.

PART TWO:
SACRED ART

Art may seem initially even less a matter of movement and measure than place. But, just as we saw the notion of place as static to be a misconception, at least where sacramentality is involved, so here with art it is proper to insist not only that measure through definition and form is of the very essence of the artist's craft, but also that its sacramental dimension necessarily introduces the question of movement. For art can only properly be described as sacramental in so far as it draws the observer into and then beyond itself, to God.

Each of the three essays which follow illustrate how this is so. Thus, whether we take the Lindisfarne Gospels, the Ruthwell Cross or Robert Campin's triptych, none was intended to be a thing of beauty in and for itself. Gospel books were adorned with all the infinite care Janet Backhouse describes because that way they could more effectively communicate and participate in the infinite care which God showed in becoming a human being in Christ. Even so, little flaws were left as a reminder that such participation could, at least in this life, never be complete. Then again, as Rosemary Cramp demonstrates, the carved crosses of the Anglo-Saxon world spoke of a world reconciled, of natural and supernatural at one, something which must ultimately be true if all the created order draws its gift of life from a single source in God. Finally, if the second essay looked at a vision writ large, it is to detail that Jan Rhodes draws our attention with her contribution: to the way in which, once a particular conception of the macrocosm has established itself, it will be natural to expect this equally to be reflected at the level of the microcosm. Accordingly, if for the Christian the incarnation really is the clue to all reality, should we not, as the medieval mind argued, find the lessons of that sacramental involvement of God in our world reinforced wherever we turn our eyes, whether it be explicitly in the sacrament of the altar or implicitly in phenomena as varied as pelicans, wine-presses, fountains and charters?

'Outward and Visible Signs': the Lindisfarne Gospels

JANET BACKHOUSE

The Lindisfarne Gospels is the finest of Britain's old books, probably dating from not long after St Cuthbert's death in AD 687. It was painstakingly and beautifully illustrated by Eadfrith, himself in due course also Bishop of Lindisfarne. Even with the aid of only an occasional illustration, Janet Backhouse's account of his work powerfully evokes the richness of its content. As a historian she is naturally reluctant to wade too deeply into theological waters; even so, she hints (on more than one occasion) at two factors which could more than justify the description of Eadfrith's work as sacramental. The first is the way in which art is used to enhance the value of religion; for Eadfrith his work is a labour of love that by sharing in the communication of the gospel shares in the incarnation itself. Then, second, by involving the animal world in its pages – even a cat's whiskers – he brings all creation into that gospel as part of God's wonderful communication of himself through the material world.

Their general character

Durham Cathedral and the Lindisfarne Gospels, two of the supreme masterpieces of English medieval art, were created within seventy-five miles of each other, each dedicated to the honour of St Cuthbert as well as to the glory of God. They are however separated by almost exactly four centuries in time, and mirror the ideals, philosophies, and spiritual needs of two very different periods in history. The cathedral, juxtaposed with the Norman castle of its bishops, reflects the essential power relationship between Church and State in post-Conquest England, sometimes in alliance, sometimes in conflict, always in some degree politically aware. The Gospels comes from the first generations after the Conversion – from the end of the seventh century – only about sixty years after St Aidan established the first Christian monastery on Holy Island. The religion which he and his companions were preaching to an illiterate pagan people was book-based and the Lindisfarne Gospels is studiedly designed to make that basic book as visually impressive as possible, gleaming with precious metals and gems on the outside and decorated inside with lively patterns and vibrant colouring. In what follows I offer some commentary on the splendid visual imagery employed in the Lindisfarne Gospels.[1]

The very first image which confronts the eye is the cross-carpet page (so called for obvious reasons) with which the manuscript begins. It is the simplest of five such pages in the book and introduces St Jerome's letter to Pope Damasus, at whose command he had carried out in the late fourth century the revision of the Latin Bible text which, known as the Vulgate, was to become standard throughout the Western church. The carpet page is accompanied by a decorated initial page, also the simplest of its type in the manuscript and lacking the ornamental framework which contains the elaborate sequence of display capitals in which the first words of text are written at the beginning of each of the four Gospels.

The opening of each gospel is marked by similar pages and by a miniature of the appropriate evangelist. To provide an introductory flavour of these major pages I have chosen to describe the sequence at the beginning of Mark. First we have the figure of the evangelist, accompanied by his traditional symbol, a winged lion which is blowing a trumpet. The figure of the saint is clearly derived from a late antique source and is labelled with St Mark's name in transliterated Greek. The lion by contrast is labelled in Latin, '*imago leonis*'. Both figures are reasonably true to life and it is interesting to note that the lion is painted in a very naturalistic tawny colour which is not featured elsewhere in the manuscript. Whether or not this is intentional and, if so, what was the source of the artist's information, is not known.

Each of the evangelists faces a blank page, on the other side of which we find the cross-carpet. In Mark the design, although based on a cross shape, is less obviously inspired by a crucifix than was the first one to which I referred. The greater part of the page is filled with purely abstract interlace and with step patterns, though there are panels of spiral designs and others of zoomorphic ornament. Opposite the carpet there is again a

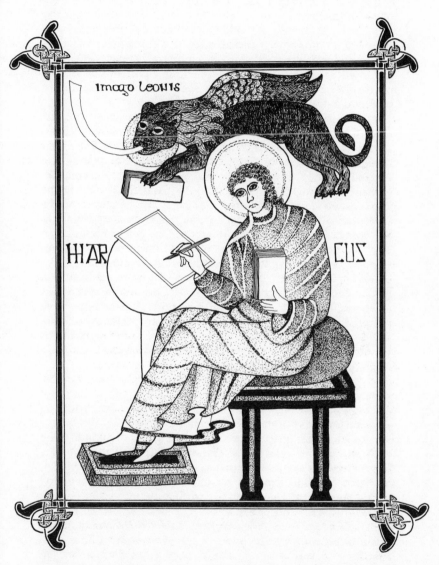

The Evangelist Saint Mark from the Lindisfarne Gospels. He is accompanied by his symbol, a winged lion blowing a trumpet and carrying a book ('imago leonis').

major initial page, on which the opening words of the gospel are written out in ornamental capitals. The colouring and elements of the ornament are chosen with care to complement the design of the opposing carpet page. Because Mark is so near the middle of the volume, this opening has been exposed for display much more than any other and has suffered a certain amount of fading and damage over the decades. It is some measure of the quite extraordinary state of preservation of the manuscript that it should seem worthwhile commenting upon this which, in most other books of comparable age, would look like almost perfect condition.

As well as the decorated pages introducing each gospel, the manuscript contains sixteen pages of Eusebian canon tables enclosed in elaborate and ingenious decorated arcades. The rather unalluring columns of figures of the tables themselves were devised in the early fourth century by Bishop Eusebius of Caesarea to provide a system whereby parallel passages in the four gospels could be located readily. It was not long before enterprising book painters found ways of integrating these into the overall decorative scheme of any de luxe gospel manuscript. The slender and elegant arcades of the Lindisfarne Gospels run in pairs, one opening having the shafts of the column and the bow of the arch filled with interlaced birds, while the head and foot of each column contains simple ribbon interlace; the next reversing the design, so that column and arch have the simple ribbons; and the odd shapes top and bottom contain acrobatically contorted animals. Variable combinations of colours add to the attractions of this delightful sequence of pages. It will help to give some idea of the minute scale of the decoration if I say that the space occupied by the animal motif at the head of any column is just one inch across at its widest topmost point and three-quarters of an inch in height, which says much for the extreme expertise of the artist's technique.

The last main element of the decoration of the Lindisfarne Gospels is a fine selection of minor initials used to introduce lesser elements of the text, such as prefatory matter before each of the gospels. The text and the initial are designed as an entity, the outline of the one modified to fit into the outline of the other. This is the sort of detail that reveals a single mind behind both script and decoration through the whole length of the manuscript, with the exception of one or two quite minor contributions such as colour patches or short titles. One cannot fail to appreciate the clear regularity of the script of the original Latin text, which is written out in a very good quality almost black ink. Between the lines of the original, added in the mid-tenth century, lies the smaller and less regular Old English text. The addition of a gloss to such a masterpiece would probably be regarded today as a form of vandalism. It is however of great interest in its own right for it offers, word by word, the earliest surviving version of the gospel text in any form of the English language. Ironically it may have been this gloss rather than the status of the manuscript as a work of art which saved it from destruction when it was removed from Durham at the Reformation. The study of the Anglo-Saxon language was high in favour with the antiquaries of Tudor England and a number of words in the first attempt at an Anglo-Saxon dictionary in 1567 are credited to the Lindisfarne Gospels.

Date and origin

Not the least amazing thing about the Lindisfarne Gospels is the very exact information which we have about its date and place of origin. We can be very precise indeed as to place since there is no apparent reason to doubt that it was indeed made in the monastery of Lindisfarne on Holy Island and, even if we still do not know with absolute certainty where that monastery stood, the possible variants do not extend over more than a few acres of land defined by sea and sand. For this precise information we are once again indebted to the 'vandal' who added his Anglo-Saxon gloss between the lines of the original Latin text in the middle of the tenth century. At the same time he added the famous colophon in which all the craftsmen who contributed to the book, including himself, are named. Just where he got the information he did not record. Possibly it was written down in connection with a cover or box attached to the Gospels and now lost. Or, perhaps more likely he derived it from an oral tradition passed from generation to generation among the guardians of the relics of St Cuthbert during their peregrinations through the north of England. Whatever his source, he named four names – Eadfrith Bishop of Lindisfarne, who made the book in honour of God and of St Cuthbert and of the other Lindisfarne saints, Ethilwald Bishop of Lindisfarne who bound it, Billfrith the anchorite who ornamented it with precious metals and with jewels, and the writer himself, Aldred, a most unworthy priest (he says!), who afterwards became provost at Chester-le-Street, where the community of St Cuthbert resided from 883 until the last years of the tenth century.

Both Eadfrith and Ethilwald are well documented in other sources, notably the writings of the Venerable Bede. Both were apparently monks of the Lindisfarne community and Ethilwald at least had been personally acquainted with St Cuthbert, to one of whose miracles he was a witness. The two men were successive Bishops of Lindisfarne, Eadfrith succeeding Cuthbert's immediate successor Eadberht, who died in 698, the year of Cuthbert's translation. When Eadfrith died in 721, Ethilwald, who had been prior of Melrose since 698, took his place. Aldred's words seem to leave no doubt that Ethilwald was personally responsible for making the binding of the manuscript 'as he well knew how to do it'. It has long since vanished, maybe removed at the Reformation for the sake of Billfrith's precious ornaments. The only contemporary evidence we have which may suggest how it could have looked is the binding on the tiny Gospel of St John found in St Cuthbert's coffin in 1104.

Eadfrith, who is credited with making the manuscript himself, is a most interesting character who emerges as the prime architect of the cult of St Cuthbert at the time of the saint's translation in 698. There is no particular reason to doubt that he was the responsible craftsman. Certainly in the twelfth century, Symeon of Durham believed it to be so. Careful analysis of the pages of the manuscript shows that both script and decoration are by a single hand, as we have already said. On only a few pages in the book can the text of the Lindisfarne Gospels be admired as its scribe originally wrote it, before the intervention of Aldred's gloss. These are the pages giving lists of gospel readings for various feast days, which was of no particular interest to the glossator, but at one point offering a very interesting indication of the possible source of Eadfrith's textual exemplar. The feast of St Januarius of Naples is included, which suggests that the book which he was copying came from southern Italy. His gospel text is in fact a particularly pure one. The most likely source for a south Italian copy of the gospels in Northumbria at the end of the seventh century is Benedict Biscop's double foundation, Wearmouth-Jarrow, home of the Venerable Bede, where we know there were many fine manuscripts imported from Italy. It seems likely that the two-column arrangement of the manuscript's text may also have been inspired by Mediterranean models. The scriptorium of Wearmouth-Jarrow went even further in emulating these imported manuscripts in the late seventh century when it produced its own three great Bibles, the Codex Amiatinus and its sisters, which are written out in a script so completely saturated in the late antique manner that only during the present century have scholars come to accept that the work is not Italian but English. Wearmouth-Jarrow seems also to have provided a model for at least one of Eadfrith's evangelist portraits. The miniature of St Ezra in his study in the

Codex Amiatinus shares its figure with the miniature of St Matthew in Lindisfarne, though the finished pages make such very different impressions on the viewer.

All four of the Lindisfarne evangelists are apparently indebted to some form of late antique model. The pages of pure decoration are, by contrast, thoroughly insular in concept, with their enormously complex fields of interlacing patterns and great variety of motifs, both abstract and zoomorphic. The Matthew carpet page is the best known and most often reproduced because the cross shape on which it is based is so very successful. The variations in texture suggested by the different patterns are very striking and the colours selected blend together and complement each other most sensitively. The palette of the Lindisfarne Gospels is unusually extensive, embracing pigments derived from sources animal, vegetable and mineral, a number of which could not have been produced within the British Isles and must have been imported from great distances. The most exotic is the blue of lapis lazuli, the only known source of which would have been the Himalayas. A detail from this page reveals one of Eadfrith's little eccentricities which have given rise to much speculation. If you look very closely into the pattern you will find that its perfection is broken by the introduction of a tiny spiral ornament on the knee joint of one of its exotic birds, though all the rest are simply filled with colour. This can only be deliberate and it is possible that our artist, like the weavers of some oriental carpet patterns even today, was taking pains to avoid absolute perfection in his artistic creation, as this would be appropriate only to the Almighty.

Opposite this carpet page comes the initial page to Matthew, the book of the generations of Christ, with Aldred's gloss squeezed off the body of the page into the margin by the sheer exuberance of the design. Here again an imperfection has been introduced. The last two letters of the first line have been left uncoloured and the ground of red dots against which they are placed is not completed. It certainly could not have been overlooked by the perfectionist who was responsible for the overall design of the page. Matthew also contains a second initial page introducing the Christmas Gospel, which Eadfrith has conceived as a quite extraordinary *tour de force* of cascading spiral designs. Here again we encounter a line of display capitals, immediately below the main initial letters, which have not been filled in with colour, though the remainder of the page is highly finished.

It would thus appear that Eadfrith had a very clear philosophy for what he had undertaken. He had procured a particularly

The Evangelist Saint Matthew from the Lindisfarne Gospels. He is accompanied by his symbol, a winged man blowing a trumpet and carrying a book ('imago hominis'), and by a mysterious figure which may perhaps be intended to represent Christ.

good gospel text from an outside source. It was to be written out on the finest of vellum, in the best of ink, and decorated to the very highest standard of which he as an artist was capable, using the widest possible range of colours procurable. But it is certainly arguable that as an artist he did not presume to claim total perfection for his human endeavours. In his colophon Aldred specifically associated the manuscript with St Cuthbert, whose relics were raised to the altar at Lindisfarne in March 698. This would indeed have been an appropriate occasion to be marked by the provision of new and splendid gospels. But such a book as this must have been an addition to the treasures of the Church, for it is inconceivable that Northumbria's premier monastery could have lacked a copy (indeed, many copies) of holy writ, which fulfilled a liturgical as well as purely academic role in the seventh century Church. This book is very deliberately a show piece, on a par with the most luxurious of altar vessels.

St Cuthbert died in his hermitage on the Inner Farne in the early hours of the twentieth of March, the Wednesday of the fourth week in Lent in the year 687, after a final illness which had lasted some three weeks. His death was expected and members of the Lindisfarne community were with him on the island during his last hours. As soon as he had breathed his last a message was flashed by torches across the sea to a watcher waiting on Holy Island, six and a half miles up the coast. The night must have been a clear one for the flames to be seen. Later on the same day the saint's body was taken in a boat to the monastery and buried in a stone sarcophagus on the right of the altar.

There was never the least doubt of Cuthbert's sanctity, even within his lifetime. According to Bede, he himself warned his brethren of the troubles they would endure from those who would flock to his tomb, were he to be buried at Lindisfarne rather than in the isolation of the Inner Farne. Events followed a predictable pattern. Eleven years passed before the elevation of his relics to the altar itself, at the end of which his bones might have been expected to appear dry, 'the rest of the body, as is usual with the dead, having decayed away and turned to dust', as Bede puts it.[2] During these years some preparations were made to improve the setting of his shrine and the wooden coffin which is still treasured in the cathedral must have been carved. The decision to translate Cuthbert's relics was finally taken and his tomb was opened on the anniversary of his death in 698. The body was found incorrupt, in final confirmation of his sainthood, and was duly raised to the altar.

I have often wondered – why 698? Why not, for example, the tenth anniversary of his death in 697? Or perhaps 700, the year marking the opening of a new century? There are three quite interesting points to favour the year which was in fact chosen. In the first place, it *was* in some sense a tenth anniversary, for the first year after Cuthbert's death is the mysterious 'lost' year, best forgotten, during which it seems that Wilfrid held his uncomfortable sway over Lindisfarne. Second, it must have been fairly obvious in the spring of 698 that Bishop Eadberht was dying. His body occupied Cuthbert's original burial place only weeks after the saint had vacated it. This suggests that it may have been regarded as the official episcopal tomb, and it is worth noting that, according to Symeon of Durham, the bones of Eadberht, Eadfrith and Ethilwald were removed from Lindisfarne along with the relics of St Cuthbert when the community fled from Viking raids in 875. Most interesting, however, is the fact that the Easter cycle in 698 exactly replicated that of 687. The day of Cuthbert's translation was not merely the anniversary of the day of his death and burial. Liturgically it repeated it in every way.

Eadfrith succeeded Eadberht as Bishop of Lindisfarne less than seven weeks after the translation of St Cuthbert. During the same year Ethilwald left for Melrose, where he remained for the next twenty-three years. It seems more likely that the Lindisfarne Gospels was the product of the period leading up to the translation, when both men were still in the monastery, than of the years while Eadfrith was Bishop. In any event, the manuscript cannot be later than Eadfrith's death in 721. Eadfrith did, however, devote much of his episcopal energy to the promotion of St Cuthbert's cult. In particular, all three of the lives of Cuthbert, the first composed by an anonymous monk of Lindisfarne very soon after the translation, are addressed to him. Both the others, one in verse dating from about 705 and the other in prose, probably written toward the end of Eadfrith's life, are by the Venerable Bede, who obtained raw material direct from Lindisfarne and whose draft prose life was reviewed and debated by the monks, including those who had known the saint, before being approved for circulation.

The animal creation adds its praise

I want to remark on just one aspect of the lives of St Cuthbert, the animal stories, because I think this has a direct relevance to appreciation of the decoration of the Lindisfarne Gospels.

Cuthbert is the only truly English saint to whom a number of miracles concerning animals are attributed, though these are fairly common in Celtic hagiography. Bede's prose life which, as we have seen, was based on material approved by Cuthbert's own contemporaries, contains just five such incidents, two of them repeated from the slightly earlier anonymous life. All the beasts concerned are perfectly credible in the context of Northumbria. Cuthbert is provided when in need with food, once through the intervention of his horse and once by a fish eagle which drops its catch in his path. A pair of little sea otters warms and dries his feet after he has been praying in the chilly waters off the sea off Coldingham. Birds which rob his corn field depart at his exhortation. Finally, birds which have been plundering the thatch of his little guest house on the Inner Farne for their nests, duly rebuked, make amends by offering him a piece of lard with which subsequent visitors were able to grease their boots. Michael Lapidge has quite recently discovered another even more locally flavoured reference in an unedited manuscript of the verse life.[3] It tells us that the seals, weighed down with the burden of pregnancy, did not dare to drop the offspring of their womb unless the saint had blessed them beforehand with his holy right hand.

The content of some of Eadfrith's ornamental pages strongly suggests that he personally was fully alert to the wildlife around him. Some extraordinarily lifelike bird and animal forms are incorporated into the decoration of the Lindisfarne Gospels. The Matthew initial for example has a fine quartet of what looks remarkably like ducks where the lines of the letters cross. Animal forms had always been a characteristic of Anglo-Saxon ornament but it is only in this manuscript that birds begin to play a major part. The tapestry-like extract from the initial page to Luke is made up entirely of birds, with curved beaks, interlaced legs and talons, and wings strongly marked with a sort of tile-like pattern. There has been much discussion about the identity of the birds most commonly used by our artist. No one should pretend that Eadfrith was setting out to provide scientific drawings in a modern sense. It is, however, hard to believe that, with all that wealth of bird life around him, his imagination would not have been inspired by creatures he could actually see for himself. My own top candidate would be the cormorant or the green shag, which has both an appropriately shaped bill and wings heavily patterned with feathers outlined like tiles. It has been objected that these birds have webbed feet while the Gospel birds have talons. It *would* be foolish to attempt to create patterns of interlace with webbed feet but cormorants and shags have extremely prominent foot bones, especially in their youth. As I have said, we are talking inspiration not science.

In just one instance however, we may have an example of direct and deliberate observation. The eagle symbol which accompanies St John is, in most early medieval manuscripts, far from the image of the real bird. But a professional ornithologist looking at Eadfrith's effort, said that its plumage was so accurately rendered and so correctly distinguished according to its relative position on the bird that it was hard to believe that it had not been copied from life. A detail of this subject underlines the distinction between the different types of feather. If we may for a moment classify the human form as wildlife, Eadfrith further emerges with credit. All four of his evangelists, for all the stylization of faces and draperies and the obsession with pattern that turns hair into an overall spiral design, remain perfectly credible seated male figures of late antique inspiration. In the case of St Luke, he is accompanied by his symbolic calf, and attached to this once again we see a magnificently observed bird's wing. By contrast, in the crucifixion miniature from the Durham Gospels, both Christ and the angels are transformed into abstract patterns far removed from natural form.

But the best and most irresistible of Eadfrith's animals is his cat. He forms the bounding margin on the right hand side of the initial to St Luke's Gospel. His tail and rear legs are in the centre of the upper part of the page. His stylized and elongated body, containing eight birds, hugs the right hand edge of the page and at the bottom his head and front paws are setting out in quest of further prey from the tapestry panel of birds on the left of the great initial Q. Of course this is not naturalistic in its entirety, but closer attention to detail reveals one very interesting thing. That cat has got whiskers, painted on so fine that they fail to show up in most reproductions of the page and have been entirely overlooked by at least one artist making a line drawing from it. The whiskers add nothing whatsoever to the general design of this page but they do prove that Eadfrith was regarding this creature at least as a recognizable reproduction of something from real life. The Luke initial page with its cat is one of Eadfrith's most satisfactory compositions.

Some contemporary comparisons

Red dot work is used to set off the display capitals in this same page, where they appear in particular profusion. Baldwin Brown once worked out that here alone there are well over ten thousand of these dots, each one a tiny blob of red lead pigment,

The Evangelist Saint John from the Lindisfarne Gospels. He is accompanied by his symbol, an eagle carrying a book ('imago aequilae').

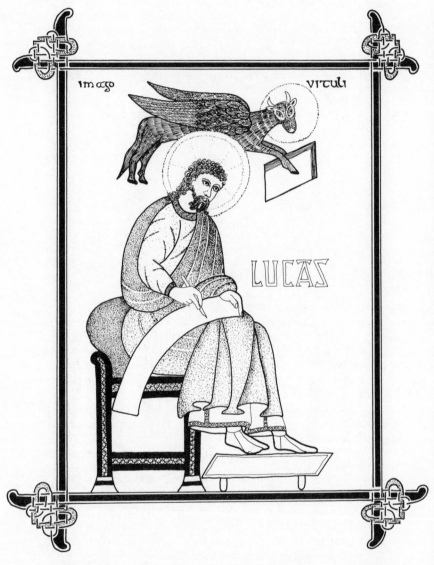

imago   vituli

LUCAS

The Evangelist Saint Luke from the Lindisfarne Gospels. He is accompanied by his symbol, a winged calf carrying a book ('imago vituli').

individually applied with a quill or fine brush point.[4] He reck-
oned that if the pigment was of a suitable consistency, the
artist's hand was steady, and the atmosphere and temperature
were favourable, to apply the dots to this single page alone
would take about six solid hours. There is actually no way of
telling how much time overall the work on an elaborate book of
this nature would consume. Julian Brown thought that two
years might be a minimum, if the work was not interrupted.[5]
However, we must assume that Eadfrith would have been
obliged to join in the worship of his community and it is also
certain that weather conditions on the Northumbrian coast in
winter would have made it impossible for such precise work to
be carried out for weeks at a time; so two years must surely be
a substantial underestimate.

To the student of Anglo-Saxon art, the Lindisfarne Gospels
is of great significance, not just as supreme example of the
achievement of its time but also for the fact that it is securely
dated and localized, with links to documented people and
places. This makes of it a touchstone for all the less well served
works of comparable content and style. Comparisons can be
made with works in a wide variety of media, for Eadfrith seems
to have been very well informed about the work of other craftsmen and borrowed motifs that are found in stonework and
metalwork as well as in other manuscripts. His cross carpet
pages may well owe something to textile work which has not
survived, but they can also be related to jewellery with overall
patterns, such as the garnet work from the Sutton Hoo ship
burial, which was deposited about sixty years before the manuscript was made. Details of the ornament also suggest a debt to
the jeweller. The centre of the Mark carpet page is occupied by
a circular design which once again features patches of colour
enclosed in a contrasting step pattern.

The complicated ribbon interlace which fills the ground of
the Mark carpet is, however, almost exactly paralleled on
the lowest panel of the face of the eighth-century cross in the
churchyard at Bewcastle, just northwest of Lanercost and the
Roman wall. Spiral patterns commonly found in enamel work,
as on the largest of the hanging bowls from the Sutton Hoo ship
treasure, appear very frequently in the Gospels. The most spectacular instance is the initial page of Matthew's Christmas
Gospel where spirals of differing diameters are woven together
to fill the area between the arms of the main letter. This is one
of the passages in the Gospels where it is hardest to imagine a
formal mathematical framework being a great deal of practical
help. The ribbon of which the initial is constructed, each one

crammed with animal ornament of truly astonishing complexity, is half an inch across.

Scholars assessing the Lindisfarne Gospels as a masterpiece of the arts of its time seldom pause to consider how it must once have fitted into a much wider pattern of manuscript production than the one we now see. Its survival in virtually perfect condition and the fact that, as we have already observed, it is so precisely dated and localized, is in itself worthy to be regarded as one of the miracles of St Cuthbert. Had the community of St Cuthbert passed over the sea to Ireland during their flight from the Vikings, as was at one time the intention, our manuscript would almost certainly never have received Aldred's gloss and revealing colophon and would be leading an anonymous life in Ireland, subject over the years to the same controversies about date and provenance as the Book of Durrow and the Book of Kells.

If you consult Jonathan Alexander's catalogue of Insular manuscripts from the sixth to ninth centuries, you will see that Lindisfarne is number nine in his chronological list and that only the Book of Durrow itself, now widely regarded as Northumbrian work, plus the mid-seventh-century fragments in Durham cathedral library, provide any evidence for the earlier comparable work from which Eadfrith's skills must have developed.[6] This includes work from both sides of the Irish sea. This is of course quite unrealistic. Vast quantities of potentially relevant material must have been lost. For instance, every seventh and eighth century religious community must once have owned a gospel book, even if of modest pretensions, though Royal ms 1B. vii in the British Library, which has a text very close to that of Lindisfarne but is decorated with a few small initials, is the only substantial survivor. Similarly there must once have been an adequate supply of essential service books, but these too have vanished, represented now by a few meagre scraps such as the recently published binding fragments discovered at Ushaw. Sometimes there are written records of things that have been lost, such as the lavish copy of the Gospels written in golden letters on purple vellum which Wilfrid commissioned for the church at Ripon. Sometimes it is possible to assume the existence of particular books, like the entire contents of the library in which Bede worked at Jarrow. But the picture we see today is a very distorted one. The fragments of a small Gospels, ms Otho C.v in the Cotton collection in the British Library, reflect one hazard which many manuscripts will variously have faced. This book was a victim of the fire at Ashburnham House in 1731, during which many irreplaceable treasures, including the unique text of the Battle of Maldon, were lost. The Lindisfarne Gospels is part of the same collection but was luckily housed in a different part of the room.

Originally, the Otho fragment must have resembled in many ways the celebrated Echternach Gospels, now in Paris, which belonged to St Willibrord's monastery in what is now Luxembourg. A family relationship between the two lions, neither of which bears much of a likeness to a real beast, is very close. The Echternach Gospels which, like the Lindisfarne Gospels, is arranged in two columns, is written in the most wonderful cursive script, probably chosen because it could be executed more quickly than the stately majuscule of Eadfrith's work. Its initials are relatively simple, probably for the same reason. It is not unlikely that the Echternach Gospels was made as a gift to be sent from Northumbria to the new fields of missionary endeavour on the continent of Europe.

The Otho fragment is also linked by its initials to the Durham Gospels, still treasured in the place where it has almost certainly been since the Lindisfarne community settled here at the end of the tenth century. This book, now only a fragment, shows every sign of having endured a long and hard life. Only the main initial to St John and the crucifixion miniature remain from what must once have been an unusually rich scheme of decoration. Otho, Echternach and Durham seem very much interrelated and there are very good reasons to associate all three with the Lindisfarne scriptorium at the time of Eadfrith. The Durham Gospels is especially interesting because it clearly includes miniatures of episodes from the life of Christ which would have placed it in a different and more ambitious category than Lindisfarne though it is now so imperfect that comparisons are difficult.

A fourth and slightly later surviving Gospels should also be compared to Lindisfarne. This is the Lichfield Gospels, some of the decorated pages in which are so remarkably similar in design to their equivalents in Eadfrith's book that it is hard to believe their artist had not been influenced by seeing the earlier manuscript. This is not of course impossible. Lindisfarne had many visitors and the Lindisfarne Gospels would undoubtedly have been a show-piece, especially if the visitor happened himself to be an artist. We do not know where Lichfield was made. At one time in its history it was in Wales, though it has spent most of its time in Mercia and could have been produced there. Like Durham it is very much worn and damaged. The unusual pinks and mauves of its colouring were once enhanced by yellows, blues and vermilions, now partly worn away. But this too was once a grander book than Lindisfarne, with a more elaborate decorative scheme and carried out in a larger format, though the book is now reduced in size because it has been cut down in successive rebindings.

It would thus appear that Lindisfarne is not in fact so very unusual when compared with its peers, could we see them restored to the full original glory which Eadfrith's work has been fortunate enough to retain. Only in one respect does the Lindisfarne Gospels far outshine these other books and that is in the matter of its range of pigments. The colouring of all these other manuscripts is very limited, mainly yellow, green and vermilion, perhaps with some purple. In the case of Lichfield the purple predominates. These were the colours easiest to obtain. But Lindisfarne, as we have already observed, employs an enormous range of colours, many of them from distant sources. The only manuscript of the period that provides anything like a comparable sense of richness is the Codex Amiatinus from the scriptorium of Wearmouth-Jarrow. It may be that here too, as in the case of his access to a textual exemplar and his choice of biographer for his patron saint, Eadfrith was directly indebted to the wide contacts and advanced skills of Ceolfrith's monastery on the river Tyne.

John says it all

We began our tour of the Lindisfarne Gospels by looking at the first and simplest of its decorative openings, right at the beginning of the book. It is proper that we should end with the last opening, which is the most complex of them all. It really does seem that the artist of the manuscript began at the beginning and went on to the end, developing his skills as he went. By comparison with that first page, the carpet page to St John's Gospel is an extraordinary composition. Here the cross-shaped elements are filled with the most minute, almost microscopic, ribbons set against a positive whirlpool of interlaced birds. Seen in close-up, the amazing precision of the painting is clear. Once again it is instructive to give the measurements. Each of the panels of ribbon interlace is five-sixteenths of an inch across. And even here the 'deliberate mistake' is not forgotten. Just one of the many birds has wings which are not broken up into tile patterns by lines drawn in ink. But that one is inescapably right in the middle of the design.

The initial page which faces the carpet is equally complex. It almost seems as if Eadfrith, reaching the end of his task, was determined to throw into this one last opportunity every single element of design that he had used elsewhere in the book. We have ribbons, we have spirals, we have step patterns, we have animal interlace, we have birds and we have little red dots. On this final initial page we also have the only instance in the entire book, except of course on the evangelist pages, where Eadfrith uses an element of the human body as a part of his purely decorative design. Here he introduces a human head with a long and flowing tail of hair as an ornament for one of his display capitals.

The Lindisfarne Gospels must be somewhere in the region of its thirteen hundredth birthday. Those thirteen centuries can be divided up into three very roughly equivalent periods in its history. For the first four hundred years the manuscript was cherished by the Anglo-Saxon Community of St Cuthbert, whether on Holy Island or, after seven years of wanderings, at Chester-le-Street or, from 995, in Durham. At the beginning of the twelfth century the newly founded Norman cathedral became its home and remained so for the better part of four hundred and fifty years. Another four hundred and fifty years have now elapsed since the Gospels was taken away from Durham to the south to be transformed into an academic and museum treasure rather than a holy relic and a glorious tribute to the message of the Gospels. But this book has never really lost what one may loosely term its relic status. Today, although it is fiercely protected from overhandling and other physical ills, it is freely available to visitors in the British Library's British Museum galleries and is visited daily by hundreds of people of all ages, creeds and nationalities. But in spite of its long absence from Durham, it is still very much a vital focus of spiritual and creative life in the northeast of England and the work of local craftsmen continues fully to testify to its inspiration.

Notes

1. J. Backhouse, *The Lindisfarne Gospels* (Oxford: Phaidon, 1991).
2. *Bede's Life of St Cuthbert*, chap. 42, from *Two Lives of St Cuthbert*, trans B. Colgrave (Cambridge: Cambridge University Press, 1985), p. 293.
3. M. Lapidge, 'Bede's Metrical *Vita S. Cuthberti*', in G. Bonner, D. Rollason and C. Stancliffe (eds.), *St Cuthbert, His Cult and Community* (Woodbridge: Boydell, 1989), pp. 80–1.
4. R. Bruce-Mitford, in T. Kendrick et al., *Codex Lindisfarnensis* (Basle and Olten: Schwitter and Walter, 1960), pp. 218–19, 238.
5. T. J. Brown, in Kendrick et al., p. 94.
6. J. J. G. Alexander, *A Survey of Manuscripts Illuminated in the British Isles, I Insular Manuscripts, Sixth to Ninth Century* (London: Miller, 1978).

Nature Redeemed

ROSEMARY CRAMP

Both literary and artistic survivals from the Anglo-Saxon world suggest that a transformation of consciousness occurred as the new faith gained a foothold. Pagan fear of the natural world was replaced by a vision of its unity under the Christian God, whereby animals became docile or even joined in worship, while a tree became the pre-eminent symbol of nature's harmony with its Creator. So thin did the veil between matter and spirit seem that the presence of angels was everywhere keenly felt. It is to this sacramental world of nature disclosing the divine that Rosemary Cramp introduces us.

Threatening nature and the saving cross

When St Cuthbert's coffin was prepared to receive his body in 698 (thus setting in train the events which led to the construction of Durham Cathedral as his shrine) the images which were considered to be appropriate were apparently not intended to make a public statement – unlike the sculptures which I am about to discuss; yet in their repertoire they are very closely related. Moreover, both the sculptured and the engraved images are remarkable within their time as a demonstration of how the newly converted Anglo-Saxon Christians had absorbed the iconographic and stylistic tradition of the late antique world.

The repertoire of Christian images chosen in the late seventh century for the coffin were as follows: the cross inside the coffin, on the inner lid; on the outer lid, Christ as he appears on the Day of Judgement surrounded with the apocalyptic beasts, who have by that time long been associated with the evangelists (Matthew the man or angel, Mark the lion, Luke the calf, and John the eagle); on one long side the seven archangels, on the other the apostles in the order of their commemoration in the Roman Mass; on one end the Virgin with the infant Jesus on her lap; on the other, two angels.[1] They are the pictorial translations of the litanies of prayer. Comparable images also occur on Anglo-Saxon relief stone sculpture of the seventh/eighth century, but to understand their import and impact we must go back in time to join together the strands of the early Christian Mediterranean traditions and those of the pagan north. Let us remember that there were still unconverted pagans in England when Cuthbert died.

We know practically nothing about the religious beliefs of the pagan Anglo-Saxons who had occupied the eastern part of this island since the mid-fifth century: the Church made a good job of obliterating them – and we have to reconstruct the little we do know from such evidence as place-names and the common Germanic stock of much later traditions.[2] Their cults, however, seem to have had much in common with those of the Celts who had preceded them on the European mainland or were their neighbours in Britain. Their sacred places were groves and pools and springs, and sacred too were certain animals and trees. For the Germanic peoples sacred trees had a particularly important role, and this is emphasized not only in eighth-century continental missionary activity,[3] but in Anglo-Saxon Christian poetry where the cross is *the* sacred tree. The fearsome centres of such cults may be illustrated by Lucan's description of a sanctuary destroyed by Caesar near Marseilles. 'And there were many dark springs running there, and grim faced figures of gods, uncouthly hewn by the axe from the untrimmed tree trunk.'[4]

Such figures may have been dressed, though to any Roman they would be crude indeed; they convey a certain malignancy, as do the stone carvings of heads found in western Britain and Ulster.[5] One such head comes from Brough and it is not without interest that the Romans planted their forts in such places as Brough or Bewcastle – the cult centre of the British god Coccidius – which like Armagh, the major pagan temple in Ulster, was later sanctified and became an important Christian centre.

The art of the pagan period is ambiguous and abstract, the main elements being exploded animal and human forms. We do not know what the animal shapes mean as they merge into the human, but perhaps the most telling image of all is the royal helmet from Sutton Hoo where the human face mask is actually composed of a flying dragon whose wing tips form the eyebrows, whilst the head of the dragon meets another animal head on the crest.[6] (On the York helmet a hundred years later the

crest is protected by a Christian inscription.) Around the crown
of the Sutton Hoo helmet are combat scenes – whether from
myths or hero legends we do not know – and these may, like the
Christian religious images on contemporary continental hel-
mets, have some protective significance. Some were struck from
the same dies as others from Öland, Sweden, which show men
in combat wearing animal masks, and it is fascinating to observe
that men in adversarial positions are not getting the better of
animals. Recently it has been suggested that some of these
images were copied and reused so that they have something of
the force of an icon.[7] This deep-rooted fear of the strength of the
animal world was sublimated by the Christian missionaries both
in England and on the continent by stressing in their hero legends
the stories of Daniel who was not subdued by the beasts, or
David and Samson who overcame them with their bare hands.
Most importantly of all they taught how Christ was (like Gilgamesh or Orpheus), lord of the animals.[8] He was recognized as
the harmonizer of creation, so that at his crucifixion all natural
phenomena were also affected and thus dislocated, darkness
displacing day (as the Bible relates).[9]

I have spent time on this hardly comprehensible background
to early Anglo-Saxon England, because I believe that it added
another dimension to popular piety, and one may remember
there was a renewed injection of Germanic paganism during the
Scandinavian invasions and settlements. Many of the customs
which Anglo-Saxon clerics inveigh against, such as offerings at
wells or trees, or feasting in churchyards, seem harmless enough,
but they may have had less harmless practices behind them.

By the time that Augustine came to England in 597, Christianity in the Mediterranean world had long lost the need to
accommodate itself to the images of the pagan past, and indeed
many of them, such as the flying geni who became angels, had
taken on a new Christian significance. The images of Christ had
also seen many guises from the young and pastoral figure of
the Good Shepherd to the mature and grave figures which came
to predominate. There was, however, a persistent feeling that
images, particularly those in the round, not only offended
against the second commandment but were a source of decep-
tion to the faithful and for that reason flat images on boards or
in mosaics and wall paintings developed. I return to this point
later.

As has often been pointed out, early medieval peoples, if they
described works of art at all, were most concerned to describe
intrinsically valuable objects such as jewelled crosses, or statues
in gold and silver rather than stone or wooden sculpture, and

there are many descriptions of such things in Anglo-Saxon texts.[10] Augustine and his monks came carrying before them 'the holy cross and the image of our great King and Lord, Jesus Christ' – an icon.[11] For many throughout the early Christian and early medieval period the cross alone carried the whole message of Christ's passion and redemption. At the centre of the cross were often five jewels which signified the five wounds of Christ, but it was also a cosmological image of the risen Christ, its jewelled arms stretching to the four corners of the globe, as described in the Anglo-Saxon poem *The Dream of the Rood*. The same poem describes how the cross borne on the breast like an amulet will mark out and protect the Christian at the Second Coming, when a great cross will fill the sky. Several humble stone crosses have heads with five bosses which presumably commemorate the five wounds; and one later carving on a slab at Lindisfarne depicts the cross accompanied by the sun and the moon which will simultaneously fall on Judgement Day. This must have been carved near to the millennium (a time when it is clear many people considered the Day of Judgement would occur).

Christian iconoclasm and the brazen serpent

Augustine's image on a panel introduced Anglo-Saxons to public representations of Christ, who like the Virgin or the apostles would have been exotically clothed in late antique dress, emphasizing to them the divisions between the earthly and heavenly worlds in a way that was not so to the earliest Christians. I have mentioned already that many could be exercised about the making of images. It was forbidden in the law of the Old Testament, and was tainted by the lifelike statues of the Greek and Roman gods, as well as the images of emperors which were part of the imperial cult. Tertullian denounced not only images but their makers: 'but when the devil brought into the world the makers of statues, portraits and every kind of image, the practice untaught as yet but fraught with disaster to mankind, took its name and its development from idols'.[12] But by the early fourth century Constantine had filled St Peter's and the Lateran Basilica with great silver images, five feet high of our Saviour seated on a throne, the twelve apostles and four angels with jewelled eyes and carrying spears.

In the fifth century Paulinus of Nola wrote excusing his decorating his church with images; he gives a reason which would also be used by St Gregory and Bede, that they were for the instruction of the unlettered. He says 'The majority of the crowd here are peasant people not devoid of religion but unable to read', and concludes that since these people have been long accustomed to cults which included feasting and drinking perhaps they could be distracted into greater austerity by looking at the pictures. It seems a rather vain hope, especially since he adds: 'If only they would not intrude into the sacred house with their beakers'.[13] Gregory the Great was perhaps wiser to counsel his Kentish missionary Mellitus to build special temporary huts for such feasting outside churches.[14]

Travellers to Rome and other early Christian centres must have been deeply impressed by the *in situ* art in the churches they encountered. I will take just one early Christian representation to demonstrate the complex symbolism which was transmitted to the infant Anglo-Saxon church. In a sixth-century presbyterium of San Vitale in Ravenna the exalted cross is borne aloft by angels, as it is in later scenes of the risen Christ.[15] A less elaborate cross below is adored by the faithful sheep (in some early scenes sheep represent the apostles). Around the exalted cross above it are the Old Testament prototypes of Christ's ministry and passion: Moses striking the rock to provide water, as the blood which flowed from Christ's side is our salvation; Abraham feeding his three angelic guests, sometimes seen as the symbols of the Trinity, sometimes as a prefiguration of the Last Supper. Abel's sacrifice is also seen as a prototype of Christ's, as is the father's willingness to sacrifice his son in the figure of Abraham and Isaac.

That such allegorical and analogical interpretations were absorbed by the learned in the Anglo-Saxon church is without question, and indeed the translation of images which reinforced these messages for the faithful is a historical fact recorded by Bede in relation to his own churches of Wearmouth and Jarrow. Bede's account of the icons which Benedict Biscop brought back to Wearmouth-Jarrow are often mentioned but I make no apology for doing so again. At Wearmouth, he provided a likeness of the blessed Mother of God with the twelve apostles surrounding the central arch and running from wall to wall, representations of the gospel story on the south wall and images drawn from the Revelation of St John for the north wall:

> in order that all men who entered the church, even if they might not read, would either look (whatsoever way they turned) upon the gracious countenance of Christ and his saints, though it were but in a picture; or might call to mind a more lively sense of the blessing of the Lord's incarnation, or having, as it were before their eyes, the peril of the Last

Judgement might remember more closely to examine themselves.[16]

On his fifth journey to Rome Benedict acquired, for St Paul's
Jarrow, paintings showing the agreement of the Old and New
Testaments. Isaac and Moses are employed as prototypes of the
Christian dispensation: Isaac as bearing his wood to sacrifice,
together with Christ bearing his cross; Moses lifting up the
brazen serpent in the wilderness, with the Son of Man lifted up
on the cross. These images were painted before the major icon-
oclastic controversy of the eighth and ninth centuries and so
established a tradition in Anglo-Saxon England. Certain themes
and images hallowed by this tradition had already been
endorsed by the weighty authority of Bede, and in his homily
on Benedict Biscop and his commentary on the Temple of
Solomon he stressed the value of such images, which must have
informed his spiritual meditations since childhood.

He argues that if it were permissible 'to lift up a brazen serpent on a piece of wood so that the Israelites who beheld it
might live why should it not be allowable to recall to the memory of the faithful by a painting that exaltation of our Lord
and Saviour on a cross?'[17] Again, if it were permissible to make
twelve brazen oxen why should it not be permissible to paint the
twelve apostles? Or again, why should it be considered contrary
to the Law to paint or sculpt on panels the stories of the saints
and martyrs of Christ? Bede's writings are recognized as being
important in justifying representational art in the West just at
the time when iconoclasm reached its peak in the Eastern
Church. The Western Church had never gone as far as the
Eastern Church in seeing art as a bridge between the earthly
and heavenly worlds. In the East the excesses whereby the more
ignorant of the faithful came to identify the image with the
model resulted in the large-scale destruction of works of art
from the mid-eighth to the mid-ninth centuries, with the virtual
extinction of sculptures and reliefs not only in the Byzantine
world but in Western Europe, but here in Anglo-Saxon England,
they survived in some quantity.

Trees of life set in stone

The plain cross image was obviously venerated at Jarrow where
the famous cross slab bears the inscription which can be read as
in hoc singulari signo vita redditur mundo (in this particular sign,
life was given to the world), and recalls the cross as Constantine's
standard of victory.[18] The Celtic church probably introduced

the wooden cross as a field monument to north Britain and recent research has proposed that the tenth-century scripture crosses reflect in their stone forms earlier wooden crosses to which metal plaques – icons – had been attached,[19] or possibly ivory panels.[20] Whether it was from this idea or crosses with busts on the arms and panels on the shaft, a cross type developed in Anglo-Saxon England in which the stone shaft was ornamented with individual panels, thus forming an open-air iconostasis. The repertoire of figural scenes is not wide in comparison with tenth-century Irish crosses, but the erection of stone crosses is a phenomenon found only in the British Isles and Ireland, and their humane and classicizing figures represent an amazing prolongation of late antique traditions which anticipates the Carolingian revival.

Certainly Benedict Biscop's icons have formed a valuable inspiration, as for instance in the repertoire on the Cuthbert Coffin: the Virgin and the twelve apostles and Christ as on the day of Judgement surrounded by his apocalyptic beasts. The themes of salvation and judgement are indeed constantly invoked in Anglo-Saxon sculpture. Recently Michael Lapidge reminded us that not only did Bede compose his most florid Latin poem on this subject but a succinct and moving Old English poem: 'Before that inevitable journey no one can be so otherwise that he will not be concerned as to the judgement of his soul, for good or ill at his death's day.'[21] At Bewcastle only one face on the cross has human images, Christ (who is labelled) in the centre, John the Baptist above, and a figure with a bird below. A further gloss on the central figure is revealed on what is the most complex and individual cross to survive, and certainly most discussed, the Ruthwell cross from Dumfriesshire. Both broad faces contain images from the life and miracles of Christ, with explanatory inscriptions. One reads '*Jesus Christus judex aequitatis. Bestiae et dracones cognoverunt in deserto salvatorem mundi.*' (Jesus Christ, just judge. Beasts and dragons in the desert have acknowledged the saviour of the world.) Christ is the judge and saviour, standing on two adoring animals and for the simple observer it must have shown the beasts in their rightful place. For all Christians it would have been a reminder of Judgement, as would the apocalyptic beasts with the figures of the evangelists on the head of the cross. The learned could have been reminded of pseudo-Matthew, where beasts and the dragons in the wilderness adored the child Jesus during the flight into Egypt, or, as in Bede's commentary on Habbakuk, of Christ recognized between two animals.[22]

The Ruthwell Cross

Bede's commentary on Luke has been a fruitful quarry for the meaning and relationships of the images on the Ruthwell cross, indeed his words sometimes seem peculiarly telling.[23] Here, for instance, is what he says of Mary Magdalene as the type of penitent sinner: 'Each individual faithful soul must humbly prostrate themselves at the feet of the Lord and obtain forgiveness of sins' whilst in a homily he says 'We anoint his feet when we proclaim with praise the mystery of the incarnation . . . we anoint his feet when we succour the poor with comforting words and urge them not to despair despite the hardships they endure. We dry his feet with our hair when from our superfluous possessions we give to the needy.'[24] This image of Mary both as the Church and as the penitent soul occurs on Anglo-Saxon crosses seeking the sacramental gift of forgiveness although one must remember that Mary the mother of God could also be seen in this position since she is seen as *the* intercessor at the feet of Christ.[25]

Despite its wealth of theological and spiritual content we must look more widely than at Ruthwell, which reflects so clearly a learned monastic world, to other crosses with other programmes. Let us glance at Bewcastle, where as well as the figure scenes a large part of the cross is taken up with more abstract imagery. The vine is a widespread symbol of Christ in the Eucharist, but on the narrow sides of both Bewcastle and Ruthwell is a tree enclosing in its branches a variety of birds and beasts, and this is an image which occurs on a number of Anglo-Saxon crosses. Such a tree nourishing creation in a harmonious Chain of Being, in which man is the head but still part of the middle material world, appealed very much to the Anglo-Saxons. The symbolism is obvious here, but what of the panels of interlace of a geometric complexity such as is found in the Lindisfarne Gospels? The provision of order through numbers and the understanding of how such numbers reflected the harmony of heaven was a part of Christian teaching at this time, and here the complex pattern is controlled from the centre by the form of the cross. It is easy to become over-fanciful when analysing such patterns today, and much has been written recently on the subject, but in a chaotic world the control of complexity must have been a solace to both artist and observer. Even quite simple patterns could appear more complex when painted, and it is clear from close observation of extant and newly excavated sculpture that it was painted.

I turn now to other figural programmes on crosses. A generation or so later than Bewcastle, and using different models, there is at Eastby in Yorkshire a mutilated but classically carved figure of Christ seated in judgement and attended by angels. He is accompanied by the twelve apostles, very different in their varied faces and postures from Cuthbert's coffin, but the theme is the same. Easby also has panels of interlace and vinescrolls, plain and inhabited with birds and beasts, while at Otley, in west Yorkshire, a fragment of a cross also has a very Roman-looking series of apostles and on the other face like the Cuthbert Coffin, a sequence of angels.[26] (If this cross were reconstructed to the same height as Ruthwell or Bewcastle, it could well have had twelve apostles and seven angels.) One panel at Otley shows a figure kneeling at the feet of the angel which could be any penitent soul, or could be a monk specifically, as is clearly the tonsured figure clasping an angel's feet on a cross head from Dewsbury. This image used to puzzle me since the monk is literally embracing the feet of the angel and looking outwards. Yet the monastic life is often compared with that of the angels in its rejection of the material world. A monk, with his rejection of fleshly ties, and a legal worldly status, did become what Brown calls 'an honorary human' and so could be said to embrace the life of the angels.[27] The veil between the material and the spiritual world was very thin in those days, and people passed easily between them, living in an intimate contact with the saints and angels in a way it is difficult for us to appreciate today. Angels, those pure intelligences who inhabited another zone in the celestial order of creation, were nevertheless considered to be literally present at the sacraments of the early Church, so much so that priests who had to spit during the service were enjoined to avoid the angels who stood beside them.[28] On a more edifying note, we can recall the anecdote Alcuin told of Bede, who might have been tempted to neglect the offices when engaged in some major work of scholarship, but is supposed to have said, 'I know that angels visit the canonical hours and congregations of the brethren. What if they do not find me among them? Will they not say, where is Bede?'[29] It is possible that the very ambivalence of the angelic creation, like the apocalyptic beasts, appealed strongly to early medieval people, but certainly angels abound on these crosses.

On the Midland crosses of the Peak district they throng on cross heads in apocalyptic scenes, and on a late cross at Halton in Lancashire we find not only Christ and the suppliant soul but the suppliant kneeling at the feet of an angel who holds up an enormous Book of Life.[30] Not all images of judgement are so peaceful, though. On the cross from Rothbury in Northumberland, which in its programme when complete must have been comparable to Ruthwell, there is not only a magnificent stern bust of Christ the Judge, but also a terrible picture of hell in which writhing serpentine creatures tear apart smaller softer beasts and overwhelm human beings.[31]

Anglo-Saxon sculpture of around AD 800 demonstrates an interest in narrative and more expressionistic group scenes. On what must have been when complete a very impressive cross from Dewsbury, Christ is shown seated in majesty, but there are also two miracle scenes which are easily related to contemporary biblical exegesis. The marriage feast at Cana with the supernatural change of water into wine is associated by the Fathers with baptism and is seen as the prefiguring of the Eucharist, just as was the translation of the loaves and fishes in the feeding of the five thousand.[32] They are depicted in juxtaposition, for instance, on the sixth-century wooden doors of St Sabina in Rome. There is also at Dewsbury a small figure of a Virgin and child, as on Cuthbert's coffin. The mysterious translation of godhead into human flesh is obviously one theme here, but also the Virgin seen as the acme of mortal intercession; for as Brown says, 'her intercessions had the infallible efficacy of a blood relative'.[33]

The ancient theme of the prefiguring of the New Testament in the Old, already noted in the Jarrow icons, achieved a new popularity on Irish scripture crosses,[34] and also occurs a generation earlier in England. A very worn cross from Masham, Yorkshire depicts two prefigurations of Christ: David playing his harp and Samson carrying off the gates of Gaza.[35] Other figures are too worn to see, but we assume that scenes from the New Testament occupied the zone above, and the fantastic animals had their own zone below. Generally, however, there are not many Old Testament scenes on Anglo-Saxon crosses, the most popular being the sacrifice of Isaac, and Adam and Eve.

Crucifixion scenes were initially placed in the shafts of crosses, and, as we have seen, the head was used to portray other scenes. By the time of the Rothbury Cross, though, the stone cross itself became a crucifix, and this continues into late Saxon times. Particularly distinctive of late Saxon England are the large scale roods which appear in churches in accordance with the reformed liturgy of the Church, which in the tenth century became more dramatic and lively. Such features as the lifesize rood to be found at Romsey could have been devotional foci, or have been used in the newly developing church drama.[36] There is a marked increase in scale in the images in late Saxon England. Two grave angels form part of a crucifixion scene which when complete must have entirely filled the east wall of the nave of the little church at Bradford on Avon. Perhaps the most dominant angel of them all is in a panel from Breedon on the

Hill in Leicestershire – swinging towards us through his arch he is nearly human size.

The renewed economic strength of the church in southern England in the tenth century produced large-scale sculptured monuments some of which, like the decorated tower at Winchester, are minutely described in contemporary texts, although all that remains today are fragments of huge limbs, heads, hair, and even eyes.[37] At this time, though, the church in the north was struggling to survive. The records of the episcopal communities at both York and Chester-le-Street (later translated to Durham in 995) testify to the unremitting problems they had to hold on to their landed possessions or to recover them after the land distributions following the Scandinavian settlements. Yet all the spiritual energy of the surviving order of the northern church could not have been dissipated in that way. There is little record of the means of conversion of the new Germanic settlers, and the only records of martyrdoms are from other areas – though even they seem to be political rather than religious killings. Yet the monuments in old Northumbria testify to conversion and the same type of emphatic links between old and new beliefs which we stressed earlier when discussing the first conversions. For example, Viking monuments at Sockburn or Heysham show two scenes of men and beasts, one with Tyr who gave his right hand to the jaws of the Fenrir wolf, in order that he might be bound until the day of Ragnarök,[38] on the other side Daniel and the lions. On one side the beasts seem out of control, on the other tamed. The famous ring-headed cross from Gosforth in Cumbria is in the shape of the world-tree of Germanic mythology, and depicts scenes from the life and fall of the gods, but there is one panel, specially surrounded by a border, which tells a different story – a figure with arms outstretched in the crucified position. This is, then, not a juxtaposition of Jewish Old Testament stories and the New Testament but of Germanic legends and the New Testament.

Among the monuments of the pre-Norman cathedral at Durham was a cross upon which Christ was depicted holding back the bound beasts in a Daniel-like way, but however useful such monuments may have been for instructing the pre-Conquest congregation at Durham they were broken up and used in the foundation of the cathedral's Norman chapterhouse. They were not great art, but the essential message is there: the Christian religion brings with it a vision of the natural and supernatural world now in unity, with nature to be seen sacramentally participating in God's purposes and no longer, as so often in pagan religion, to be feared.

Notes

1. E. Kitzinger, 'The Coffin Reliquary', pp. 228–80, plates vii–x of C. F. Battiscombe (ed.), *The Relics of St. Cuthbert* (Oxford: Oxford University Press for the Dean and Chapter of Durham, 1956).

2. D. Wilson, *Anglo-Saxon Paganism* (London and New York: Routledge, 1992).

3. C. H. Talbot (trans. and ed.), *The Anglo-Saxon Missionaries in Germany* (London: Sheed and Ward, 1954), p. 54, pp. 274–301.

4. S. Piggott, *The Druids* (London: Thames and Hudson, 1968), p. 86.

5. H. Hickey, *Images of God* (Belfast: Blackstaff, 1977), pp. 7–30.

6. For the fullest account of this remarkable object see R. Bruce-Mitford, *The Sutton Hoo Ship Burial* (London: British Museum Publications, 1978), vol. 2, pp. 138–239; and for another view of animal offerings in pagan graves see J. D. Richards, 'Anglo-Saxon Symbolism' in M. O. H. Carver, ed., *The Age of Sutton Hoo* (Woodbridge: Boydell, 1992), pp. 131-47.

7. M. Alkemade, 'A History of Vendel Period Archaeology' in N. Roymans and F. Theums (eds.), *Images of the Past: Studies on Ancient Societies in Northwestern Europe* (Amsterdam: Institut voor Pre-en Protohistorische Archeologie, 1992), pp. 267–98.

8. According to the Epic of Gilgamesh, the hero of that ancient Mesopotamian epic destroys the evil forces of nature, whereas pre-Homeric Orpheus, a legendary poet, charms even wild beasts with his lyre.

9. Matt. 27.45.

10. C. R. Dodwell, *Anglo-Saxon Art: a New Perspective* (Manchester: Manchester University Press, 1982).

11. Bede, *Ecclesiastical History of the English People*, B. Colgrave and R. A. B. Mynors (eds) (Oxford: Clarendon, 1969), p. 75.

12. Tertullian 'On Idolatry' in S. L. Greenslade (ed.), *Early Latin Theology* (Library of Christian Classics London: SCM Press, 1956), vol. 5, section 3 p. 84.

13. C. David-Weyer, *Early Medieval Art 300–1150* (Toronto: Toronto University Press, 1986), p. 19.

14. Bede, *Ecclesiastical History*, p. 109.

15. W. F. Volbach and M. Hirmir, *Early Christian Art: the Late Roman and Byzantine Empires from the Third to the Seventh Centuries* (London: Thames and Hudson, 1961), plates 159 and 160.

16. Bede, *Lives of the Abbots* in *Historical Works* Loeb Edition (Cambridge Mass.: Harvard University Press, 1933), vol. 2, section 6, pp. 405-7.

17. W. Levison, 'The Inscription on the Jarrow Cross' *Archaeol. Aeliana*, Series 4, xxi (1943), pp. 121–6.

18. R. Cramp, *Corpus of Anglo-Saxon Stone Sculpture 1 County Durham and Northumberland* (Oxford: Oxford University Press, 1984), pp. 112–13.

19. D. Kelly, 'The Heart of the Matter: Models for Irish High

Crosses', *Journal of the Royal Society of Antiquaries of Ireland* 121 (1991), 105–45. See also footnote no. 34.

20. A. Goldschmidt, *Die Elfenbein-Skulpturen aus der Zeit der karolingischen und sächsischen Kaiser* (Berlin: Cassirer, 1914).

21. M. Lapidge, *Anglo-Latin Literature 900–1066* (London: Hambledon, 1993), p. 341.

22. E. O'Carragaín, 'Christ and the Beasts and the Agnus Dei: Two Multivalent Panels on the Ruthwell and Bewcastle Crosses' in P. E. Szarmach (ed.), *Sowers of Anglo-Saxon Culture* (Studies in Medieval Culture 20, Kalamazoo: Medieval Institute 1986), pp. 376–403.

23. M. Shapiro, 'The Religious Meaning of the Ruthwell Cross' in *Late Antique, Early Christian and Medieval Art. Selected Papers* (London: Chatto and Windus, 1980), vol. 3, pp. 151–95.

24. These passages are fully explored in a recent article by P. Meyvaert, 'Ecclesia and Vita Monastica' in B. Cassidy, (ed.), *The Ruthwell Cross* (Princeton: Princeton University Press, 1992), pp. 110–12.

25. R. Cramp, 'The Position of the Otley Crosses in English Scuplture' in *Studies in Anglo-Saxon Sculpture* (London: Pindar, 1992), plate 15 (1).

26. The same. Plates 13 (4) Easby; 6, 7, and 8, Otley; 12 (3) Dewsbury.

27. P. Brown, *Society and the Cult of the Holy in Late Antiquity* (London: Faber, 1982), p. 319.

28. This extract from the *Rule of the Master* is again quoted by Brown, as above, p. 319.

29. C. Plummer, *Bedae Opera Historica* (Oxford: Clarendon, 1896), vol. 1, pp. xii–xiii.

30. R. Cramp, 'The Position of the Otley Crosses', plate 14 (2).

31. The same, note 18, illustration 1224.

32. W. G. Collingwood, *Northumbrian Crosses of the Pre-Norman Age* (London: Faber and Gwyer, 1927), p. 73, figure 91.

33. P. Brown, *Society and the Cult of the Holy*, p. 271.

34. P. Harbison, *The High Crosses of Ireland* (Bonn: Habelt, 1992).

35. Collingwood, *Northumbrian Crosses* note 32, figure 55. Both these images are present in George Herbert's poetry. See p. 139 of J. Rhodes' essay in this volume, quoting 'Easter'. And on Samson, see Herbert's poem 'Sunday':

> The rest of our Creation
> Our great Redeemer did remove
> With the same shake, which at his passion
> Did th'earth and all things with it move.
> As Samson bore the doors away,
> Christ's hands, though nailed, wrought our salvation,
> And did unhinge that day.

Cited from J. Tobin (ed.), *George Herbert: The Complete Poems* (London: Penguin, 1991), p. 69.

36. A full discussion of the liturgical and literary associations of these Roods is to be found in B. Raw, *Anglo-Saxon Crucifixion Iconography* (Cambridge: Cambridge University Press, 1990).

37. R. N. Quirk, 'Winchester New Minster and its Tenth Century Tower', *Journal of the British Archaeological Association* Series 3, 24 (1961), 16–54.

38. See S. Sturluson (trans. A. G. Brodeur), *The Prose Edda* (London: Oxford University Press, 1929), Section 21 of *Gylfaginning*, pp. 44–5.

Ways of Seeing:
Christ in Everything

J. T. RHODES

For the medieval mind not only was the Eucharist a natural extension of the sacramentality of the incarnation, images of Eucharist and passion were detected everywhere. In the second part of her essay Jan Rhodes examines some of these, including a number which have all but passed from the Christian consciousness, such as Christ as charter or harp. The first part, however, focuses on what made this riot of imagery intelligible – not only medieval biblical exegesis but also specific theories of perception and even physiology.

The body of Christ dominated late medieval spirituality. Scenes from his life were pictured in carved work, stained glass, embroidery and painting and in manuscript and printed books, and they occurred in some domestic as well as ecclesiastical settings. They spanned the time from his nativity, with the infant being held in his Mother's arms, to the wounded body of the Passion scenes, the dead body of Jesus held in his Mother's arms (the Pietà), and the resurrected body of his post-resurrection appearances (and disappearances). All these scenes embody Jesus who was both Son of God and Son of Mary.

Churches in general, especially the chancels, were particularly saturated with Passion imagery. There was the Rood or crucifix that dominated the chancel screen; the East windows and the retable behind the altar often represented scenes from the Passion and the priest's chasuble frequently had a crucifixion embroidered on the back. More symbolic representations, notably the instruments of the Passion, known as the *Arma Christi*,[1] might decorate just about every surface.

The body of Christ was also seen by the faithful in another

way; when they gazed on the consecrated host raised between the priest's hands at Mass or presented to their view in a monstrance.[2] Usually, in the context of the chancel, the symbolic body of Christ represented by the host was juxtaposed against more historical images: crucifixes and scenes from the Passion pictured in the stained glass and on the celebrant's vestment. The many allegorical interpretations of the Mass that were popular throughout the Middle Ages also served to relate the symbolic actions of the liturgy to the historical narrative of the Passion.[3]

Already, two broad questions are posed by what has been said. The first is about the kind of seeing implied by these representations. The second concerns the sort of history we are considering.

Ways of Seeing

There are many different ways of seeing, from rose-tinted spectacles to poetic and artistic vision. George Herbert's well-known lines remind us that:

A man that looks on glass
On it may stay his eye
Or if he pleaseth, through it pass
And then the heaven espy.[4]

In his diaries Gerard Manley Hopkins gives a detailed drawing and description of a bluebell. He concludes the entry: 'I do not think I have ever seen anything more beautiful than the bluebell I have been looking at. I know the beauty of our Lord by it.'[5] The physical reality of the bluebell has become a bearer of God's presence.

Although I am going to distinguish between what I call 'prophetic' and 'symbolic' vision, the two are complementary and interdependent ways of envisioning; together they affect the kind of reality we see in Christian history.

Prophetic vision

The prophet is someone who sees beyond present realities to things yet to come and to far distant places, as far as hell and its demons and to the glories of heaven. The prophet or visionary is not restricted to physical space and historical time. The Old Testament has its prophets who engage in symbolic actions and utter cryptic words. Many of those words were interpreted as prophecies about the Messiah, and Jesus often talked of himself and his actions in terms of those prophecies: 'everything written about me in the law of Moses, in the prophets and in the Psalms, has to be fulfilled' (Luke 24.44). The very next verse reads: 'He then opened their minds to understand the Scriptures', as he had done shortly before with the two disciples on the road to Emmaus.

The life of Christ was, in one sense, to be read out of the Old Testament. F. P. Pickering[6] and J. H. Marrow[7] have shown how literary and pictorial elaboration of the details of the Passion narrative in the later Middle Ages was not just imaginative invention, but practically every detail can be traced back to the Old Testament via patristic exegesis and the liturgy. In late medieval vernacular writing about the Passion (prayers, meditations and verses), certain Old Testament texts recur, such as Isaiah 1.6 'from the sole of his foot to the crown of his head there is no health in him'.[8] Other references are more allusive and require considerable knowledge of patristic exegesis. Take the Easter day psalm 57.8, 'Awake, lyre and harp'. Pickering goes so far as to describe the harp 'as the most influential of all the medieval symbols of the crucifixion',[9] and it is interesting to note that George Herbert was still in touch with this and other instances of medieval imagery in the early seventeenth century when he wrote 'Easter':

> Awake, my lute, and struggle for thy part,
> > With all thy art.
> The cross taught all wood to resound his name,
> > Who bore the same.
> His stretched sinews taught all strings, what key
> Is best to celebrate this most high day.[10]

If the details of Christ's life and Passion are to be read out of the Old Testament, medieval writers and artists make it clear that Jesus and his Mother read the Passion back into the whole of his incarnate life. In *The dialogue between Our Saviour Jesus Christ and a sinner* (c.1539) Jesus states: 'truly, I received the cross of my bitter Passion in the womb of my Mother, and bore it continually in my heart and established it in my body with great austerity'.[11] The same point is made in pictures of the Annunciation where a homunculus (little man) holding a cross descends from heaven to enter the womb of Mary, or when instruments of the Passion are included in nativity and infancy scenes and in the symbolic juxtaposition of the lily of the Annunciation with the crucifix in the lily-crucifixus images.

Symbolic vision

Typology was a pervasive way of seeing in the Middle Ages. The Old Testament was not just prophetic, it was also symbolic of the events in Jesus' life.[12] The typological method was most clearly encoded in the series of woodcuts and quotations from the Old and New Testaments known as the *Biblia Pauperum*[13] and in numerous stained glass glazing schemes, including King's College Chapel.[14]

Once one has become accustomed to seeing symbolically, medieval art is seen to carry meaning beyond what is actually pictured. For example, eucharistic significance can be read out of (or is it into?) a great deal of medieval art.[15] Both the infant Jesus lying on an aureole of hay and the head of John the Baptist on a dish (an extremely popular image) may represent the host lying on the paten.[16] In Robert Campin's famous annunciation painting the room can be read as a sanctuary: the niche is a piscina, the table with its candle and liturgical-looking book an altar, and the angel is dressed as a deacon; at the same time it is a tabernacle enclosing Christ as Mary's flesh is to enclose her son and as an oven or fireplace encloses the baking bread of the host.[17]

Symbolic vision is more than observing what is; it is a way of 'reading' and interpreting what is seen. To begin to understand the world of late medieval spirituality we have to learn to see in a richer, more allusive and symbolic way. The ability to see beyond or through the immediately present by means of typology, symbol, allegory and metaphor was apparently much more widespread and certainly more explicit in the Middle Ages; Chenu calls it 'the symbolist mentality'.[18] Our more literary culture seems also to have become more literal.[19]

Concern for historical detail

Yet in other ways the medieval approach to the Passion seems to be very literal. Medieval Christians were keen to know the exact length of Jesus' body on the cross, the exact size of the cross and the nails, the precise number of wounds on his body and the details of all his sufferings. So we find representations of the cross that claim: 'This cross fifteen times moten is the length of our lord Jesu Christ' and whoever carries it with them will be protected from dangers such as evil spirits, thunder and lightning. Similarly Pope Innocent promises seven gifts to anyone who carries on them 'the length of these nails saying daily five Pater Nosters, five Ave Marias and a Creed'.[20] Many representations of the measure of the wound of Christ's side survive[21] and calculations or statements of the total number of his wounds, usually set at 5475,[22] were widespread. This kind of verisimilitude was important precisely because the Word became flesh and lived among us.

Places and things associated with Christ's earthly life were believed to possess power and were venerated accordingly.[23] The goal of all pilgrims, attained by few, was to reach the Holy Land and there see, touch and carry away a physical contact and continuity with his presence. For those who could not go there in person various substitutes were available,[24] such as relics and reproductions of relics. In England pilgrims travelled to venerate the holy rood at Bromholm in Norfolk,[25] or carried scale drawings of the cross or nails. But the cross was more than just a static relic, it was an effective sign:

> A shield of red, a cross of green
> A crown wreathed with thorns keen
> A spear, a sponge, with nails three
> A body bound to a tree;
> Whoso this shield in heart will take
> Among his enemies he shall not quake.[26]

The sign of the cross was made to gain divine protection and to invoke a blessing.[27]

The historical cross on which Jesus is supposed to have been crucified turns out to be reproduceable. Its power, derived not from the physical constituents of the wood but from its significance, is transferable to words, drawings and gestures. Notions of a single, physical reality or of a linear, chronological history are inadequate tools with which to approach medieval images of the Passion.

The devotional present

The most widely advocated way of 'seeing' in medieval devotional texts is what I call 'the practice of the devotional present'.[28] Imaginative descriptions (heard or read) and visual images that evoked an emotional response helped to make the past events of the Passion real to the individual's present experience. Over and over again medieval authors invited their audiences to behold, see, take heed, consider and imagine that they saw Jesus before their very eyes. In *The vii. shedynges of the blode of Jhesu cryste* of 1509 the meditation on the scourging helps the audience to see:

> the bare and naked bones, the flesh rent from the bones with many and fell strokes of the knotted scourges dyed with his

precious blood. Think also that thou hearest him groan, quake and tremble for anguish and wonderful pain . . . and that with the strokes of the scourges a part of his blessed flesh or a drop of his precious blood falleth or droppeth on thy face or on thy clothes.[29]

The past becomes present reality to the senses, sight, hearing and feeling, of the meditator who is drawn into the scene and reacts accordingly. Julian of Norwich's revelations, which start from the sight of the crucifix held before her eyes, are probably a consequence of this practice,[30] and St Ignatius Loyola formally built the practice into his famous *Spiritual Exercises*.[31]

Seeing, hearing, feeling, tasting and smelling are implied by incarnation (I John 1.1).[32] It is worth remembering how very tactile Jesus' earthly ministry was and how strong the tactile-sensual component was in the sacraments of the medieval church. This would be the more striking in a society where music, sweet smells (incense), colours, lights, pictures and images were not generally available in a domestic setting.

In addition to what John Fewterer, writing in 1534, calls 'inward hearty remembrance' of Christ's Passion, or the practice of the devotional present, he recommends physical *ascesis*, such as 'kneelings or pain-takings', 'taking disciplines or scourging'[33] and he adds: 'so continue until thou have gotten the grace of tears'.[34] Devout beholding or the practice of the devotional present was far more than a passive, detached observation of events. Tears were the recognized and desired signs of compassion, the goal of so much medieval devotion; and with compassion repentance became possible, leading to amendment of life and greater love of God. Julian of Norwich prayed for true compassion producing a longing for God.[35] For some, love-longing for God had physical consequences like the *calor, canor, dulcor* (warmth, song and sweetness) experienced by Richard Rolle (c. 1295–1349) or the spiritual inebriation of the mystics.[36] A very few, whose compassion and love of Jesus was of extraordinary intensity, like St Francis and St Catherine of Siena, experienced his actual wounds in their own bodies. Compassion, suffering with the Lord, could not be more real than this.

The visual image

Ancient theories of sight thought that a physical ray was projected from the eye of the beholder to touch its object. An impression of that object then travelled back along the visual ray to be imprinted on the soul and preserved in the memory.[37] The practice of the devotional present, whether through visually graphic descriptive language or by means of a representational image such as a crucifix, was a means of imprinting the events of Christ's life and Passion on the soul, so that they left an indelible impression in the individual's experience and memory. To paraphrase Mitchell: authentic images do not just represent but trigger a transaction which is transforming.[38]

Different versions of a set of prayers on the instruments of the Passion, usually illustrated, suggest some of the ways in which images were considered to be effective. The vernicle, the image of Christ's face impressed on St Veronica's cloth on his way to Calvary, is one example of a transforming image:

> The cloth he set over his face,
> The print he left there of his grace,
> His mouth, his nose, his eyen two,
> His beard, his hair he did also.
> Shield me Lord, for that in mine life
> That I have sinned with mine wits five . . .
> Lord of heaven, forgive it me
> *Through virtue of the figure that I here see.*[39]

The representation of the suffering face of Christ puts the beholder in touch with a power, Christ's redemptive suffering, that makes it a means of forgiveness. One version of these *Arma Christi* verses is prefaced by lines that describe how memory of the Passion can help to purge vices:

> O glorious Jesu redeemer of mankind
> which on the cross hung full of compassion
> Grant of thy grace, with my heart and mind
> Wholly to remember the arms of thy Passion
> Engrave good Lord, thy grievous pains strong
> Deep in my thought avoiding all sin
> And purge the vices that been in me long
> With contrite heart these verses to begin.[40]

Another version concludes with the verses:

> These instruments that here portrayed beth
> In memory of thy bitter death
> They helpen them to do thy Passion
> They help us to our salvation.[41]

These illustrations of the instruments of Christ's Passion can be a means to forgiveness, a way to purge sins and help towards salvation. They are effective, or transforming images, not because of what they are as physical objects or historical realities, but because they represent aspects of the redemptive sufferings of Christ.

Since the Passion of Christ was the means to forgiveness and redemption, the idea of images (the crucifix, the *Imago Pietatis* or image of piety which is discussed later, the *Arma Christi*, the Pietà) that represented those sufferings as agents of forgiveness becomes more intelligible. Remembering that devout beholding implies more than 'just' looking, we find many problems like: 'Who so ever devoutly beholdeth these arms of Christ hath 6755 years [of pardon]'.[42] More often, there is a double requirement, both devout beholding and the recitation of a few familiar prayers: 'To them that before this image of pity devoutly say five Paternosters, five Aves and a Credo, piteously beholding these arms of Christ's Passion, are granted 32,755 years of pardon.'[43] No wonder they were popular images! Where there was devout beholding, the image could be transforming: the viewer responded with compassion, repentance, conversion of life and increased love of God. However, images as effective as this were almost an invitation to superstition and abuse.

The sixteenth-century Reformers were quick to seize on such superstitions to give public credibility to their iconoclasm. But their determined opposition to medieval imagery, like the crucifix, the Pietà, the Image of Pity and the Mass tacitly acknowledged that these were effective images. Imagery is a powerful way of expressing belief, especially in a society that is not highly literate, and images cannot be divorced from theological understanding and doctrinal teaching. If the Reformers' doctrines were to be implemented, the Catholic imagery had to be destroyed.[44]

Specific Images

I shall concentrate on a selection of visual images, but it is worth noting that there was also a very rich array of literary images relating to Christ's Passion and the Mass. They tend to be more overtly doctrinal, for example Christ the lure or bait as a figure of the process of redemption. Some are developed from patristic exegesis, such as Christ on the cross as a harp or bow.[45] Many are pervasive, like Christ as the physician or as medicine.[46] A quality they tend to have in common is that they are graphic, frequently seen or experienced things or processes. For example, Richard Rolle likens the scourged body of Christ to heaven full of stars, to a net full of holes, a dovecote full of nesting boxes, a honeycomb full of cells,[47] a book written in red ink and a meadow full of sweet flowers.

The image of Christ crucified as a book was very widespread in the Middle Ages[48] and it endured into the sixteenth century.[49] The related image of the charter of Christ[50] had doctrinal implications; it emphasized the contractual obligations of those who wished to receive the charter of their redemption. This unique charter was written not on sheepskin but on the body and skin of Christ himself, with hard nails, a sharp spear and sore pricking thorns instead of pens. 'The wounds upon that blessed body and sweet skin of Christ were instead of letters and as clerks say, and specially St Anselm, there were upon the blessed body of Christ open wounds by number 5475. This is the number of letters with which our charter was written.'[51] In the whole concept of the book or charter of Christ his physical body is, again, emphasized but his symbolic, sacramental body is also implied.

The imago pietatis

The Image of Pity was one of the most common book illustrations of the Passion;[52] it also occurred in stained glass, on alabaster and brasses, and in paintings. It is a symbolic image, not a historic one. The wounded body of Jesus, often accompanied by instruments of the Passion, usually stands in or by a tomb, as if not yet risen. It is chronologically ambiguous; it provides a synchronous representation of the totality of Christ's sufferings during his Passion.

The image was particularly associated with the Mass of St Gregory. There are different versions of the story, but the point is always to prove to a member of the congregation who doubted it, that the body of Christ is physically present in the consecrated host. In one account, St Gregory describes how, as he consecrated

> our Lord's body
> Christ Jesu in form of bread . . .
> I saw a sight I was adread
> A naked body in a tomb of stone
> full of wounds bleeding sore
> His face all pale, his colour was gone
> His skin, his flesh was all too tore
> A spear was put through his body
> In every hand a nail was thrusted
> . . . A wreath of thorn upon his head
> The pricks through his brain ran

he looked as he had been dead
His eyes, his lips, were all wan
His hands were crossed him before[53]

Thus the *Imago Pietatis* can be a visual realization of a doctrine
that was widely defended and 'proved' in vernacular writings,
often by means of miracles such as bleeding hosts.[54]

The pious pelican

Thomas Aquinas' description of Jesus as 'pie pelicane' in his
widely known hymn *Adoro te devote* may have helped to popularize the image,[55] but the legend of the pelican, reviving her
dead chicks with blood torn from her own breast, goes back to
the *Physiologus* of about AD 200.[56]

The pelican his blood doth bleed
Therewith his birds for to feed
It betokeneth upon the Rood
Our Lord fed us with his precious blood.[57]

The image was widely represented on bench-ends, misericords,
bosses and tiles and occasionally occurred as a lectern. It is not
coincidental that it occurs on the arms of both Corpus Christi
colleges; Richard Foxe, founder of the Oxford college, was
formerly Bishop of Durham (1494–1501) and used it as his
personal badge where it may still be seen in the Castle.

William Bonde in his *Pilgrymage of perfeccyon* of 1531 makes
the eucharistic connection overt:

Never forget that most tender loving pelican which would
not only suffer death to save his birds but over that he hath
ordained his blessed flesh and blood to be our sustenance
and daily food, ministered and consecrated in the Mass, in
the most gracious and glorious sacrament of the altar, signi-
fying the most precious death and passion of our merciful
saviour and redeemer Jesus Christ.[58]

Elsewhere Bonde explicitly links the figure of the pelican with
that of Christ as heavenly physician.[59] And if Christ is a heavenly
physician it is natural to regard the consecrated elements as
medicinal to soul and body: 'preserve thy body and soul to ever-
lasting life'.[60] The simultaneous physicality of the Real Presence
in the consecrated elements and the ever closer identification of
the body of Christ with the redemption he effected, led to an
exaggerated respect for the host itself and opened the way to
superstitious abuses.[61]

The wounds of Christ

From the fourteenth century the physical sufferings of Jesus in his Passion became increasingly prominent in literature and art.[62] The outpouring of his blood and his wounds received greater emphasis. In part this needs to be seen in the context of a society accustomed to gross disfigurement, where physical pain and agonized death processes were inescapable. In part it was a deliberate attempt to elicit an affective response from the audience and to arouse compassion.

Bynum has demonstrated that 'late medieval texts were awash in references to the blood of the lamb'.[63] Whether in devotional texts like *The vii shedynges of the blode of Jhesu cryste* of 1500 and 1509, or in narrative descriptions and illustrations of the Passion, the great rivers of blood that flowed out of Christ's wounds and fountains are prominent.[64] One only has to think of Julian's revelations. Saints like Catherine of Siena were privileged to drink the blood flowing from the wound of his side.[65] This maternal, nurturing aspect of Christ was the more apparent because medieval physiology believed that a mother's milk was derived from her blood.[66] Christ's blood was also healing; the blind Longinus who pierced Jesus' side on the cross recovered his sight on contact with the blood.[67]

There were also numerous relics of the precious blood that were the focus of pilgrimage as at Hayles in Gloucestershire,[68] and this despite Thomas Aquinas' doubts about whether any of Christ's blood could remain on earth after his resurrection and ascension. Given that the precious blood was believed to be really present at every Mass, relics of it are a somewhat puzzling phenomenon. More characteristic were the angels carrying chalices to collect the blood flowing from his wounds on the cross, or representations of the Mass of St Gregory where blood flows directly from the wound of his side into the chalice on the altar. A further elaboration, that goes back to patristic sources,[69] was to see the wound of his side 'as the door whereby the sacraments of the Church come from Christ to us'.[70] This was graphically represented in those seven-sacrament compositions which showed the figure of Christ, often as an *Imago Pietatis*, with blood-red lines running from his wounds to illustrations of each of the seven sacraments.[71]

The wounds as fountains and wells

The Latin word *fons*, of course, signifies both a fountain or spring that bubbles up from its source and a well sunk down into the earth from which water must be drawn up; the former was more attractive to artists. Life-giving springs and wells are significant in Scripture[72] and Paradise was often pictured with a fountain.[73] But, as Schiller has shown, these images 'are not merely *topoi* for the Paradise of creation and the future Paradise, but were related . . . to the sacrificial and redemptive death of Christ'.[74] Thus, Bellegambe's early sixteenth century *fons vitae* is filled with blood flowing from the figure of Christ on the cross and the basin of the fountain is reminiscent of a chalice or a font.[75] Banderoles (ribbon-like scrolls) carry texts from Isaiah 12.3, 63.1–2 and Revelations 7.13–14, all of them familiar 'types' of the Passion and Eucharist. Another, more explicitly eucharistic *fons vitae* representation, includes among the multiple figures of the suffering Christ one of him in the (wine) press of the Passion, a fulfilment of Isaiah 63.3 'I have trodden the wine-press all alone'. The figure survives widely in written texts such as the last of the *XV Oes* (the set of prayers attributed to St Bridget), where Christ is addressed as 'the plenteous vine' whose blood is shed like a ripe cluster of grapes when 'they pressed thy blessed body . . . upon the press' of the cross.[76]

The visual realizations of the wounds as wells tends to be more or less symbolic. The dismembered hands, feet and heart were depicted, often as *Arma* mounted on a shield, on numerous fonts, bosses, benchends and pulpits. Sometimes the sacred monogram was added, a visual expression of the way in which the popular devotion to the Holy Name of Jesus[77] was assimilated to the dominant contemporary emphasis on the Passion. The frequent addition of a chalice to the compositions, as on the banner carried by the Pilgrims of Grace in 1536, made the eucharistic implications of the wounds explicit. There were also more abstract representations of the wounds as on the brass to Robert Hacombleyn (d. 1528) in Winchester and in a quarry of fifteenth-century glass surviving at Sidmouth. The crowning and labelling of the wounds as well of mercy, well of pity, well of grace, well of comfort and well of life was quite widespread;[78] the seventh of St Bridget's *XV Oes* begins 'O blessed Jesu, well of endless pity'.

In addition to being the sources of mercy, pity, grace etc., the wounds represented safe places to hide. In them sins could be safely hidden:

> O Jesu which for me . . . would have thy left hand digged and bored with a nail and fastened to the cross, grant me that I may ever put and hide all mine adversities and temptations in the most sweet wound of that left hand and that I may find in

it a sure and wholesome remedy against all manner of tribu-
lations.[79]

They also offered a refuge to the sinner in which he could
hide himself from the fear of death and the Judgement that
haunted medieval Christians. 'O blessed Jesu, deepness of endless mercy' implores the eleventh of St Bridget's *XV Oes*:

> I beseech for the deepness of thy wounds . . . that thou vouch-
> safe to draw me out of sin and hide me ever after in the holes
> of thy wounds from the face of thy wrath unto the time that
> thy dreadful doom be passed.[80]

The wound in Christ's side

The wound of Christ's side attracted particular attention. It was
represented in a variety of ways, the most widespread probably
as a heart either on its own or with the wounded hands and feet.
A wound was often marked on the heart. Sometimes it appeared
on its own, usually in the context of other Passion-related imagery, as a kind of red slit with or without a 'measure', the kind of
'scale' we have met before in connection with the cross and
nails. Or the heart and slit/measure might be combined, as in
the late fifteenth-century Capesthorne commonplace book:
'This is the measure of the wound of our Lord Jesu Christ that
he suffered on the side for our redemption'.[81]

It was not only sins that could be hidden in Christ's wounds,
the sinner himself was encouraged to seek refuge there through
devout remembrance of the Passion.[82] As one author put it, the
opening of his side with a spear grants us entry, to join our heart
to his heart.[83] Fewterer, paraphrasing from one of St Bernard's
most influential sermons on the *Song of Songs* (2.14),[84] declared:

> O good Jesu, thy side was wounded and opened, that we
> might have entrance or way to come to thee . . . It was also
> wounded that by that visible wound we might see the invis-
> ible wound of thy love . . . therefore this bodily wound doth
> show to us his spiritual wound of love . . . Arise therefore thou
> spouse of Christ, as a dove building thy nest . . . in the deep-
> ness of the hole or wound. Join or put thy mouth to that
> wound: that thou may suck or draw the water of health from
> the fountains of our Saviour. This is the well that springeth in
> the midst of Paradise, which doth make fruitful the devout
> hearts and plenteously doth water all the world.[85]

As we have seen, compassion is an expression of love and gratitude to the Redeemer, the desire to suffer with him. 'Let thy

pain abound in me as much as it abounded in thee' runs the refrain to a set of prayer-meditations on the Passion. The significant thing about this particular set of Passion meditations is that they are the earliest English ones I know addressed to the precious heart of Jesus and the other refrain that runs through them is: 'and all for love'.[86] The language of the heart is the language of love, and the highest human experience and expression of love points beyond itself to the source of all love. I close with the words of Godfrey Ashby:

> In the heart of God, sacrifice is the eternal offering of mutual love of the persons of the Holy Trinity. In the world the offering of sacrifice takes and has taken many forms. All these forms, we believe, find their final expression . . . in the perfect sacrifice, racked with the suffering caused by the world's alienation from its Creator, of Jesus Christ, the anointed King. This the church sets forth and acts out in all its members upon and for the world, until it will finally be taken up into the sacrifice of the Trinity in mutual love.[87]

Notes

1. R. Berliner, 'Arma Christi', *Müncher Jahrbuch der Bilden Kunst*, 6 (1955), pp. 35–152.
2. cf. J. T. Rhodes, 'The Body of Christ in English Eucharistic Devotion 1500–1620', in R. Beadle and A. J. Piper (eds.), *New Science out of Old Books* (Aldershot: Scolar Press, 1995). This essay treats in more detail the issues raised in the text.
3. Dating back at least to Amalarius of Metz in the ninth century, sixteenth-century versions of these allegorical interpretations were available in print e.g., in Bk. 2 of Gararde's *Interpretacyon and sygnyfycacyon of the Masse*, 1532 (available as no. 11549 in A. W. Pollard and G. R. Redgrave, *A Short Title Catalogue of Books Printed in England, Scotland and Ireland 1475–1649*, 2nd edn, 1976, hereafter abbreviated as *STC*).
4. 'The Elixir', lines 9–12.
5. Diary entry, 18 May 1870.
6. F. P. Pickering, *Literature and Art in the Middle Ages* (London: Macmillan, 1970), ch. 4.
7. J. H. Marrow, *Passion Iconography in Northern European Art of the Later Middle Ages and Early Renaissance* (Kortrijk: Van Ghemmert Publishing, 1979) passim.
8. Some of the most frequent are: Pss. 22 and 57 (AV numbers) both used extensively in the Holy Week liturgy; Isa. 53.2–5 and 63.1–3; Lam. 1.12, *O vos omnes*, on which see R. Woolf, *The English Religious Lyric in the Middle Ages* (Oxford: Oxford University Press, 1968), pp. 42–5.

9. Pickering, op. cit., pp. 285–301.

10. J. Tobin (ed.), *George Herbert: The Complete English Poems* (London: Penguin, 1991), p. 37.

11. *STC* 14548.

12. M. -D. Chenu, *Nature, Man and Society in the Twelfth Century* (Chicago: University of Chicago Press, 1968, reprinted 1979), ch. 4; B. Smalley, *The Study of the Bible in the Middle Ages* (Notre Dame: University of Notre Dame Press, 1962, repr. 1970), ch. 3; R. Tuve, *Allegorical Imagery* (Princeton: Princeton U. P., 1966), ch. 4.

13. See A. Henry, *Biblia Pauperum* (Aldershot: Scolar Press, 1987).

14. H. Wayment, *The Windows of King's College Chapel, Cambridge* (London: British Academy, 1972); É. Mâle, *The Gothic Image* (London: Fontana, 1961), pp. 140–6.

15. B. G. Lane, *The Altar and the Altarpiece* (New York: Harper and Row, 1963) passim.

16. Lane, op. cit., p. 59; M. Rubin, *Corpus Christi* (Cambridge: Cambridge University Press, 1991), p. 315.

17. Lane, op. cit., pp. 41–5.

18. Chenu, op. cit., title of ch. 3.

19. e.g. R. A. Alves, *The Poet, the Warrior, the Prophet* (London: SCM Press and Trinity Press International, 1990), chs. 4–6.

20. e.g. Durham, Ushaw College MS 29; and widespread in books of hours. See C. Buhler, 'Prayers and charms in certain Middle English scrolls, *Speculum 39 (1964), pp. 270–78*; and E. Duffy, *The Stripping of the Altars* (New Haven and London: Yale University Press, 1992), ch. 8 and plates 110, 112.

21. Oxford, Bodleian Library, MS Latin misc. c. 66 fo. 129: 'This is the measure of the wound of our Lord Jesu Christ that he suffered on the side for our redemption.' D. Gray 'The five wounds of our Lord II', *Notes and Queries* 208 (1963) and E. Kuryluk, *Veronica and her Cloth* (Oxford: Blackwell, 1991), p. 50.

22. e.g. Oxford, Bodleian Library, as above: '. . . five thousand and four hundred three score and fifteen full "grithe" were God's wounds to save us with' and numerous Latin and English versions of 'A woman devout and solitary'; cf. E. Duffy, *Stripping of the Altars*, pp. 254–6.

23. cf P. Brown, *The Cult of the Saints* (Chicago: University of Chicago Press, 1981), ch. 5; J. Bentley, *Restless Bones* (London: Constable, 1985), chs. 1 and 3.

24. e.g. the development of the Stations of the Cross: H. Thurston, 'The stations of the cross', *The Month* (1900), pp. 1–12, 153–66, 282–93.

25. D. J. Hall, *English Medieval Pilgrimage* (London: Routledge and Kegan Paul, 1966), ch. 9 'The Holy Rood of Bromholm'; F. Wormald, 'The Rood of Bromholm', *Journal of the Warburg and Courtauld Institute* 1 (1927–8), pp. 31–45.

26. Cited by D. Gray, *Themes and Images in the Medieval English Religious Lyric* (London: Routledge and Kegan Paul, 1972), p. 133.

27. e.g. the widespread use of the formula 'Per crucis hoc signum +
     fugiat procul omne malignum et per idem signum + salvetur . . .'
     (Through this sign of the cross let all evil flee far from me and
     through this same sign let me be saved.) This was sometimes
     combined with the Holy Name of Jesus, in the popular prayer-
     charm: '+ Messias + Sother + Emanuel + Sabath + Adonai + . . .'
     cf. Duffy, op. cit., p. 273.
28. cf. B. Pelphry, *Christ our Mother; Julian of Norwich* (London:
     Darton, Longman and Todd, 1989), pp. 113–18; J. Hirsh, *The
     Revelations of Margery Kempe* (Leiden: E. J. Brill, 1989), pp.
     87–91; M. Miles, *Image as Insight* (Boston: Beacon Press, 1965),
     p. 143f.
29. *STC* 14546.
30. Julian distinguishes three ways in which she 'saw' her visions: in
     actual vision, in imaginative understanding, and in spiritual sight,
     Revelations, ch. 9.
31. See L. Martz, *The Poetry of Meditation* (New Haven: Yale
     University Press, 1962), pp. 27–32.
32. The sufferings of Jesus in all his senses are noted. See, for exam-
     ple, in the popular *Golden Legend* section on the passion, e.g. *STC*
     24879 fo. 15ᵛ.
33. John Fewterer, *The myrrour or glasse of christes passion*, *STC* 14553.
     Also L. Gougaud, *Devotional and Ascetic Practices in the Middle
     Ages* (London: Burns Oates and Washbourne, 1927), Pt. II, ch. 3;
     R. Kiekhefer, *Unquiet Souls* (Chicago: Chicago U. P., 1984), pp.
     118–21, 147–9.
34. Fewterer op. cit., fo. 5. There is a huge literature concerning tears
     from the Middle Ages including *A Tretys to Lerne to Wepe*, cf.
     Hirsh, op. cit., pp. 76–7 and S. McEntire, 'The doctrine of com-
     punction from Bede to Margery Kempe' in M. Glasscoe, *The
     Medieval Mystical Tradition* (Cambridge: D. S. Brewer, 1987).
35. *Revelations*, ch. 3; Kieckhefer, op. cit., pp. 91–4.
36. e.g. W. Hilton, *The Goad of Love*, ed. C. Kirchberger (London:
     Faber and Faber, 1952), chs. 26 and 27.
37. M. Miles, op. cit., pp. 45, 95f.
38. N. Mitchell, *Cult and Controversy* (New York: Pueblo, 1982), p.
     377.
39. *Early English Text Society, original series* 46 (London, 1881), pp.
     170–1 (my italics), hereafter referred to as *EETS*. On the vernicle,
     E. Kuryluk, *St Veronica and her Cloth* passim.
40. Princeton, Taylor MS 4.
41. *EETS* 46, p. 195.
42. York Minster MS XVI. k. 6; E. Hodnett, *English Woodcuts* (Oxford:
     Oxford University Press, 1973), no. 2512.
43. Hodnett, op. cit., no. 2513. c. 1500.
44. M. Aston, *Lollards and Reformers* (London: Hambledon Press,
     1984), ch. 5 'Lollards and Images'; C. Davidson and A. E. Nichols
     (eds.), *Iconoclasm vs. Art and Drama* (Kalamazoo: Medieval
     Institute Publications, Western Michigan University, 1989); J.

Phillips, *The Reformation of Images* (Berkley: University of California Press, 1973). Interestingly, England did not develop the kind of popular Reformation art that flourished in Germany: R. W. Scribner, *For the Sake of Simple Folk* (Cambridge: Cambridge University Press, 1981).

45. Pickering, op. cit., pp. 285–307.

46. R. Arbesmann 'The concept of Christus Medicus in St Augustine', *Traditio* 10 (1954), pp. 1–28; W. Riehle, *The Middle English Mystics* (London: Routledge and Kegan Paul, 1981), pp. 78–9.

47. cf. Joseph of Arimathea, *EETS* 44, p. 50; like Christ he is also a 'ghostly physician'.

48. E. R. Curtius, *European Literature and the Latin Middle Ages* (London: Routledge and Kegan Paul, 1953), ch. 16; D. Gray, *Themes and Images*, pp. 129–30; R. Woolf, op. cit., p. 253, n. 2.

49. e.g. Bonde's *Pilgrymage of perfeccyon*, 1531, fo. 59; Fewterer's *Myrrour*, 1534, fo. 9; John Fisher's *Spirituall Consolation*, 1578.

50. M. C. Spalding, *The Middle English Charters of Christ* (Bryn Mawr, 1914); Rubin, op. cit., pp. 306–8.

51. Spalding, op. cit., pp. 100–2.

52. E. Panofsky, 'Imago Pietatis', *Fetschrift für Max J. Friedlander* (Leipzig 1927), pp. 261–304; R. Woolf, op. cit., Appendix E. The term 'Image of Pity' often referred to the Pietà, e.g. in Lydgate *EETS* 107, p. 297, but not always as T. E. Bridgett claimed in *Our Lady's Dowry* (London: Burns and Oates, 2nd edn 1875), p. 264.

53. *The lyfe of saynt Gregoryes mother*, c. 1536, STC 12353.

54. e.g. N. Love's *Treatise on the Sacrament*, in his *Mirror of the Blessed Life of Jesus Christ*, ed. M. G. Sargent (New York: Garland, 1992), pp. li–lvi, 225–41; R. S. Wieck, *Time Sanctified* (New York: George Braziller, 1988), pp. 107–8; proof verses like: 'It seemeth white, yet it is red', R. L. Greene, *The Early English Carols* (Oxford: Oxford University Press, 2nd edn, 1977), nos. 318.2, 319.2.

55. Text and English translation, *The Penguin Book of Latin Verse*, ed. F. Brittain (Harmondsworth: Penguin, 1962), pp. 257–8.

56. E. Kuryluk, op. cit., pp. 132–3.

57. *EETS* 46, pp. 172–3.

58. Bonde, op. cit., fo. 261; cp. Rubin, op. cit., pp. 310–12.

59. Bonde, op. cit., fo. 107 and 168.

60. cf. G. Dix, *The Shape of the Liturgy* (reprinted London: Dacre Press, A & C Black, 1964) and P. Camporesi, *The Fear of Hell* (Cambridge: Polity Press, 1990), pp. 186–9.

61. K. Thomas, *Religion and the Decline of Magic* (Harmondsworth: Penguin, 1973), ch. 2 'The magic of the medieval church'.

62. Marrow, op. cit., ch. 4; É Mâle, *L'art réligieux de la fin du moyen âge* (Paris: Librarie Armand Colin, 3rd edn, 1925), Part I, ch. 3; P. Thoby, *Le crucifixe* (Nantes: Bellanger, 1959), chs. 7–8. E. Kuryluk, op. cit., p. 209, notes contemporary interest in and knowledge of anatomy as a contributory factor.

63. C. W. Bynum, *Holy Feast and Holy Fast* (Berkley: University of

California Press, 1988), p. 56 and on the symbolism of blood: E. Kuryluk, op. cit., index 'blood'.

64. Fewterer, op. cit., fo. 116. For verses on the seven sheddings: Hirsh, op. cit., pp. 57–9.

65. Bynum, op. cit., pp. 157–9; Kieckhefer, op. cit., p. 109.

66. Bynum, op. cit., pp. 269f.

67. Fewterer, *Myrrour*, 1534, fo. 135ᵛ.

68. St Clair Baddely, 'The holy blood of Hayles' in *Transactions of the Bristol and Gloucestershire Archaeological Society*, 23 (1900), pp. 276–84; J. C. T. Oates, 'Richard Pynson and the holy blood of Hayles', in *Library* 13 (1958), pp. 269–77. See also V. Lagorio 'The evolving legend of St Joseph of Glastonbury', *Speculum* 46 (1971), p. 219.

69. e.g. Chrysostom, *Instructions to the Catechumens* 3.24–7.

70. Fewterer, op. cit., fo. 136.

71. e.g. windows at Doddiscombsleigh, Devon; Crudwell, Wilts; Melbury Bobb, Dorset; Llandyrnog. See A. E. Nichols, *Seeable Signs: the iconography of the seven sacraments 1350–1544* (Woodbridge: Boydell, 1994), pp. 59–68.

72. e.g. Song of Sol. 4.15; Isa. 12.3; Jer. 2.13; Ezek. 47.1, 12; John 4.10–14; Rev. 2.16.

73. e.g. Ghent altarpiece, *Très Riches Heures*.

74. G. Schiller, *Iconography of Christian Art* vol. 2 (London: Lund Humphries, 1972), p. 133.

75. Marrow, op. cit., pp. 84ff; also E. Underhill, 'Fountain of life: an iconographical study', *Burlington Magazine* 17 (1910), pp. 99–109.

76. cf. George Herbert, 'The Agonie': 'Sin is that press and vice which forceth pain/ to hunt his cruel food through every vein'; on the *XV Oes* see Duffy, *Stripping of the Altars*, pp. 246–56.

77. e.g. R. W. Pfaff, *New Liturgical Feasts in Later Medieval England* (Oxford: Oxford University Press, 1970), ch. 4; J. Hughes, *Pastors and Visionaries* (Woodbridge, Boydell, 1988), p. 266f; P. Revell, *Fifteenth-century English Prayers and Meditations* (New York: Garland, 1975).

78. W. Billyng, *The Five Wounds of Christ* (Manchester, 1814) – a late fifteenth-century prayer roll, now lost; also in prayers to the five wounds in *The Mystic Sweet Rosary* of 1533 (*STC* 21318) and in many other literary references. Illustrations so labelled include Billyng and Hodnett, nos. 675, 676 and 677.

79. Fewterer, *Myrrour*, fo. 114 – the actual prayer is a translation of Jordanus, see J. T. Rhodes, 'Prayers of the Passion: from Jordanus of Quedlinburg to John Fewterer of Syon', *Durham University Journal* 85 (1933), pp. 27–8.

80. cf. the very popular prayer: 'Lord Jesus Christ, Son of the living God, Saviour of the world, King of glory, place your passion, cross, death and pity between your judgement and my soul' (e.g. *STC* 15987 fo. 65), and the similar Marian image, 'Mother of Mercy', where her cloak shelters her petitioners. It was also

believed that at the Last Judgement the instruments of the Passion were displayed, to reassure the faithful but convict the guilty; cf. *The XV tokens afore the drefull daye of iugement* (*STC* 793.3), in which the crown of thorns convicts the proud, the nails the covetous, the lance the angry etc.

81. Oxford, Bodleian Library, MS Lat. misc. c. 66; W. Sparrow Simpson, 'On the measure of the wound of Christ's side', *Journal of the British Archaeological Association* 30 (1874), 857 0 74.

82. e.g. *The Dyetary of ghostly helthe*, 1521, *STC* 6834; or the words of the well-known prayer *Anima Christi*, 'within your wounds hide me.'

83. Cambridge University Library MS Dd. 5.55 fo. 102; cf Cardinal Newman's motto 'Cor ad cor loquitur' (heart speaks to heart).

84. Sermon 61 *On the Song of Songs III* (Kalamazoo: Cistercian Publications, 1979), p. 144. See E. A. Matter, *The Voice of My Beloved* (Philadelphia: University of Pennsylvania Press, 1990), pp. 137f.

85. Fewterer, *Myrrour*, fo. 136 including references to Song of Sol. 2.14, and Isa. 12.3.

86. Cambridge University Library MS Dd. 10.21. cf. V. Bainvel, *Devotion to the Sacred Heart* (London: Burns Oates and Washbourne, 1924), pt. III, chs. 1–3.

87. G. Ashby, *Sacrifice* (London: SCM Press, 1988), p. 135. Reprinted by permission of SCM Press Ltd.

PART THREE:
SACRED MUSIC

Movement and measure are of course what determines the impact of music upon us; the varying length of the notes, the speed with which the piece is played, the continuity of key signature, the development of the underlying theme. What may nonetheless make some resist acknowledgement of its potential as sacramental is music's apparent insubstantiality: it cannot be touched or tasted. Is it, then, part of the divine creation at all, or only very indirectly so through human creativity? Each of the three pieces which follow help us to answer that question. Music may not be as essential to life as the water used in baptism or the bread for the Eucharist, but the same sacramental principle applies, of things in the creation communicating, and participating in, something very different from themselves, the eternity of the divine life. Thus, just as perishable things such as bread and wine can convey the gift of eternal life, so can the noise and changes within a piece of music successfully speak of the peace and changelessness of God.

Music does so, our first two contributions argue, by functioning iconically. The distinguished composer, John Tavener, puts it very forcefully; it is only when, like the icon painter, the composer ceases to be self-absorbed with his own creative genius and instead allows himself to be used as a vehicle for divine grace that divine realities can then be communicated through him. The movement and measure, without ceasing to be what they are, then become a window to another, very different reality, a reality in which the listeners can also participate, will they but attend. The fact that music can achieve this, no less than the essentials of life which God has built into the creation, according to James Lancelot, displays the marvellous generosity of the Creator. We discover ourselves to be living in a world that overflows with the sacramental, once we open our ears as much as we do our eyes.

The Iconic Function of Music

TERENCE THOMAS and ELIZABETH MANNING

Paul Tillich made much of the importance of the relation between religion and culture. In pursuing the issue of how this affects music and the Church the two authors prefer the aesthetic term 'iconic' to 'sacramental', but admit overlap in meaning: like an icon the 'iconic' partakes of some of the qualities it communicates. Though insisting that ultimately the final judge must be each individual's personal response, they note some of the reasons why plainsong has traditionally proved effective, as well as some of the conspicuous successes and failures of subsequent generations.

Religion and culture

It is only fair to point out at the very beginning that the study we are engaged in is not theology, nor purely musicology, nor, to use a term that we have discovered recently, theomusicology. If a term is to be invented it might be religiomusicology. On the side of the study of religion we are engaged in the history and phenomenology of religions, on the side of music we are engaged in a kind of musicology. In both respects we are engaged in a study of the relationship between religion and, broadly conceived, culture, more specifically cultural forms or expressions.

The theologian Paul Tillich was very concerned to see religion and culture as two sides of the same existence.[1] His aphoristic statement, 'religion is the substance of culture, culture is the form of religion' was often quoted by him in different contexts, and is often quoted to express something that was fundamental to Tillich's way of doing theology. If the statement is examined closely it is not as simple as it appears at first sight. It can be argued that what Tillich meant to say was 'religion ought to be or will be, when the Kingdom of God is come, the substance of culture; culture is now, and historically, in many civilizations, has been the form of religion.' One half of the aphorism is a theological statement, the other half is a historical statement. We will not go into the question of civilizations in which religion and culture are indistinguishable. Suffice it to say that in the broadly European and American civilizations that we are most closely acquainted with the aphorism is to be interpreted in the way that has been suggested. Religion is always clothed in cultural garments. We want to suggest that in this case as in many others – 'the clothes make the person'.

It is very clear, then, that religions are culturally expressed, even culturally conditioned. Religions do not exist in a human or cultural vacuum. The languages of the different world religions are specific to different cultures. If the language of one religion were to be used in the presentation of a different religion, that is, in a language alien to the particular religion, then the religion would not take root nor would it flourish. This is not to say that the basics of one religion cannot be explained to a certain degree in a different cultural milieu. If this were not so then the teaching of world religions in our institutions would have to cease. However, it is always the case that the terms used in one religious milieu to explain religious terms from a different milieu always only proximate to the indigenous meanings of the terms.

In describing the relationship between religion and culture we would want to go further and suggest that religions are, in fact, culturally determined. Religions may be founded on what is called revelation. Revelation is understood as the receiving of a message, understood as an expression of eternal and ultimate truth. Revelatory claims are claims to an experience of something new, authentic, received, through intervention from outside the immediate human realm, therefore, in a sense untainted by base human thoughts or ideas. As such, revelatory claims in themselves cannot be investigated. They can only be investigated if they are transmitted by the receiver of the revelation. When the revelation, the message, is transmitted, we find that the claims to intervention from outside the human realm are at best ambiguous and ambivalent. For the simple fact is that the revelation has to be expressed in terms that are understood within the cultural environment of the receiver of the revelation. So Tillich would argue, as against the Barthian position, for instance, that all revelation becomes religion the moment it is transmitted, and it is on this fact that he bases his statement about culture being the form of religion. We would go further and maintain that not only is the religion culturally expressed, it is culturally determined, and also that the revelation, in so far as we can determine what a particular revelation is, is culturally determined.

To make such a statement in a theological environment may seem unduly contentious. However, the statement should be considered carefully as to what has been said and what has not been said. It has not been said, for example, that because a revelation is culturally determined it is therefore not true or should not be believed. To claim that a certain revelation may or may not be true is for the individual to decide. It is a matter of faith, and the statement regarding the culturally determined nature of religion is not a statement regarding faith. To say that a revelation is culturally determined is to say something that is merely observably true. There were those who heard Jesus of Nazareth preach who thought he was mad. Imagine what their reaction would have been if instead of saying 'I and my Father are One', he had said 'I and Krishna are One'.

What has been largely concentrated upon has been the use of language and cultural imagery to make the point about the intrinsic nature of the relationship between religion and culture, religion being, for our purposes, the result of revelation. But the range of cultural forms which determine the way a religion is expressed are manifold and complex. This is especially the case where a religion, and Christianity is perhaps a classic example, expands and moves into new cultural areas and adapts itself to the new cultural environment. The other classical example is Buddhism. Islam is less so, though it is too simple to suggest that Islam is not as adaptable as the other two mentioned. Of course Christianity has not always been and is not always now so adaptable. Experiences of Christianity in India lie behind much of what is expressed here about the intrinsic relationship between religion and culture. In the case of India the prevailing ethos of Christianity is one of cultural alienation. It is also as well to remember that there are cases in which an expanding religion has not adapted itself to a new cultural environment but has, often with tragic results, destroyed and replaced the existing culture with its own imported cultural forms.

If we are able to argue successfully the intrinsic relationship between religion and culture to the point where we find religion culturally determined then we are able to proceed to the point at which we examine the ways in which different cultural forms or expressions operate in the religious context or environment. We have already seen how language and cultural imagery operate in the religious context. What about music or dance or painting or sculpture or architecture? What part do they play in the religious action? At this point we want to turn to talking more specifically of ritual action. What part do cultural forms play in ritual action? We would argue that they play a part so intrinsic, due to the way in which religion is culturally determined, that cultural forms or expression when brought into or associated with the ritual action are not mere add-ons or embellishments or aids to piety or worship but become part of the ritual action. They become vehicles for whatever the worshipper or devotee is expecting, seeking and receiving in the way of divine blessing, grace or power.

Music as iconic

The term for describing materials which become vehicles of divine grace, power and blessing is that they are sacramental. We are suggesting that cultural forms and expressions are likewise sacramental. However, we have chosen to avoid the term sacramental because it is expressive of only one religious tradition and what we are examining is the universal way in which cultural forms and expressions function. We have chosen rather the term *iconic*, because it is a term that is used outside the immediate religious context. It is a term which can be used without specific religious content. It is in this sense a term of neutral application, especially since it is related to the term iconography which is constantly used in religious contexts other than Christianity. The word 'icon' is used quite generally today to speak of certain artefacts which express the 'spirit' of a historical period. It is often used these days even of persons. The term *iconic* is used especially by art historians.

The following quotation will help illustrate our point:

[The term] *iconic* derives from the Greek word *eikon*, meaning 'image'. In art history, *icon* is most frequently used to denote a Byzantine – that is, a Christian Greek – representation, usually of Christ, the Virgin, or saints and angels, painted in a highly conventional way. In Byzantine thought, the icon partakes of some of the qualities of the original it represents, so that the devout Christian venerates the original through its representation. An *icon* embodies the essence of the personage by representing his or her significant attributes and status, but not at any particular moment or in any fleeting state of mind or being. *Iconic*, as used in art history, refers to this kind of representation . . . *Iconic* imagery (always using the word in its art-historical sense only) is concerned with the status of the personages it represents, and some particular aspect of their being, as it were frozen in time or outside time altogether . . . *Iconic* art aims to elicit veneration and awe . . .[2]

The art historian contrasts iconic art with narrative art and makes the point that the line between iconic and narrative art is not always clearly defined, as for instance in the case of the crucified Christ, which may be seen as a narrative of what happened on Good Friday or as an icon in its own right. This may be seen also in the way in which composers approach religious themes.

We want to refer especially to one section of the art historian's description of the use of the term 'iconic'. Among other things she says: 'the icon partakes of some of the qualities of the original it represents, so that the devout Christian venerates the original through its representation. An icon embodies the essence of the personage by representing his or her significant attributes and status.'[3] If we rephrase this and apply it to music in the Latin Mass we will get something like this: 'the music partakes of some of the qualities of the original message it represents, so that the devout Christian venerates the original message through its representation. The music of the Mass embodies the essence of the ritual by representing its significant attributes and status.' That is what we are arguing in this presentation: that the music is an intrinsic part of the action of the Mass, not an embellishment or decoration or an aid to worship, but part of the whole action of the Mass when music forms part of the celebration. However, this is an over-simplification of what we wish to examine.

While we would argue that where music is used with purpose in the ritual setting it is part of the ritual experience in an essential way, music is not essential to the full ritual experience. We would suggest that for the full ritual experience as applied to the Latin Mass certain core elements need to be present. These core elements consist of a sacred text and sacred materials, with sacred action, read and performed by a sacred person. Ideally the action should take place in a sacred space, i.e. a ritual space set aside for the sacred action, a space which, traditionally, would only be occupied by ritually prepared persons. These core elements can be amplified so that the sacred text is not just read but chanted, the sacred person is identified by particular dress and the sacred space takes on certain well defined characteristics amounting to highly stylized and decorated architecture. Finally there is added music. The music is included in such a way that it harmonizes with the actions and the text and becomes part of the whole. When everything is put together it is referred to as High Mass, as opposed to Low Mass when some of the elements are missing, and by the description High giving it a status which is of an enhanced nature. And music is part of that enhanced status.

For all the elements to work for the desired ends the music has to be of such a kind that it meets certain traditional requirements; possibly, it should also meet the expectations of the ecclesiastical authorities; and finally it should meet the needs of the congregation of worshippers. Therefore for the music to work as part of the whole ritual experience there has to be collaboration between the composer and the ecclesiastical authorities and clients. When the desired ends are fully met or as fully met as possible we would say that the music is performing an iconic function. Music which is deemed inappropriate by the ecclesiastical authorities or clients would not operate in an iconic fashion. It is one of the interesting features of music in the Christian tradition that one style of music will be iconic for one set of clients and not iconic for another set and vice versa.

One of the problems in dealing with the kind of music we are now discussing is that over a span of time the music composed for the ritual setting will be performed in a concert or entertainment setting. What do we say of the music in the alternative setting? We cannot say that the music composed for the ritual setting but performed in the concert setting is inappropriate for the alternative setting. The appropriateness is determined by a different set of clients. In saying this it should not be forgotten that for some of the clients of the ritual setting the music may perform an entertainment function, i.e. not be iconic in the way we have suggested. We would meet these questions by suggesting that there is nothing absolute about iconicity. It is a variable status. The same problems apply to artefacts which are removed from the ritual setting to the museum or the drawing room. In Hinduism, artefacts which have specific power in one setting are deemed to have lost the specific power in another setting. We think that something similar can be applied to anything that belongs to the ritual space and action which finds its way into another setting. We would say that when the ritual object or action, including music, is functioning with iconic power in the appropriate setting it is functioning with manifest iconicity. When the object or action, including music, is removed from the ritual setting, then it will not necessarily lose its iconic power completely but will function with latent iconicity.

This is what we wish to argue: that music functions in an iconic way when brought into ritual action, in this case the Latin

Mass. In order for it to function iconically the music must be composed in accordance with the expectations of the ecclesiastical authorities and clients. Given that music functions in this way, it is part of the action which is a vehicle for divine grace, power and blessing and not a mere appendage. But can we go any way to proving what we argue?

Some specific examples

Composers in the medieval period are not likely to have thought of themselves as artists. The Church as their main employer paid them not just for their compositions but for other services too, such as those of priest and singer. Leonin and Perotin, working at Notre Dame in Paris in the twelfth century, are good examples of this. The music they supplied had therefore to be acceptable to the church authorities. But what was considered acceptable? In other words, what did the Church at that time consider sacred music to be?

No doubt the most highly regarded musical style was plainsong, which is characterized by simplicity, its single melodic line ensuring the clarity of the text. Purity is another word one could use to describe it, but it is beyond the scope of this paper to examine the meaning of this word in the musical context. A quotation from St Bernard of Clairvaux from the twelfth century is typical of the many references made to plainsong: it is 'full of gravity – sweet, yet without levity'. It is significant how frequently and regularly similar views have been expressed since: the aim of the St Cecilia Society, for example, which was formed in the nineteenth century, with ten thousand members throughout Europe and the USA, was to 'lead back sacred song to simple ecclesiastical form', and this meant cultivating 'Gregorian or plain-chant everywhere'. Bruckner was a prominent member of this society. Elsewhere, Gounod praised the 'timeless' quality of plainsong, an interesting word seeing that the form still survives in use today after many centuries and can thus be said to reflect the timeless nature of the liturgy. Two twentieth-century popes have referred to the appropriateness of plainsong: Pius X described it as being 'the highest model of all sacred music' and Pius XII said that it possessed 'dignity and solemnity'. Olivier Messiaen, the great French composer and organist, whose whole output reflected his deep Roman Catholic faith, wrote, 'There is only one: plain-chant . . . it forms the daily bread, other musics are garnishes.'

So the purpose of these medieval craftsmen was to provide appropriate music – based on plainsong – on demand, and this music would also meet the expectations of the worshipper. Their music was deemed to be sacred by their patrons, the Church authorities, and came to be accepted as such by those who heard it. The listener, or in this context, the worshipper, meets it 'half way'. This is still the case: this style of music is instantly recognizable as 'sacred music'. It is part of our cultural tradition and has the added power of association. As Stockhausen has said of plainsong: 'it smells of the Church'!

Just as painters of the Renaissance were imbuing their works with greater realism and humanity, so did composers, particularly in the fifteenth and sixteenth centuries, begin to push back the boundaries of expression. In the context of the present discussion there is evidence of word painting in the Mass. For example, if one takes the *Et incarnatus est* section of the *Credo* of Josquin des Prés *Missa Pange Lingua* (c. 1530) it is very apparent that he treats the text very differently from the preceding passage. The relatively florid counterpoint gives way to a sombre chordal texture, the voices are in their lower register with long held notes and meaningful pauses and rests. Such a change is not only effective musically and dramatically but it indicates how important Josquin felt this part of the text to be. He, as an artist, as opposed to a mere craftsman, had the freedom to express the words as he felt they should be expressed.

Josquin was thus developing means to make his music more expressive. By the beginning of the seventeenth century other influences were being felt, notably those of opera. Opera, at the very least, provided an opportunity for individual expression through melody (as opposed to counterpoint) and colour through the use of instruments. The effect of this on church music was immense and caused problems for the authorities, as it continues to do now.

Music now was a vehicle for expressing emotion and composers were looking for opportunities to do so. There were also an increasing variety of ways in which to convey it. (It is interesting to note that one of the reasons why Gounod favoured plainsong was because it avoided 'emotionalism'.) As a result, sacred music was associated with the secular (or, according to Pope Pius X, the 'profane, vulgar or theatrical') and this presented further problems. It was music that could be enjoyed for its own sake, independent of its context – and function – becoming, for want of a better word, *entertainment*. Another implication here was that there was a danger of the text becoming of secondary importance to the music. It was now less easy instantly to recognize such music as 'sacred'.

The papal authorities have from this time periodically done

battle with their progressive musicians, trying to assert their views on what is acceptable or not. The Council of Trent in the sixteenth century was the most notable stand taken against the new trends which were said to 'delight the ears more than the mind . . . which is seen to excite the faithful to lascivious rather than religious thought'. It is not surprising too that many of the liturgical settings of the eighteenth and nineteenth centuries were (and are) not acceptable to the authorities. It was only in 1947 that Pope Pius XII commented on the exception taken to the 'liturgical unfitness' of composers such as Mozart, Haydn and Rossini.[4] It is significant that sacred music formed only a relatively small part of the output of these composers, and the Church was only one of their patrons.

If we focus on the music of the eighteenth and nineteenth centuries, it is not surprising that, particularly with its frequently operatic style, it is not thought to be acceptable; a view, we suspect held just as much without as within the Church. It is our view, however, that the style is immaterial to its function. As stated earlier, if music is performed in the ritual setting it has an iconic or sacramental function.

The are one or two caveats to this rather broad assertion. Firstly, the music must accord with each individual's *taste* otherwise the effect on the worshipper is not iconic. Someone who prefers to worship today with the aid of guitars and tambourines is unlikely to be moved by Beethoven, and *vice versa*. It should also be pointed out that, although it is commonly felt that the sacred involves the separation from the profane world and that high art music is the more appropriate medium for expressing the inexpressible, we do not restrict our argument to high art music. James Livingston, for instance, in his recent book *The Anatomy of the Sacred* refers to the ambivalence of sacred power which can be felt in a wide variety of responses.[5] Secondly, the music needs to match each individual's interpretation of the text, to fuse into one iconic action. In the mainstream classical repertoire, for example, it is likely that the composer's intentions are understood by the listener. This happens because of the employment of certain stylistic conventions; thus it is possible to convey emotions and states of mind such as joy, serenity, rage which are readily understood as such. In a simple experiment conducted with groups of people, some with a musical background, some not, we played a long instrumental introduction from a section from a late Haydn Mass without saying what it was and asked those present to note down adjectives they would use to describe the piece. It was striking (although perhaps not surprising) how similar the responses were. It must surely be assumed that if the vast majority considered the music to be 'peaceful' then this was Haydn's intention. For one person only did the music convey something completely different. He thought it was 'triumphant'. If, on hearing the complete movement, which was the *Agnus Dei*, he believed that the text should not inspire a triumphant setting, then the music would not be iconic for him. (It follows, too, that if any of the rest did not agree with the 'peaceful' interpretation of the words, the music would not have an iconic function.) Music is a language with a recognizable vocabulary – depending, of course, on one's cultural traditions and expectations. It is therefore quite possible to compare settings of the Mass over time, and in the remainder of this essay we will attempt to explain further our ideas on the iconic function of music, through a number of case studies.

If you were asked how you would go about setting to music the words of the opening of the *Gloria* – a hymn of praise – we suspect that the answers would be similar. If you had a lot of instruments at your disposal you would probably choose to use many of them together to create a large sound; the dynamic level would be loud; you would tend to use the whole chorus instead of a soloist and it is likely that you would decide to exploit the whole pitch range available to you. A survey of Mass settings from the eighteenth and nineteenth centuries confirms this: it was customary to have a fast tempo, a busy accompaniment, a homophonic or chordal choral texture (as opposed to counterpoint) which would have greater impact, a loud dynamic level and a noticeably rising melodic line. Such conformity could be said to be explained by tradition, yet this is not the whole explanation because if this is so why is it that other parts of the Mass are given very different settings, often by the same composer? The following words of the *Gloria* – *et in terra pax* – are also treated uniformly with a drop in vocal range, and lowering of activity in the accompaniment and dynamic level.

Other sections of the Mass can be set in different ways, as we have suggested above (just as in paintings, biblical scenes such as annunciation and crucifixion are given very different interpretations). The *Sanctus* provides a good example of this. The words from the book of Isaiah can elicit feelings of dread or awe or humility, and there may be other interpretations. Mozart in his *Mass in C minor* (1782) chooses to separate each utterance of the word *Sanctus*, each one higher in pitch than the last. The tempo is also slow, as is the harmonic movement generally. Assuming that worshippers receive similar messages from this musical interpretation, it could be said that such treatment of the words elicits feelings of awe. It could be pointed out at this point too, that Mozart places great emphasis on the next words, *Dominus Deus Sabaoth* which he achieves with a dramatic crescendo, enhanced by a prolonged tonic pedal. If these lines of the text are compared with what Schubert did in his *Mass in E flat* (first performed after his death in 1829), the similarities are immediately apparent. Again the words are separated and the melodic line rises, but here there are also sudden changes of dynamic level and completely unexpected, increasingly dark harmonies which add a sense of dread to that of awe. This is not because Schubert had a wider range of musical 'tools' at his disposal; Mozart could have depicted dread equally successfully had he chosen to do so. Beethoven, on the other hand, gives a very different interpretation in both his *Missa Solemnis* and the earlier *Mass in C* (1807): both sections are headed *Mit Andacht* (with devotion). Humility is achieved through the use of the quiet woodwind in the orchestral introduction (there is no introduction in either the Mozart or the Schubert); the chorus is *piano* and at a fairly low range and significantly unaccompanied (said by some to reflect Palestrina's influence!). If, therefore, any or all of these musical interpretations matches those of the worshipper, then again the effect is iconic and the music provides a channel for the receipt of divine power, grace and blessing.

It is interesting to note where composers place special emphasis in their word setting. Let us take again the *Et incarnatus est* section of the *Credo*, for example. This is a narrative section of the Mass, so it is particularly important for the words to be heard to allow the worshipper to 'follow the story', so to speak. Haydn in his *Nelson Mass* (1798), for example, as he does elsewhere, treats the whole section as one musical paragraph, whereas Bruckner in his *Mass in F minor* (1867–8) places great emphasis on the words *Maria Virgine* and *passus* (suffered). In the latter case the word is frequently repeated with static harmony, maybe to allow the worshipper to meditate on the word. Other repetitions are less felicitous. Schubert's decision to repeat the whole *Et incarnatus est* section and the following *Crucifixus* in the *Mass in E flat* may point to his unorthodox Christian belief. (One of his friends actually queried whether he had one at all – certainly it would appear that he composed Masses in order to provide a range of compositional genres in a portfolio for prospective patrons without being particularly committed to what he was composing. It is outside the scope of this paper to consider in detail the implications of the reasons for the commissioning of individual Masses. This is a whole other dimension: for example, if a work is composed to celebrate a victory or a patron's birthday, then the occasion must be reflected to a greater or lesser extent in the mood of the music without compromising its iconicity.) To return to the Schubert example, such a manipulation of the liturgical text shows either a misunderstanding of the ritual or a preference for musico/ dramatic effect at the expense of the iconic.

An example of a piece which we consider to be clearly *not* iconic is the opening of the *Kyrie* from Mozart's *Mass in C major* (1776). It seems to us in no way to reflect the penitential mood of the text. The major key is in itself no problem, but it is the combination of this with the spritely rhythms and catchy fugal subject which undermines the effect and does not succeed in matching the worshippers' expectations. If this setting is compared with what Mozart did in his later *Mass in C minor* (1782) (is it significant here that this latter work was not commissioned but composed for himself?) the difference is startling. The mood in this case is sombre: the dark colours of the orchestra emphasized by the exploitation of the lower instruments and trombones, the slow tempo, the descending chromatic lines and dissonant harmonies. Yet it is likely that this is exactly the kind of music which is frowned upon for being too operatic, for the soprano soloist who enters with the words *Christe eleison* has a role which is straight out of the theatre with its virtuosic line. However, her first notes could not be more simple and direct and thus to many wholly appropriate in reflecting a more personal supplication to God the Son as opposed to the Father. The ensuing virtuosity is Mozart's way of conveying a sense of yearning which is entirely appropriate to the requirements of the text and therefore iconic.

Inevitably we have only given a very few musical illustrations, and these have been taken from the familiar 'classical' repertoire where composers in general employ similar conventions which are readily understood and met half-way by the worshipper. It is significant that there are relatively few very modern settings of the Mass. This may be for various reasons – the increasing secular society and composers' concerns elsewhere; the way in which the arts are patronized, for instance – but there is the problem of the inaccessibility of many modern styles which contradicts the role of the Church as a social institution. Some composers, such as Jonathan Harvey, write complex music in an uncompromising style which aptly reflects the 'striving in the dark' aspect of worship. Others, like John Tavener (albeit in the Orthodox tradition) and Arvo Pärt, have returned to the primitive simple style of the medieval period which is where we started.

Notes

1. P. Tillich (ed. R. C. Kimball), *Theology of Culture* (New York: Oxford University Press, 1964), p. 42.
2. E. Langmuir, *Introduction to Art History* (Milton Keynes: Open University Press, 1986), pp. 31–2.
3. ibid., p. 32.
4. R. F. Hayburn, *Papal Legislation on Sacred Music 95 AD to 1977 AD* (Collegeville, Minnesota: Liturgical Press, 1978), p. 340.
5. J. C. Livingstone, *Anatomy of the Sacred: An Introduction to Religion* (New York: Macmillan, 1989), p. 49.

Towards a Sacred Art

JOHN TAVENER

As a Christian composer, John Tavener laments the Romantic notion of the artist as creative genius, and the disintegration of culture and tradition which has gone with it. Instead, in a way which parallels the icon painter, he sees the composer required to operate within a sacred tradition – in his case the eight Ortho-dox tones. Thereby God is enabled to work through him, and instead of contributing to the concert hall, like an icon his music can help us participate in the mystery of Christ, our God, and his Mother's response.

Working within a tradition

My subject is the sacred in art – art that is *athanatos*, without death, without change, without beginning and without end. This is so difficult to discuss in a time when human beings seem to have lost their belief not only in God, but also even in them-selves. We live in a culture in ruins.

The modern concept of the artist as creative genius differs radically from the divinely inspired artist of Plato:[1] any artist who produced a work of sacred art could never think of himself as a creative genius in the modern sense of the word. The artists of the sacred con-creates or reproduces, and must submit to the discipline of practising, through endless repetition of a given form, until he has mastered all of it, so that its original tran-scendence begins to flow through him; no longer a matter of external copying or repetition, but a matter of directing the forces of primordial inspiration, of which he is now the vehicle, into formal patterns that long practice and meditation have allowed him to master both inwardly and outwardly. I would say that the 'dictum' for all sacred Christian art must be as St Paul

172

expresses it in another context: 'yet not I, but Christ liveth me' (Gal. 2.20 AV).

As a composer, living and working in these secular times, I work of course in a small area which does not seem to concern many people. My increasing concern for the sacred needs some explanation. For an artist to work in a sacred tradition, he must first believe in the divine realities that inform that particular tradition. This is a *sine qua non* – not of course a guarantee of great art – but it is absolutely essential. Second, he must know the traditions of the art that he works in. He must know the tools, so that he can work with material that is primordial, and therefore not 'his'; not his or her expression, but the tradition working through him.

The artist concerned with the sacred must make an act of faith. In my own case, it was a commitment to the Orthodox Church. First and foremost a commitment to Christ our God as expressed through the eyes of the Orthodox Church. This is 'radical' in the purest sense of the word and demands a gradual losing of self through a work of endless repentance, constantly falling, but picking oneself up, pointing ever more God-wards, to provide the vehicle through which the only Creator can work. There is nothing 'pie in the sky' about this; the task is daunting, awesome and exigent, and at the end of the day one can expect nothing but crucifixion and failure, because our strength, uniquely as Christians, lies in our weakness, our frailty and our vulnerability.

Not only is the task daunting spiritually, but it is daunting in specific musical terms. This is because if an English composer wishes to write music within the Orthodox tradition, he must, like an icon painter, renounce any ideas of his own, and adhere to a strict discipline based on a system of tones – tones 1 to 8. Each tone is different, somewhat like the Indian ragas, somewhat like the Gregorian modes, but unlike these in so far as every Orthodox country has developed its own tone system. For instance, there are eight Greek tones, eight Russian tones, eight Coptic tones and so on. All these tones have probably evolved from the dawn of civilization. Indeed, one can see many connections between the Greek tones and the Indian ragas. It would take a lifetime to become fully acquainted with even one of these tone systems. If in Byzantine times a melodist was asked to set anything to music, he would first have to set it in the appropriate tone or melody. The music is as much part of the tapestry and strict discipline of the Church as is the iconography. If for instance a composer was asked to set a text to the

Mother of God, he would first have to know on which feast day this was proposed, because all eight tones may be needed for one single text, depending on whether the text is to be sung in Lent, Easter, Pentecost or any other day in the Church's year. My *Lord's Prayer* was written in tone 1 of the Byzantine system.

I often wonder why the sacred music of any age should sound very different. The answer is that it should not. If composers in the West concerned with sacred tradition were trained in the disciplines of Byzantium, sacred India, music of the Sufis, Judaic chant or any of the Orthodoxies, instead of learning about Schoenberg's *Innovations* they would become aware that innovation has nothing to do with tradition. That is why no innovatory art can possess the magisterial, primordial beauty emanating from the divine, making us creatures through which a theophany could pass.

People talk about composers finding their own voice; this is another totally misleading concept; not misleading if the composer does not believe in the divine realities; then of course he can be totally promiscuous in his artistic pursuits, and there is nothing wrong with this. It only becomes wrong if he believes in divine realities, and, at the same time, digs from the endless so-called innovations from the last three hundred years.

You can perhaps begin to see why the Orthodox find the concept of an anthem or a hymn totally incomprehensible. To us it holds up proceedings, and instead of encouraging congregational participation in the Liturgy, it seems to introduce the idea of an 'entertainment' or a 'concert' into the middle of a sacred ceremony. No wonder Stravinsky referred to Mozart's Masses as 'operatic sweets of sin'.

The composer as icon-painter

The icon is a supreme example of Christian art and of transcendence and transfiguration. It possesses simplicity, transfigured beauty and austerity: austerity because the manner of painting has remained unchanged since the first mandelion (or 'icon not painted by human hands') bearing the face of Christ miraculously imprinted on a piece of material and was sent to the King of Edessa.[2] Icon painting is a strict discipline, requiring fasting and constant communion. An icon does not express emotion (it is geometric and its colour palette is severely limited) and yet to the believer it inspires awe, wonder and the reverence of kissing. The icon is in one sense beyond art because it plunges us straight into liturgical time and sacred history. But what makes a great icon? I believe that it is the Holy Spirit working through the painter, and that is a total mystery.

How far can the art of icon painting relate to music? I will suggest some ways on which the composer may meditate. If the composer knows something of the sacred tones of the Orthodox Church he will have the material. If he understands the significance of the 'ison' or drone, then he will have some clues. The composer may dance out of or back into the tone, but it must always be somewhere present. He must also limit the tonal and colour palette, but always knowing where he must insert the divine archetype by a fully assimilated knowledge of the tones. All this has at any rate given me some ideas for the small patch that, as a composer, I feel compelled to work.

The Church is no longer the wise patron that she was in the Byzantine period, the medieval Western period, or in Bach's Protestant Germany. As artists, we literally write or paint into a vacuum and into an apparent spiritual void. The point of any sacred art, however, is that it should be functional. Think of Egyptian wall paintings, Muslim architecture, Bach Passions, Byzantine icons, the Cathedral of Saint Sophia, the Taj Mahal – all once functional and now in danger of becoming museums: out of the church, into the concert hall; out of the church, into the art gallery; out of the temple, into the greedy anonymous hands of dealers, along with the terrifying devastation of God's world. This is all part of the desecration of the sacred. Surely all creation, in all its fullness, is the necessary expression of divine Life, with all the absolute freedom and spontaneity of God's being.

Contrast all of this with Mary's 'Yes' at the annunciation: without her there would have been no Christ, no salvation, no life, no restoration of the unity of creation. That is why the Mother of God is so important for me and it is this that I have tried to express in my setting of a hymn to her from the divine liturgy of St Basil the Great. It speaks of her cosmic power and beauty over a shattered world – '*all* creation rejoices'.

I see the act of re-creating in the end as a miracle. After the ascetic pain of labouring to find the best way that I can to depict the subject, then this 'miracle' happens. But also each new piece is an act of repentance, stripping away unessentials, ever more naked, ever more simple – one might even say ever more foolish. One tries in one's work to follow the life of the saint, even if it appears completely unobtainable. Through ascetic struggle the saint reintegrates himself into the paradisaical life. Again and again his or her life is associated with a variety of forms of reconciliation to nature, to trees, to plants, to climate: the enduring of heat and cold, the eating with no ill effects of noxious weeds, friendship with wild animals. This is the traditional view of the saint, common to all great Orthodoxies. So you can imagine how thrilled I was at the opportunity of being able to contribute something to the memory of one of the great Celtic saints of the West; St Cuthbert of Lindisfarne, whose relics lie in Durham Cathedral, with my *Icon of St Cuthbert*. Here, contained within the conventional symmetry of the Orthodox Matins Canon, together with the familiar repetition of the invocation to the saint to pray for us sinners, comes the life of a truly great saint of the Western world.

Recovering memory in a disintegrating present

Now comes a more practical problem. How does one communicate to a world that has forgotten and has little time for repentance, simplicity or foolishness – the foolishness of Christ our God, the foolishness of the Mother of God and the foolishness of all the crowds of martyrs, saints and holy fools? I said, however, that the world had forgotten, and this seems to me to be the operative word; otherwise, why has there been such a return of the memory in the resurgence of sacred art towards the close of the millennium? Think of Yeats, Eliot, Arvo Pärt, Messiaen, David Jones, Eric Gill. This seems an appropriate place to mention a short piece which sprung from the death of a beloved friend, Cecil Collins, who spent his life devoted to the sacred painting of fools and angels. He was always outside any religious tradition, but he used the world of archetypes that he considered to be more universal. He would take from the Sufi tradition, the early Christian tradition, the Hindu tradition, and indeed any sacred tradition what he felt to be relevant to his art. 'Eonia' is a piece which came to me already fully grown – I think of it as an essence, a fragrance, a haiku,[3] but above all a tribute to the man I loved and whose frail, iconographical art touched me deeply.

Yet we are also at the same time witnessing a profound amnesia of simple, primordial and eternal truths, in favour of an insane, technological, materialistic, psychological, intellectual culture. What we have is a culture and spirituality in ruins; devoid of *gnosis*, as T. S. Eliot predicted, a civilization that rejects what it cannot diminish. If, as I say, the operative word is 'forgotten' then there must be a ray of hope. To reawaken the primordial consciousness that lies dormant in all of us, somehow we have to provide a *temenos* or sacred space in which to work. The concert hall, the opera house and the art gallery are all glaring reminders of how fragmented and dislocated we have become. Stockhausen has said that the churches will become the concert halls of the future, and there is more than a ring of truth about this. To move the temenos back into the cathedrals and churches, not to popularize and desanctify even more, but to allow sacred art to breathe gently on these ancient stones. Let the great medieval cathedrals of England be used to breathe back anew the medieval thought or gnosis that formed them.

And if the Christian Church is to offer a positive response to the challenge of the sacred and to the ecological crisis, it must understand the colossal significance and implication of the incarnation, in all its amplitude and magnificence. As the Orthodox Christmas service of Compline proclaims, 'God is *with* us, understand ye nations, God is *with* us'.

Adherence to primordial tradition requires a very deep humility; a humility that at the end of the day says 'we know nothing'; a humility that requires a complete dismantling of the whole present scientific, psychological, popularist, profane and radical dehumanization of our society, which has of course dislocated the whole cosmic realm. Theology in the Orthodox East has always been regarded as an expression of a given reality. But in the West, instead of the Platonic elements which had served early Eastern theologians as a vehicle for expressing an understanding of man confirmed through a life of prayer and contemplation, largely due to the disastrous teachings of Aristotle, its thought entered a ruinous epoch of abstraction and theory. In the West, art has become abstracted and removed from its eucharistic function, removed also from nature, from its sacramental roots and finally removed from life itself.

I believe that we are in an abnormal state, split between imagination, reason, art and metaphysics. Our art is separated from sacred cosmology and the teachings of the Fathers on the anthropological aspects of the sacramental nature of creation. Out on a limb from the sacred, English hymns have references to God and the saints, but they have nothing to do with sacred art. A great deal of art expresses intimations of the divine, aspirations of the divine, glimpses of the divine, either in the human soul or in the world of nature. However, the quality that distinguishes a work of sacred art and that sets it apart from other works of art, is one that can only be described by a word such as 'knowledge' or 'gnosis'. As Dante writes: 'Ye that are of good understanding, note the teaching that is hidden under the veil of the strange lines'.[4] Indeed this invites us to seek out 'the intellect of love' – a disposition of being that induces and permits the God that constantly desires to reveal himself (if only we could see in our soul) and desires our power of vision. This is the only way out of the spiritual, theological, ecological and artistic catastrophe that faces us at the close of the twentieth century.

I am neither philosopher nor theologian, but my work – my work of repentance that may or may not lead me towards a sacred art – can be judged only by how near the music I write comes to its task. This is my work within the small area from which I must continue to dig and labour and to try to resituate the modern mentality as a whole within the framework of metaphysical values and wisdom from which it has been so disastrously uprooted.

I would like to end, however, on a more apophatic note; perhaps you might even say on a more apocalyptic note, at any rate on a question mark. How childlike, and how deep must be our trust in God in the face of the apocalyptic events that are happening around us day by day? How childlike and how immeasurably deep must have been the faith of the Mother of God when the Archangel appeared to her and she exclaimed, terror-struck, 'How can this be?' (Luke 1.34 RSV).

No amount of writing, philosophizing, poetry, music or painting can in the end give any absolute answer. Faith and doubt go hand in hand, and we love both the faith and the doubt equally. The Mother of God trusted, you might say madly, blindly, insanely at the prospect of God entering into her womb. We try hard and continue to follow her example in the joy of believing and yet not knowing, and the piercing agony of watching her Son crucified day after day, hour after hour, and forever asking her question, 'How can this be?'

So we proceed, as the Mother of God did, with joy and sorrow in our hearts, singing with her our joy and sorrow songs of the cross and of the empty tomb, until one day we may perhaps be able to grow up out of our spiritual adolescence into the resurrection.

Notes

1. Plato in his earlier writings insists that art is never self-generated but is always the result of a divine inspiration or 'madness'. Compare for example *Phaedrus* 265 A, 10ff.
2. The story is recounted in *The Story of Addai*, dating probably from the fifth century. The topic can be pursued at greater length in E. Kuryluk, *Veronica and her Cloth* (Oxford: Blackwell, 1991), especially pp. 38ff.
3. A 'haiku' is a Japanese poem that manages to condense all it wishes to say into three lines.
4. Dante, *The Divine Comedy*, *Inferno*, Canto IX, lines 61–3, trans. J. D. Sinclair (Oxford: Oxford University Press, 1961), p. 123.

Music as a Sacrament

JAMES LANCELOT

Taking his cue from the Prayer Book definition of a sacrament James Lancelot argues that music may naturally be seen as such, as a sign or symbol which imparts spiritual grace. Strictly speaking music was unnecessary as part of creation, and so is a powerful symbol of the overflowing generosity of divine love, most powerfully expressed in the incarnation. As such it can also draw us out of ourselves, and so help every aspect of our lives to be lived sacramentally. It is for this reason that its sacramental function cannot be confined to purely sacred music, and indeed why some 'secular' sounds can sometimes function successfully in a sacred way.

God's sacramental generosity

What is a sacrament? The Catechism in the Book of Common Prayer tells us that it is 'an outward and visible sign of an inward and spiritual grace given unto us, ordained by Christ himself, as a means whereby we receive the same, and as a pledge to assure us thereof.' According to St Thomas Aquinas, it is 'a sign of a sacred reality in as much as it has the property of sanctifying human beings'.[1] Originally a *sacramentum* was a soldier's oath of allegiance, but the Latin New Testament used the word to render the Greek *musterion* or mystery. Both Eastern and Western churches now commonly accept seven sacraments, of which baptism and Holy Communion alone are accounted as 'generally necessary to salvation'. So where does music come in?

I think that the answer to this becomes plain – or plainer – if one can learn to see life itself as something to be lived sacramentally. If we shut the seven sacraments in church and fail to see their significance in our everyday lives, then we are up against it – and perhaps we have lost a vision of what life is

179

about. Long ago in Iona, the monks would take the remainder of the eucharistic bread out into the cloisters after Mass, and break it with each other; a custom which is observed again on the island today, where one is given a piece of bread to break with a stranger in the cloisters after the service. The point of this was, and is, to emphasize the extension of the sacrament and of Christ's indwelling presence into the whole of our lives. Perhaps one of the reasons why the world today often seems so godless is that Christians have not been clear enough in spelling out to the world that life is not divided up into some sort of pious sacred compartment and some sort of secular compartment, but rather that what is not actually profane is instead sacred – or capable of being made so. The Celtic monks of Iona saw this so clearly and expressed it wonderfully in their literature and in their manuscript decoration. How much of this vision we have lost over the centuries! And surely when one starts to see life from that sort of standpoint, music takes its place alongside many other of God's gifts as part of a theory of sacramental spirituality.

To be fair, the Church has never lost sight of the importance of music in worship – not just as a practical vehicle but also as an enhancement of the liturgy and as spiritual refreshment. I would go further than that and say that I think music offered in worship can have an eternal significance. John Casken, composer and Professor of Music at the University of Manchester, to whom we shall return later, has spoken of his feeling that the sounds cling to the stones. Many of us must have felt, as the echoes of an anthem or whatever have died away, that we have been, as it were, in the presence of angels.

Church buildings of great architectural splendour surely cry out for music to articulate the rhythm of the architecture and to complement it, to express the glory of God just as the building itself expresses it. To return just once more to Iona and to quote from the morning service used a few years ago by the community there: 'If we were to keep silence, the very stones would cry out loud' (an extension of Luke 19.40).

Yet it seems to me that music was not an absolutely essential part of creation; I suppose some inflections of pitch are necessary, for example to allow living creatures to distinguish the calls of each other and of their offspring, to warn of danger and so on; but the specific construction of music and its mathematical workings is something altogether beyond that. Surely it is a powerful symbol of a Creator whose love overflows, for it seems to have been given to us purely for the worship of God and for our own delight and comfort. It has a long and honourable history in the Old Testament: Job (38.7) speaks of the morning stars singing together, and the allusions in Psalm 150 are well known. There is also a lovely verse in Psalm 32 which we ought always to remember when we are tempted to despair: 'Thou art a place to hide me in, thou shalt preserve me from trouble: thou shalt compass me about with songs of deliverance.'[2]

Perhaps I have said enough to show how music can become *analogous* to a sacrament as we observed it so defined earlier. It combines a powerful symbol of God's love (creation of music and indeed of the human voice) with human creative skill (in finding out tunes and in making musical instruments). Here also we find reinforcement of a truly incarnational theology: God becoming man, God using human means to further his will. Look at it another way: we make music, but God uses the music to move our minds if we are receptive.

Now that begs an enormous question. For while sacred music should act beneficially on a receptive hearer and while much other music will, there is no doubt that music can also be used to deprave and corrupt. That does not detract from the value of music *per se*, for all of the most valuable things in life can be abused, and the evil of their abuse grows in proportion to their value when cherished and used aright. Much more difficult is the question of where one draws the line. If we accept that all of life is sacred and that all human work offered in the right spirit can be redeemed, then the great works of the repertoire are all safely gathered in; and I suspect that we shall find that the line gets drawn in places we did not expect. For example, I would never have expected to be so strongly moved by the use of music by Duke Ellington in worship as I have now twice been. I expect many of us could think of other examples in our own lives of where we have been surprised and perhaps jolted out of our preconceived ideas.

For centuries plainsong complemented both liturgy and the buildings in which that liturgy was celebrated. Someone who understood perfectly the need for such complementarity was the sixteenth-century composer, Thomas Tallis. One piece of his has come to illustrate very clearly for me the sacramental aspect of music: *O sacrum convivium* ('O sacred feast'). Musically its construction is relatively simple; it can be taken to pieces and analysed pretty easily. But that – while it may be useful – is to miss the point: the point is that it sets a text which talks of the Blessed Sacrament as a *pignus* or 'pledge' of future glory. And the music not only underlines the words but transcends them, putting the work on an altogether higher plane. It seems to be reaching, reaching out towards something outside itself – just as

Eucharist helps us reach out hands to heaven to grasp something of the eternal reality of the Christ who is hidden in bread
and wine.

A generosity reflected in music's variety

Now a theology based solely on music – if such a thing were
possible – would be an extraordinarily fragile house of cards. Yet
for me that work by Tallis does render the veil between earth and
heaven exceedingly thin. In fact I would go further and say that
in my more mystical moments I find the mere fact that such a
piece as that can actually exist to be sufficient proof for me of
the existence of a loving Creator and of the promise of eternal
life hereafter with that Creator – in other words sufficient proof
that all shall be well with the soul. If the whole universe were
just a random collection of atoms, such music could not exist –
and nor could a whole host of other things; at least, I cannot
believe so. Of course, it is not always that easy for me or anyone
else to believe. However, I hope this rather personal account will
help to illustrate what I mean by music's ability to be sacramental in being the outward sign of an inward grace which is
mediated to us.

I am not suggesting that that is enough – that somehow being
in love with music and being prepared to be moved by it is going
to be enough to live by. But I do suggest that as part of a
rounded and complete faith it is one of the many signposts
which God gives us towards himself, if we have eyes to see and
ears to hear. And at the same time I have to say very emphatic-
ally that it is quite right and proper that there will be many
more to whom the particular music I have mentioned does not
speak – or, indeed, no classical music at all. That does not
matter; and it is very good for our humility as musicians to realize that. God has many different ways of getting hold of us, and
we are none of us alike.

Let me try to reinforce my earlier point by referring to
another piece: a setting of Campion's famous poem 'Never
weather-beaten sail' by Hubert Parry, who died in 1918. I would
love to enlarge on the life and work of Parry, but it would be
pure self-indulgence; I would also try to explain the musical
means whereby Parry communicates feelings of longing, of
ecstasy, and of resignation; but while that might explain the
emotional effect which this music may have on us, it would not
help to explain the spiritual and sacramental significance of the
fact that music can solemnize us. Parry's music is very much of
its time and place – probably more so than Tallis's. But like all

the greatest music it also transcends the narrow bounds of its origins and speaks to new generations in new places – maybe not to all, but nevertheless to many who can hear it afresh in the new light of a different time and background. That is why in our cathedral worship we should try to use the best music of many different periods and at least a few different countries. Of course, some of it is bread-and-butter material; we cannot always live on the heights, and we would mis-shape the liturgy if we were to try to. But compared to the monks of old, we probably live on an astonishingly rich diet – in more than one sense!

So far, we have concentrated exclusively on music that was written specifically for use in worship – indeed, music that sets sacred texts. But if what I have suggested about the secular being redeemed by the sacred is true, it must follow that much other music has about it some quality of the sacramental. And when I say 'much other music', I am flinging wide the doors of our rather narrow compartment of (mostly) English church music and letting in the mainstream of Western music as millions of people understand it – music which includes some of the greatest achievements of Western civilization. It is sometimes said that Western art has forgotten God and that it needs to rediscover its ancient roots. I have spoken of music's capacity to depress and degrade, when used in the wrong hands. Inasmuch as all composition is a human endeavour, it must be tainted with the fall of Adam. But in elevating the greatest compositions and in thanking God for them, are we ennobling the work of human hands unduly? I think we can only fall back on the claim of Genesis that man and woman are created in the image of God, and on the New Testament claim that, when God wanted to show us more of himself and to redeem us from our sin, he sent us his Son, who came to us in human form. No, we are not playing at being God, or ignoring God and elevating human endeavour to equal divine creation; we are acknowledging that spark of the divine which God has placed in each one of us, acknowledging that in Adam all must die, but joyfully accepting that in Christ all shall be made alive. Musicians, along with writers, painters and architects, must accept some of the blame for the state of the world today and for the depressing quality of so many of our cities. But how much we can be thankful to them too for their contribution over the centuries to the ennoblement of our spirits.

One composer of this century who has very specifically sought to relate his music to the Christian faith is Olivier Messiaen – a man who has done much to reinforce the stature of the organ as an instrument to be taken seriously and one which has contributed quite enormously to the liturgy of the Western Church. Thoroughly versed in Western music, Messiaen also showed himself open to oriental influences, in addition to his use of birdsong in later works. His organ music, nearly all of it tied to particular theological concepts and seasons of the Church's year, is strongly didactic in that it takes us deeper into the mysteries of God. An early organ work is *Le banquet céleste*, a meditation on the Blessed Sacrament. Subtitled 'He who eats my flesh and drinks my blood abides in me, and I in him', it is like an incandescent jewel, radiant in its intensity. Like much of Messiaen's music, it achieves a good deal of its effect by means of an almost timeless slowness which challenges the man-made busy-ness of our cluttered lives and forces us to be still and to recollect ourselves.

The Church has traditionally been a generous patron of the arts, and this is right. The Church as a whole needs artists, not least musicians, if it is to continue to enhance its worship both as it has traditionally done and in new ways, of which the Messiaen piece is such a fine example. And the sacramental quality of its music will always have much to do with the spirit in which it is offered. It is obvious to anyone who studies our great cathedrals that it has mattered to generations of craftsmen that whatever handiwork they did was done well; it has to be right. It is more than ever important that the way we offer our worship is right, not only because we are offering the best of what we can do to God, but because worship goes to the very roots of what we are and why we were created in the first place. It is fatally tempting to relax into the comfort of an established church, with centuries of history behind us. Are we not rather in the front line of the battle between good and evil, the battle which will assuredly be won, that God may be all in all? If, as I believe, we are, then everything that we do in church, including music, is brought into ever stronger significance, and the sacramental quality of what we do is sharpened.

I will end by mentioning a piece that is in the very best tradition of church patronage – a work composed by John Casken as a gift to Durham Cathedral, to celebrate its nine hundredth anniversary. It continues and enriches what we have inherited musically from the past, so that the tradition is passed on to the next generation, not only alive but also active and fertile. The composer has set a poem by Sylvia Townsend Warner, entitled 'Sunrising'. The poem tells of Mary Magdalen's first encounter with the risen Christ (John 20). Poem and music marvellously combine to achieve an integrated sacramental effect. For in the poem the transformation of nature is used as an image to convey the transforming power of Christ, to which the music then adds its own characteristic grace:

Hearing him speak thus,
Each dewdrop shone
Enfranchised diamond.[3]

Notes

1. St Thomas Aquinas, *Summa Theologiae*, 3a, Q. 60, art. 2.
2. Psalm 32.8. I have quoted the verse according to the form choirs are accustomed to sing from the Book of Common Prayer.
3. Sylvia Townsend Warner, *Collected Poems*, ed. C. Harman (New York: Viking Press, 1982), pp. 5–6. Reproduced by permission of Carcanet Press Limited, Manchester.

PART FOUR:
SACRED TIME

Earlier in the book we observed how traditional understandings of pilgrimage sought to transcend the notion of time: by retreading the place, the pilgrim's aim was to abolish the temporal distance which separates the present from the time of the original divine disclosure. The Christian liturgy has also often been understood in this way; there is an anamnesis or remembrance of the past which, however understood, brings Christ's sacrificial death and the promise of new life disclosed in his resurrection into the here and now. Combined with this there has also been an anticipatory element, that the Eucharist is a foretaste of a perfect consummation which is yet to come. Whether the primary focus is on the past or on the future, both alike speak of a sacramental participation in a different order of time, of a divine reality that remains eternally valid. Yet it cannot be denied that very different theological understandings are generated depending on where the greater stress is laid. Should we sanctify the past as enabling us to be what we now are, or should we rather see ourselves as called out of our present to a very different future? This is a tension which carries obvious parallels to one we noted earlier when considering sacred space, that between place and movement.

The two essays by Terence McCaughey and Christopher Rowland very effectively highlight this tension. Terence McCaughey attributes the success of the Celtic mission to the way in which it sacralized existing Irish social structures, while for Christopher Rowland the Christian message is about liberation from existing social realities through anticipation of a transformed future. Put thus, the contrast is of course too crude; Christopher Rowland also looks backwards to the Bible, while equally Terence McCaughey by no means suggests that the Celtic missionaries endorsed every aspect of the existing Irish social world. But if both aspects are required, and we should accept our temporal situatedness, our existing social world, as both gift and a summons to go beyond it, how is the right balance to be struck? Our modern prejudice is to look to the future for our critiques, and no doubt this is often right, but may not neglected aspects of the past be of equal, if not greater, force? After all, if God is outside human time, then he is as much related, sacramentally, to past as to present or to future.

Social World as Sacrament

TERENCE McCAUGHEY

Terence McCaughey begins by challenging two common assumptions about Celtic spirituality: that it is a single, integrated phenomenon, and that it had a distinctive attitude to the natural world. Instead, he locates the decisive contribution of early Irish Christianity in the way in which it used its existing social world sacramentally, to communicate the truths of the gospel. To illustrate this, he gives four examples: the understanding of grace in terms of the relation between patron and client; the notion of 'fasting against'; 'Be thou my vision' as modelled upon going berserk in battle; and 'fosterage' as the best image for the believer's relation with Christ.

A common Celtic spirituality?

There is undoubtedly a tendency in some quarters, when speaking of Celts – whether it be with reference to their military achievements, their arts or their religion – to speak of them in the past tense. Thus we hear that the Celts 'were' such and such, or that they 'used to' do this or that. If, however, one adopts a narrowly linguistic definition of the word 'Celtic', i.e., as referring to people who speak a Celtic language, then the present tense is as appropriate as the past. Under these circumstances, the word 'Celtic' must necessarily refer to those who (in however sadly diminished numbers) habitually use Breton, Irish, Welsh or Scottish Gaelic when writing or speaking in any period right up to the present. 'Celtic' spirituality may refer to the spirituality of people living in places as far apart as Bangor and Patagonia, Inverness and Cape Breton, or alive at any time between the arrival of Christianity and the introduction of writing into Ireland and Britain by the first missionaries, on the one hand, and the spirituality of the present day, on the other.

The term 'Celtic Church' has, of course, been employed more narrowly than this, it should be said. It is usually confined as a term to refer to the native church of Britain or Ireland – often represented as upholding an early and purer formulation and practice in the face of subsequent missions from Rome, the introduction of the diocesan system and the new Roman discipline in the twelfth century. But this hardly fits: for Mael Sheachlainn (Malachy) who instituted these reforms in Ireland, or Malcolm III, who backed up his wife's plans for a similar reform in Scotland, were Gaels and Celts just as surely as those who opposed them. The same can be said for the fifth Earl of Argyll who spearheaded reforming ideals and practices in the highlands in the sixteenth century, or for the Evangelicals of the eighteenth. It is one of the merits of a recent collection of essays aiming to introduce the reader to 'Celtic Christianity', that it acknowledges this wider and more accurate understanding of the term 'Celtic', particularly in the chapters on Scotland and Wales.[1]

It has sometimes been alleged that there is, in fact, no real continuity between the faith and practice of the church of the first centuries after the arrival of Christianity and the faith and practice of more recent times. There are, of course, senses in which this is very obviously true. Few today, for instance, would draw the naïve and even crude parallels between the church of Patrick and the faith and practice of the nineteenth- or twentieth-century Church of Ireland, or between the church of Columba/Colmcille in the sixth century and the Church of Scotland in the twentieth, as was quite often done in the past.[2] Most people today recognize the discontinuity, the chasm of difference which yawns between the fifth century and the present. However, continuity there is – sometimes of a surprising kind.

The devotions associated with 'patterns' and the holy wells of Ireland survived what has been called the 'devotional revolution' of the mid-nineteenth century associated with the ultramontanists. Many of these go back centuries – some of them at least touch hands with pre-Christian religious practice.[3] And even in Scotland, where successively the Protestant Reformation and the Evangelical movement cut so many links with the past, there is to be discerned a continuity with the pre-Reformation past which can take us by surprise. In a recent paper, John MacInnes has drawn attention to the fact that a number of the sites used for the great highland open-air Communions are also sites with strong pre-Christian associations.[4] While, of course, the terrain itself may have rendered these obvious as gathering places, one is tempted to trace what MacInnes calls 'some vestige of memory that these were traditionally gathering-places'. One such in Gairloch, Wester Ross, was *Leaba na Bà Bàine* – the 'Bed of the White Cow' (the cow goddess of tradition) – while another, in the Isle of Skye, *Beul Átha nan Trì Allt* – the 'Ford of the Three Streams' – is still associated with witches and fairies, and during the Land agitation of the 1880s, was used for mass meetings as earlier it had been for the open-air services of Maighstir Ruairidh (1794–1868) the great Evangelical.[5]

Some of what was peculiar had a way of surviving. It is important, however, in speaking of this material, to distinguish what exactly is peculiar from what is shared with the world outside of Ireland or Gaelic-speaking Scotland.

Natural or social sacramentality?

Over the past decade or more there has been a strong tendency on the part of ecologically conscious people, often with only a slight grasp of the Gaelic tradition and language, to use the texts of the 'Celtic Church' and especially the collection of prayers and charms made by Alexander Carmichael in the early years of this century, to show that there was a time in these islands when Christians were closer to nature than they are today. They discern in these texts a theology and a devotion which, it is alleged, has been missing from what is held to be the altogether too cerebral tradition of Western theology in general. Certainly it is easy to adduce texts to confirm this contention.

But, leaving aside the consideration that everyone in any part of Europe was more affected by the changing seasons and lived in more familiar proximity to their domestic animals and in fear of the wild ones than anyone does today – and that this was not peculiar to the Celts – it should be noted that modern scholarship questions the link between the so-called 'nature poetry' of the eighth and ninth centuries and any group of hermit poets. D. Ó Corráin, in a recent article, denies that this body of verse is in any sense the literary expression of the ideals of the eremetic movement or the 'ingenuous product of the primary emotions and experiences of the hermit life', but are rather a commentary on the religious life as seen through 'the conceits and tropes of scholarly men writing to meet the needs and tastes of a cultural élite.'[6]

What these poems of the Old Irish period (c. 700–c. 900) do illustrate is the way in which Old Irish church people (mostly within monastic communities) often interpreted the faith and structured their life and devotion by critical reference to the society in which they lived. The structure of this society was gradually changed by Christianity, which was itself transformed by it to some extent in the process.

In the remainder of this essay, I propose to examine, with reference to some Old Irish literary remains, some of the ways in which the people of that time took the data of social organization around them and deployed them as models or means by which to address and even understand ultimate realities. Our subject-matter, therefore, becomes the social world as (flawed) sacrament of the relationship with the transcendent.

It may be alleged, with reference to the early Irish church, that it came to be too uncritical of the social order. Whatever the justice of that charge, it is nevertheless an extraordinary fact of early Irish history that, during this first mission of the Western church outside the bounds of Empire, the church insinuated itself into 'barbarian' society without violent dislocation of its structures. There is no evidence that any of the early missionaries were martyred. We can only guess at the reason for this, but it is tempting to seek at least part of the explanation in the character and policies pursued by the person recognized by the tradition as the most significant of the fifth century missionaries, that is, Patrick, author of the *Confessio* and the *Letter to Coroticus*.[7] This remarkable man was taken away to Ireland as a youth from his home on the west coast of northern Britain – possibly in Cumbria. There he served Irish masters for six years, after which he escaped and returned to his native country, only to return to Ireland again after an indeterminate number of years. But the man in holy orders who returned to Ireland had as a youth acquired a worm's-eye view of the society to which he now returned. This product of immediately post-Roman Britain returned to an Ireland which had certainly been in touch with the Roman province to the east, both through trading and raiding, as archaeological research also shows, but into which the legions had never marched and which remained firmly outside the frontiers of the Empire. The fact that Christianity established itself in Ireland without causing major social dislocation or the population suffering martyrdoms, may perhaps be attributed to the sensitivity of Patrick to the social ambience of the country and the detailed knowledge of it he had gained when a slave.

He seems to have travelled widely, especially from the plain of Meath right across to the west and also into the northern half of the country. To do so he had to pass the 'frontiers' of many *túatha*, the tribal areas of which it is calculated there were between one hundred and fifty and two hundred at the time.[8] Most people (even including the kings) did not cross these, but one class of person was free to do so, that is, the *filí*, the learned class. Its members, usually accompanied by a *dámh* or retinue (in the historical period at any rate using the language of their class) could and did travel freely from the north of Gaelic Scotland to the southern tip of Ireland. No doubt Patrick the British slave-boy noticed this 'diplomatic immunity'. It is no surprise, therefore, that in one of the few glimpses he gives us of his way of life in Ireland as a priest, he describes himself as travelling with a retinue of young men (chiefs' sons), whom he maintained with a stipend.[9] It is perhaps worthy of note that in one of the early law tracts, written in the seventh to eighth century when the church was well established, the honour-price (*enech*) of the king of a single *túath*, of a poet and that of a bishop were the same.[10] Whatever the significance of that, it does appear to be the case that the missionary used the experience of the slave in order to slot the faith into a pastoral, tribal and patriarchal society without urban communities (*civitates*) or any of the attendant infrastructure which the church had found it safe and convenient to use in Gaul and Britain.

Certainly in the monasteries, which from an early period came to be the bastions of Irish Christianity, the abbatial succession follows the pattern established for royal succession. The latter was, of course, not that of primogeniture.

Legal terms as models

Patrick has left us no other writings than the *Confessio* and his *Letter to Coroticus* – no catechisms, no sermons, no hymns.[11] But from the Old Irish period (AD c. 700–c. 900) there survives written evidence in Irish of the creative way in which the church a century and a half later was using the terminology of the laws and the social structures in order to speak meaningfully of the primary experiences of Christian faith. One cluster of such terms may serve to illustrate, that is, *rath*, *flaith* and *céle*.

The modern Irish word used to translate the Greek *charis* and the Latin *gratia* is *grás* and indeed this term occurs as early as the *Passions and Homilies*.[12] (There can be no doubt that from the beginning this was a concept of the first significance in a church which was consolidated and expanded during a period when the orthodox of Gaul and Britain were determined that Augustine's rather than Pelagius' theology would prevail). But the earliest term for 'grace' to be found in Old Irish even in glosses on the Latin text of Paul's epistles, is not one formed from *gratia*.[13] It is *rath*, a native legal term used for a fief of stock or land advanced by a superior (Ir. *flaith*) to his client (Ir. *céle*) in return for food – rent, winter hospitality or various other ser-vices. Over a period of years the *céle* was expected to pay back the original fief plus what we might term 'interest'.[14] One early law-tract lays down exactly the time-scale for this. Already in the corpus of law-tracts (*Cáin Lánamna*, 2) the relationship between *flaith* and *céle* is deployed as a simile for other relationships, for example, that of a husband and wife, that of teacher and pupil and that of a church to its monks. The Old Irish poet Bláthmac compares it to the relationship between God and the Jewish people in particular, but the use of the term *rath* in Old Irish glosses certainly extends its application beyond the relationship between Yahweh and Israel to that between God and believers in general.[15]

According to the Old Irish jurists, there were various cate-gories of *céli*, each relating to the superior in a particular way. Possession of at least five of each category is what gives the superior his noble status. Three benefits accrue to the *céle*: 1) the *céle* uses the advance, i.e. *rath* in order to live; 2) the *céle* may look to the superior for surety in future contracts. It is clear that each of these was potentially and actually susceptible of theological application. Other legal terms, too numerous to dis-cuss here, were pressed into theological service, but these may suffice to make the point that legal terms could be given clear theological application.

Social custom as model

The late Professor James Carney, who discovered and later edi-ted the poems of the eighth-century poet Bláthmac, has drawn attention to the use to which the poet puts contemporary social practice.[16] In the first of his two poems to the Virgin Mary, Bláthmac calls on Mary to 'keen' (mourn) her son with him:

With you I may beat my two palms for your son.[17]

Elsewhere he speaks with dry humour of the soldiers at the cross of Jesus offering him 'a drink for the road (*deoch séto*), in eager-ness for his speedy death'.[18] The implicit image is of hosts, impatient to be rid of a guest of whom they have wearied, giving him 'one for the road'.

Another poet makes creative use of the practice of 'fasting against' someone in order to be heard in one's petition. The writer of *Saltair na Rann* (c. 985) portrays Adam, on expulsion from Paradise, fasting against God in order to get God to for-give him.[19] According to this poet, not only did Adam himself fast, he actually persuaded the river Jordan to do so too, which it obligingly did by refusing to flow. Indeed, so earnest was Adam's entreaty that the fish and the animals joined the river and the man. It should be noted, in this connection, that one law-text states that a noble person who holds out against a justified and properly-conducted fast then loses his entitlement to be paid for any offences that may have been committed against him. The implication with reference to fasts against *God* is that God is bound to accede to a justified and proper fast.

A famous Old Irish poem beginning *Rob tu mo boile* is usually translated into English 'Be thou my *vision* . . .' and appears in many hymnals. Certainly, there can be no doubt that the word *boile* can and does on occasion carry that meaning, with some of the connotations borne by the word *vision* in English. However, equally certainly, the word *boile* is used to indicate the heightened awareness of those who are possessed by battle frenzy, becoming *beserk*. In the *Táin Bó Cualgne*, the great saga of the Ulster cycle, we read: *Rot gab baile is búadre* ('Madness and frenzy have seized you').[20] *The Egerton Glossary* 20, gives *boile* as a synonym for three other words which mean 'provocation', 'foraying' and 'mad rage'. The word occurs also in the title of the saga *Buile Shuibhne*.[21] This saga tells of one Suibhne, King of Dál nAraide, who fled out of the battle of Magh Rath (Moira) in 637, maddened by the clash of the weapons in the battle. He remained mad, living in desert places, even taking on the physical attributes of a bird. His madness (which may in the end be 'saner' than the fury of warriors) is a kind of critique of the battle fury of warriors. The *boile* for which the author of the poem *Rob tu mo boile* prays is of a similar kind. The poet asks to be filled with *boile* and, consistent with that, he asks (stanza 5) that God should be his battle-shield and sword (*rob tu mo cathsciath, rob tu mo cloidem*) and (stanza 6) his shelter and fortress (*mo didiu . . . mo daingen*). Stanza 14 speaks of victory (probably as won by piety), but this is a victory in which the victor laments as well as rejoices:

> Beloved Father, hear my lamentation;
> timely is the cry of woe of this miserable wretch.

> (stanza 15).

> O heart of my heart, whatever befalls me,
> O ruler of all, be my battle frenzy.

> (stanza 16).

The warrior in this battle does not seek loot or power over others:

> Be my noble and wonderful estate!
> I do not seek men or dead wealth.

> (stanza 10).

In his frenzy in this battle, the poet hopes to see things as they really are.

The translation of *boile* as 'vision' is therefore inadequate and misleading. *Boile* signifies 'frenzy' like that of those who go into battle (and flee out of it) as the military and battle imagery of much of the rest of the poem suggests. The poet is making a critical use of contemporary 'beserkr' practice in order to speak of the frenzy he himself will require in the holy war, the battle of faith.

Another very different example concerns the Celtic practice of fosterage under which parents 'farmed out' their offspring to a foster-mother who then played a key role in the child's education. It is a practice which dates back to the Old Irish period and indeed survived into seventeenth-century Ireland and Gaelic Scotland. It is presupposed in much of the literature and is also deployed as a means of understanding our relation to God and of Christ's to the believer. Again the evidence is too extensive (and sometimes too complex) to be treated adequately here, but it may suffice to say that, almost certainly under the influence of Luke 8.21 ('My mother and my brethren are these which hear the word of God and do it' AV) an Old Irish writer could identify Brigid as mother of Christ, and Brendan as his brother, and state that every dedicated virgin shares in Mary's motherhood.

However, the idea that the saintly may become the 'foster-parents' of Christ is exploited for the insights it may yield. In a catechetical poem, embedded in the text of the *Tripartite Life of Patrick*, is a poem which includes the following:

Question: Who is God and where is God?
of whom is God
and where is God's dwelling?
Is God ever-living?
Is God beautiful?
Was God's son fostered by many?[22]

Behind the last question is the assumption that the son of 'the great King' would have been fostered at more than one house. So basic were the bonds between foster-parents and their foster-child (*dalta*), that the names for foster-father (*oide*) and foster-mother (*muime*) are in fact baby-words. In both Irish and Scottish Gaelic, moreover, the word for education today is derived from *oide*, that is, what one learned from the fosterer.

The most striking use of this imagery is probably the lyric *Ísucán* (a diminutive of *Ísu*, or Jesus) attributed to *Íte* who appears in the poem to be at once wet nurse and *muime* to the baby Jesus. She says, among other things:

Ísucán –
I nurse him in my lonely place;
tho' a priest have stores of wealth,
all is lies except Ísucán.

The little boy fostered in my house
is no son of base-born churl;
Jesus comes with heavenly host
to my breast each evening.[23]

The foster-child (*dalta*) was normally of higher status than the fosterer but their function (certainly during the lifetime of the *dalta*) served to raise their status. The potential for theological development is obvious, and it is exploited in this poem and elsewhere. Not surprisingly, many of the most moving laments in later Gaelic tradition are composed by the *muime* of the deceased – one whose emotional attachment was usually deep and whose own status might now be expected to drop, as a result of the death lamented in the song.

In conclusion, the evidence adduced here must leave one in no doubt about the extent to which the early Irish Christian tradition makes use of the existing social structures as a way to understand and speak about realities which transcend them.

Notes

1. J. Mackey (ed.), *Introduction to Celtic Christianity* (Edinburgh: T & T Clark, 1989). Reprint 1994.
2. See K. Hughes, 'The Celtic Church: Is this a valid concept?' in *Cambridge Medieval Celtic Studies* 1 (1981) pp. 1–20. The Rev. T. Roe, in his pamphlet *The Church of Ireland before the Reformation* (Belfast: Phillips and Sons, 1866) is a nineteenth-century representative of this point of view, but its roots lie in the writings of James Ussher. Roe's pamphlet was first printed privately in Enniskillen in 1845, and the later version was published in response to the disestablishment movement. See N. Canny, 'Why the Reformation failed in Ireland' in *Journal of Ecclesiastical History* 30 (1979) pp. 423–50.
3. See P. Harbison, *Pilgrimage in Ireland: the Monuments and the People* (London: Syracuse University Press, 1992).
4. J. MacInnes, 'Religion in Gaelic Society' in *Transactions of the Gaelic Society of Inverness* 52 (1980–1982) pp. 222–42.
5. R. MacLeod, 'The Bishop of Skye, the life and work of Rev.

Roderick MacLeod (1794–1868), Minister of Bracadale and Snizort' in *Transactions of the Gaelic Society of Inverness* 53 (1982–1984) pp. 174–209.

6. D. O. Corráin, 'Early Irish Hermit Poetry?' in D. O. Corráin, L. Breatnach, K. McCone, eds., *Sages, Saints and Storytellers: Celtic Studies in Honour of Professor James Carney* (Maynooth: An Sagart 1989) pp. 251–67.

7. Translations of these are to be found in Liam de Paor, *St. Patrick's World* (Dublin: Four Courts 1993), pp. 88–114. Latin original and translation in A. B. E. Hood (ed. and trans.), *St. Patrick: His Writings and Muirchú's Life* (London: Phillimore, 1978).

8. For meaning and usage of the word *tuath* (sing.) see F. Kelly, *A Guide to Early Irish Law* (Dublin: Dublin Institute for Advanced Studies 1988), p. 323 *et passim*.

9. Section 52 – *Interim praemia dabam regibus praeter quod dabam mercedem filiis ipsorum qui mecum ambulant . . .* See Hood, *St. Patrick*, p. 33 or de Paor, *Saint Patrick's World*, p. 107.

10. See Kelly, *A Guide*, pp. 40–1, p. 310 *et passim*.

11. The so-called 'Breastplate of Patrick' is certainly of later date than the fifth century.

12. R. Atkinson (ed.), *The Passions and Homilies from the Leabhar Breac: Text, Translation and Glossary* (Dublin: Royal Irish Academy Todd Lecture Series 2, 1887).

13. E.g. the Würzburg Glosses (Wb. 3d. 16) where *rad* (= *rath*) *Dé* = *gratia Dei* or Wb. 5d. 6 *amal romboí cuit cáich din rath diadu* = *secundum gratiam quae data est nobis*. In the Old Irish Glosses from Würzburg *rath* is also (significantly) used to render Latin *charisma* often with a defining genitive, thus: Wb. 12b. 21 – *rath dénma ferte = gratiam curationum*, or Wb. 12b. 29 – *rath precepte*, or Milan Glosses 89c. 15 – *rath somailse*.

14. Kelly, *A Guide*, pp. 26–33.

15. See *Contributions to the Dictionary of the Irish Language* (Dublin), under *rath*. See note 16, following.

16. J. Carney (ed.), *The Poems of Bláthmac, son of Cú Brettan, together with the Irish Gospel of Thomas and a Poem on the Virgin Mary* (Dublin: Irish Texts Society), 1964.

17. Carney, *The Poems*, pp. 2–3. For further information on 'keening' (*caointeoireacht*) see A. Carmichael, *Ortha nan Gaidheal* (Edinburgh: Oliver and Boyd, 1954), v. 338–67 and vi. 29.

18. Carney, *The Poems*, pp. 20–1. In Scottish Gaelic there is a saying *Deoch an dorais, deoch an dorais!* (drink for parting, literally 'drink at the door').

19. *Saltair na Rann* is a poem of the end of the tenth century. See D. Green and F. Kelly (eds. and trans.) as *The Irish Adam and Eve Story from Saltair na Rann* (Dublin: Dublin Institute for Advanced Studies, 1976), vol. 1. Vol. 2 is a commentary by B. O. Murdoch.

20. E. Windisch (ed.), *Táin Bó Cualgne* (Leipzig: Irish Texts Society), 1905.

21. J. G. O'Keefe (ed.), *Buile Shuibhne* (Dublin: Stationery Office 1931), reprinted in *Medieval and Modern Irish Series* 1 (1952).
22. Kelly, *A Guide*, pp. 86–90.
23. J. Carney, *Medieval Irish Lyrics* (Dublin: Dolmen, 1967), pp. 3–7. Reprinted by permission of Colin Smythe Limited. Also E. G. Quin, 'The Early Irish Poem *Ísucán*' in *Cambridge Medieval Celtic Studies* 1 (1981) pp. 39–52.

Eucharist as Liberation from the Present

CHRISTOPHER ROWLAND

Taking three liberation theologies as his starting point, Christopher Rowland finds all three concerned in their discussion of the Eucharist to stress its eschatological dimension: as an anticipation of the overcoming of human division as expressed in class, poverty and social structure. He then tests that vision against the New Testament, among other things arguing against the common narrow ecclesiastical interpretation of 'brother' in Matthew 25, and for a very open reading of the Epistle to the Hebrews. He ends by suggesting that for the Christian the Eucharist is the equivalent of the German philosopher Jürgen Habermas' 'ideal speech situation': the ideal of maximum openness and reconciliation towards which all thought and action should be tending.

Eucharistic theology and the cries of the poor

What I want to do in this essay is to consider three authors and how their writing typifies the character of liberation theology in Latin America in so far as it concerns the setting of the Eucharist in present and prospective time (eschatology). Gustavo Gutiérrez is a priest and theologian who has for years divided his time between University, adult education and parochial ministry in one of Lima's shanty towns. Leonardo Boff, until recently a Franciscan professor of theology, has similarly been involved with the grassroots church in Petropolis just south of Rio. Jon Sobrino, for many years a target of the death squads who eventually succeeded in bringing about the death of six of his colleagues, was a close friend of Oscar Romero and heads theology at the University of Central America in El Salvador. Because

200

liberation theology is a contextual theology and has a distinctive flavour depending on its origin, there are many differences of emphasis. The writers I deal with are all men writing out of a Western Catholic tradition, necessarily influenced by trends in wider European theology. The form of their theology is typical of the compromises which are at the heart of so much of the liberation theology with which we are familiar; in which the conventional theological genre is infused with the reality of oppression and suffering of the majority, on whose behalf these theologians feel themselves called to articulate a case. After outlining facets of their work which, I hope, raise several different themes relating to time and the Eucharist, I shall examine some of them more closely from my particular perspective as a biblical interpreter.

In *A Theology of Liberation*, Gutiérrez briefly speaks of the Eucharist.[1] He sees it as having a pivotal place in the mission of the Church. Celebration of the Lord's Supper and human brotherhood are indissolubly joined, leading to opportunities for annunciation and denunciation. Gutiérrez quotes with approval a statement from his friend Camilo Torres (who died in Colombia after giving up the priesthood to join the guerrillas to fight for a more just society): 'The Christian community . . . cannot offer the sacrifice in an authentic form if it has not first fulfilled in an effective manner the precept of "love thy neighbour"'.[2] Not surprisingly, Matt. 5.23 is quoted in support. Gutiérrez argues that a necessary precondition for participation in the Eucharist is fraternal charity.[3] *Koinonia* (communion) must characterize the Church's life in three ways: union with God; union with Christ; and the common ownership of the good necessary for earthly existence. For Gutiérrez, to remember Christ is more than the performance of an act of worship. It means living under the sign of the cross in the hope of resurrection. It is to accept the meaning of a life that was given over to death, at the hands of the powerful of this world, for the love of others. Hence identification with the Crucified One means a contemporary identification with those given over to death and the denunciation of the processes which bring death and dehumanization.

In Leonardo Boff's *Jesus Christ Liberator* there is a more overt eschatological strain.[4] The Eucharist is set in the context of a wider christological discussion about Christ's presence in the world. He accepts the view that according to the New Testament the future creation is already initiated in Christ, in whom the future destiny of humanity is discovered. That means that we can no longer be content to analyse the world and accept creation as it is as our starting-point. We must comprehend it *sub specie finis*, that is from the perspective of its end. In Jesus, God appeared in a concrete form assuming our human condition; so each human being reminds us of the perfect human being, Jesus. To accept a poor person is to accept the poor Jesus.[5] Whoever rejects the poor rejects Christ, the very image and likeness of God, who identifies with them. Boff's view is inclusive:

> wherever people seek the good, justice, humanitarian love, solidarity, community and understanding, wherever they dedicate themselves to overcoming egoism to make this world more human and fraternal, in opening themselves up to the normative transcendent for their lives, there we can say that the resurrected one is present, because the cause for which he lived, suffered, was tried and executed is being carried forward.[6]

This broader context offers the one in which the Eucharist is to be understood. The Eucharist celebrates the giving and self-communication of the Lord. It is there that the eschatological future is anticipated and the values of the new creation celebrated. It is a commitment to life, the life of Christ outside the worshipping community in daily life. Those who share in the Eucharist are a sign of the presence of Christ, the particularities and partiality of whose life are celebrated in eucharistic worship. So the Eucharist cannot be inward-looking. It looks forward to the future consummation and outwards to others in whom the resurrected Lord is to be glimpsed.

Jon Sobrino, in another of the classics of liberation theology, *Christology at the Crossroads*, echoes the views of those who see in earliest Christianity a transition from groups looking forward expectantly to a new heaven and new earth to an inward-looking cultic worship.[7] The latter, he suggests, involves distinctions between priests and laity and generates privileged opportunities of access to God. As it developed, the Church began to see itself as *the* mediator of salvation. Sobrino regrets this process, particularly the effect on giving priority to the cult over other obligations of discipleship. In contrast, Sobrino juxtaposes the refusal of the Epistle to the Hebrews to turn nascent Christianity into a cultic religion. In the exposition of Hebrews he argues that there is no separation of the realm of the sacred and real-life history. Jesus' work of mediation takes place in the profane realm of real history, 'outside the camp'. Jesus, a layman living in the profane world, manages to do what priests had vainly been trying to do, namely, to render present among human beings God's love and the desire for human solidarity. In addition, the retrieval of the historical Jesus is an important corrective to cultic representations of the risen Lord's death. The way to communion with God is to follow in the footsteps of the historical Jesus. It is he who shows us how we are to lead a Christian life. To quote him, 'we can celebrate his life and journey with doxologies, but it is even more important to follow in his footsteps.'[8]

In his later *The True Church and the Poor*[9] he echoes some of the themes of Gutiérrez and Boff's presentations. Conformity with Christ demands of the Church that it becomes poor and is of the poor. It must accept a real *kenosis* or self-emptying in order to be truly a sacrament of salvation, and be in solidarity with the poor. The eucharistic celebration with its meeting with the Christ who offered the kingdom to the poor and persecuted means acceptance of poverty. Sobrino, as befits one brought up on the *Spiritual Exercises* of St Ignatius Loyola, affirms that there is something inherent in poverty that enables human beings to glimpse something of the meaning of the Kingdom of God. The presence of the poor shatters assumptions about what it is to be human and provides a basis for a response to the questions, 'what is love, who is the neighbour and most fundamentally, who and where, is God?'

This brief survey indicates why the perspective of liberation theology is so important for eucharistic theology. The concern with identifying God's presence and serving God in the contemporary world is a fundamental theme of Latin American liberation theology. Yet although that clear assertion that the presence of Christ lies beyond the gathered community to include the poor at the gates seems to suggest the breadth of their horizon, Latin American liberation theology still has a trace of the Christendom mentality. Gutiérrez, for example, consistently stresses that Latin America is both oppressed and Christian. So relief of suffering and oppression is a mark of fellowship which already exists, for the oppressed are brothers and sisters in Christ, baptized members of Christ's Body. This situation contrasts markedly with those exploring liberation theology in the context of patriarchy or where non-Christian religions predominate. In those situations appeals to solidarity in the Body of Christ are inadequate. The critique of patriarchy and the emergence of feminist theology cuts across religious affiliations. In Asian civilization there is the quest to be identified with the liberative elements in all religion, the promotion of human dignity and the struggle against mammon. In all this, identification with the poor and humble is the key.[10] That will mean that Christians will put themselves alongside all who seek solidarity with the poor.

In this, of course, there are significant parallels with the experience of Latin American churches in the nineteen sixties and seventies. While it may be formally correct that all those who became part of the grass roots movements under the aegis of the Church were baptized, in fact, the vast majority of them had turned their backs on it. They saw it as being in alliance with the corporate state, dominated by the hierarchy and cut off from the life and misery of the majority of the population. On the other hand, the experience of the military dictatorship in Brazil in this period led many disenchanted Catholics back to the Church. There they found an opportunity to join hands with practising Christians in working to ameliorate the conditions of the vast majority who had not benefitted from Brazil's economic miracle, and to promote human rights. The experience was of mutual benefit. The pastoral openings offered by Vatican II and Medellín (the Conference of Latin American Bishops in 1968) allowed a more eclectic approach to evangelization, and the political activists themselves were drawn into a fellowship of reflection and struggle in which the Christian tradition was found to be a resource which informed their approach to politics and everyday life. That point is a reminder of one of the fundamental features of liberation theology as it has emerged in Latin America.

Living the Eucharist: the tensions of the present

Discussion about the idea of liberation theology and the Eucharist may be an interesting theoretical exercise, and yet a concentration on the *writings* of the theologians encapsulates only a fraction of what they seek to communicate by the central experience of the Eucharist and its ramifications in ordinary life. Extracting material from the books of the liberation theologians cannot adequately convey what liberation theology has become. Even if we admit that its genesis lies in the emergence of a form of political theology at a peculiar juncture in Latin American history, what is has become depends almost entirely on the intimacy of its links with the Church at the base of society. That experience of being the Church has many facets. A brief discussion of them is a necessary part of identifying liberation theology's contribution to eucharistic theology.

The context in which eucharistic theology is carried out is central. Liberation theology, as we have come to know it, is identified with the life of the people at the base of society. Base communities are the driving force of liberation theology. These are the groups in a locality which share their sufferings, for a community rooted in worship, reflection on Scripture and celebration remains at the heart of the struggle for land and human dignity, which are seen as the necessary concomitant of fellowship. The recital of God's saving work (a significant part of the Eucharist) is not merely an evocation of the past but a demonstration of what is true in the present also. Such identification between the paradigmatic story and contemporary story is typical of the way in which the Bible is read in these base communities. The liberating acts of the past are appropriated and lived out in the land occupations and the attempt to obtain release from the oppression of the present, through agitation for better health and education. The assertion that 'We are Abraham and Sarah' and the resultant identification with their life of wandering, so different from the settled life from the surrounding civilization, is typical of base communities. It is this to which liberation theology returns again and again. As a result, the boundaries between biblical and modern story are blurred, as the reading of the former is conditioned by the latter, sometimes insightfully, at other times stretching the limits of the First World observer's credulity.

The reality of the experience of the majority is the presupposition of any adequate eucharistic theology, for if the Eucharist is cut off from life, this will mean participants being blind to the appalling conditions of the poor made worse by the ideological reinforcements of present patterns of social and economic life. The Latin American experience of sharing in the Eucharist is one that takes place in the midst of poverty of mind, spirit and body. The socio-economic deprivation is matched by an ecclesiastical scarcity too. Put bluntly, there is a shortage of priests and consequently for people in rural areas the Mass has become an occasional office like baptisms or weddings – eucharistic deprivation is now added to the economic. Every three months or so, the priest will appear to fulfil a round of priestly functions. What this is doing to the priestly vocation one can only speculate, particularly for those who are seeking a more participative ecclesiology. In terms of the eucharistic life of many it means that at the official level at least sharing in the body and blood of Christ is not part of a regular pattern of devotion. The pattern of religious life becomes frequently non-eucharistic, at least officially, though rumours abound of lay presidency in the light of the shortage. The staple fare of the worship is lay led – something that may be a mixed blessing. One occasion I attended in the far north-east of the Brazilian countryside was at one and the same time remarkable and rather depressing. It was remarkable for its organization and originality in worship organized without any recourse to priests or religious by those who live and work in the fields as casual labourers, but it was for me depressing because of the way in which this lay occasion (formally similar to the eucharistic liturgy without sharing of bread and wine) so closely mimicked conventional eucharistic worship in the dynamics of the liturgy, the identity of its participants, and the climate of dependency created between celebrants and congregation. Although women were not entirely excluded, the main liturgical activists were men. In addition there was a central core of active worshippers and a circle of vaguely interested onlookers. This anecdotal evidence typifies the problem.

In short, lay people are obliged to take responsibility for their worship. In their gatherings they receive from Christ and offer to him their thanks. Week by week this happens without a normal Eucharist, and leadership and pastoral ministry are worked out in the context of the particularity of the church in that place. Let me be clear. These were no dissidents. In so far as I can judge, there is enormous respect for the authority of the Church and its patterns of ministry. How often those people feel the disjunction between the local, regular pattern and the occasional incursion of official representative into their worship (which is so striking to an outsider) I cannot say. Theologically, it is certainly a problem which several liberation theologians have confronted, Leonardo Boff among them, itself one of the main reasons for his clash with the teaching authority of his Church.

Insiders and outsiders: the future pressing on the present

I have pointed out that the emergence of base communities coincided with periods of repression in which the Church offered an umbrella for all those who sought to resist oppression and to work for human dignity. That ecumenical spirit is one which has always typified their activity. Admittedly, there was a sectarian stance to the degree that there was a clear rejection of any ideology which merely maintained the *status quo*, but within the groups variety of opinion and degrees of commitment are entirely typical. That experience bids a biblical commentator reflect in the light of the New Testament. Many would endorse the view that early Christian groups are best understood in the light of a sociology of sectarianism.[11] Refinements of Troeltsch's rough church/sect classification have made us aware of the possibility of differences of sectarian strategy lying behind different

New Testament documents. Compared with much of Judaism, Christian groups appear to have been more exclusive. The existence of a penumbra of sympathizers with Judaism who might continue in that position without ever converting contrasts with what we know of the early Church. Yet for all the exclusiveness there are contrary indications in the New Testament texts which suggest inclusiveness and offer a surprising lack of reassurance to insiders about their ultimate destiny. Indeed, in texts where the boundaries and contrasts seem to be most clear and the sectarian spirit pronounced, the assurance offered to those who might suppose themselves to be insiders (as for example in Revelation) is far from certain.

Such indications should make us pause before we assume too quickly that early Christian rites like the Eucharist encouraged a sense of certainty in salvation. Even in 1 Corinthians, which is particularly concerned with the life of the gathered community, the Eucharist is no ideological glue for group identity. The recollection of the words of institution in chapter 11 start with the admonitory note struck by the theme of betrayal by one of Jesus' intimate circle. The occasion itself elicits a level of moral reflection which challenges lack of concern. One has very little sense here of a ritual occasion which was seen as the messianic banquet reserved only for the elect, cut off from the struggles and misdemeanours of ordinary life. Paul's task seems to have been to remind his readers that their participation in the Eucharist was not just another cultic occasion but a meeting with Christ (1 Cor. 10.16f) which challenged the assumptions and practice of participants.

Even in the most overtly interested sectarian texts in the New Testament, the Fourth Gospel and the Johannine epistles, there is curiously little of that sense of certainty and belonging which one might expect from a self-confident enclosed group. The references to the coming of the Spirit-Paraclete in John 14—16 are in the context of intimate discourses vouchsafed to the disciples alone. All the superficial indications are that such intimate connection with the divine is found only in the circle of followers, but here too in these discourses a note of division and betrayal is sounded. The coming of the Spirit is after all conditional: 'if you love me, you will keep my commandments' (John 14.15 RSV). But that does not mean that the presence of the Spirit-Paraclete in John 14—16 is ultimately dependent on the disciples. The world cannot receive the Spirit, but that does not confine the presence of the Spirit to the realm of the Church; it was exactly the same with the divine Logos ('He came to his own and his own received him not' (John 1.9). Those who did receive him became children of God. That work and witness before the world is the Son's mission which carries on even in the face of rejection. Similarly, the continuation of this work by the Spirit-Paraclete is ultimately independent of the disciples, though they have a role to play in sharing that witness through identification with the world's final judgement (as is suggested by John 16.9f). Baptism and participation in the flesh and blood of the Church are, as David Rensberger has pointed out, not private initiation rites but public demonstrations of commitment.[12] Within the highly charged struggle between Jewish groups they are socially costly acts of changing sides – ways of being identified with a mission which leaves one outside the synagogue. Consequent on that public demonstration is a life of service. As Gutiérrez points out, it may be no accident that the account of the institution is replaced in John by foot-washing: 'John seems to see in this episode the profound meaning of the eucharistic celebration . . . the Eucharist appears inseparably united to . . . the building up of real human brotherhood.'[13]

In all of this we are a long way from a ritual occasion serving as a gathering point for all those discontented with contemporary politics. Yet equally there is little sense here of a ritual which served only to bind the participants in assumptions about their destiny or indeed inure them against wider concerns. Even if the Body of Christ is identified with membership of the *ecclesia*, the identity of the group is not allowed to mask either the costliness of participation in social terms or the activity of God in history. However great the pressures might have been to allow the divine to validate the community and its interests, that was on the whole not allowed to happen. The Eucharist was a place where this could be announced, celebrated and explored.

But was the presence of God to be so confined to the communion of the like-minded? Or is there a demand that one looks beyond ecclesial boundaries to include the outsiders, so that the charity demanded in the treatment of insiders is extended to others? The answer to that question has often centred around the interpretation of Matt. 25.31ff. This is a passage which has, not surprisingly, loomed large in many treatments of the option for the poor in liberation theology, and forms a central plank in the argument in the recent papal encyclical on social justice *Sollicitudo rei socialis*.[14] Gutiérrez in *A Theology of Liberation* sees in the passage a stress on communion and brotherhood as the ultimate reality of human life (thereby anticipating central themes he enunciates with regard to the Eucharist later in the book), the insistence of love being manifested in concrete actions; and the inescapability of human mediation as necessary to reach the Lord.

In Matt. 25.31ff the heavenly son of man sits on the throne of glory, a scene parallel to a contemporary Jewish text, *The Similitudes of Enoch*, where the heavenly son of man sits on God's throne of glory, exercising judgement and vindicating the elect. But in contrast to the Jewish text, Matthew's scene does not describe an expectation confined to some eschatological event. In the parable of the sheep and the goats we find that the vision of the glorious theophany is attainable in the mundane circumstances of human need. Thus, to their astonishment, the righteous learn that they have in fact met the glorious son of man who occupies the throne of glory in the persons of the naked, the poor, the hungry, the sick and those in prison. Judgement is determined at the moment of reaction to those who appear to be nonentities and who are making claims upon us from a position of weakness. There are parallels to all this in the Jewish tradition where respect for the human person created in God's image, irrespective of nation or religious affiliation, is to be found. Most akin to Matthew's sheep and goats is 2 Enoch 42.8ff. where clothing the naked, feeding the hungry, looking after the widows and orphans, and coming to the aid of those who have suffered injustice are criteria for blessedness.

Although there is little doubt about the universal application of the criteria in the text, debate has raged over the identity of Jesus' brethren in the parable of the sheep and the goats. Is it right to see in the verse, 'As you did it to one of the least of these (my brethren), you did it to me' a reference to all the poor, naked, hungry, sick and imprisoned, or is it not the case that, in Matthew's gospel at least, they are references to followers of Christ, particularly to those Christian missionaries who might need shelter and care? Whatever the meaning of the words on the lips of Jesus, or the meaning which a contemporary reading of Matthew might offer, powerful arguments have been marshalled for the view that Matthew intended the phrase 'Jesus' brethren' to refer exclusively to poor Christians and not to the poor in general. Such arguments adduce the fact that Jesus' disciples are referred to as 'brethren' elsewhere in the Gospel. In the discussion of the identity of the brethren in Matthew 25, however, there is one issue which I believe has not received enough attention in the debate. While an identification of the disciples with the little ones may possibly be found earlier in the Gospel, the picture of the disciples becomes progressively less positive. After the revelation granted Peter at 16.17 concerning the true nature of Jesus, Peter becomes the embodiment of Satan and a *skandalon* to Jesus, while his remonstration with Jesus in chapter 26 ('Though they all fall away because of you, I will never fall away' (v. 33)), is followed by his emphatic denial of Jesus later in the same chapter. After the descent from the Mount of Transfiguration the disciples understand the significance of John the Baptist (17.13), but some are almost immediately reproached for being a faithless generation (17.17 cf. 16.4 and 21.20). Despite the words of Jesus about the blessedness of the children they rebuke the children who come to Jesus (19.13), they are indignant with the woman who anoints the head of Jesus (26.8), and they are astounded by the implications of Jesus' teaching (19.10 and 19.25); they are blind also to the humble way of the Messiah and desire places of honour (which is not disguised by their mother acting as their agent, 20.20ff). They remain attached to the old order (24.1), and like the Pharisees want to know what signs will usher in the new age (24.3). Judas betrays Jesus and his closest disciples fail to watch with him (26.40–45), while their readiness to use the power of the old order to resist Jesus' arrest is rebuked by Jesus in a statement of spiritual principle peculiar to Matthew's account: 'All who take the sword will perish by the sword' (26.52). Even after the resurrection, when the eleven disciples go to Galilee to meet Jesus on the mountain, 'some of them doubted' (28.16).

I wonder whether a case can be made for seeing the second half of the Gospel as being one in which the ideal of discipleship ceases to be embodied in the group of disciples. It is not that they are failures but that other paradigms are needed. This is seen most clearly in chapter 18 where the child is set over against the twelve as the type of true greatness. Although Peter has had his moments of insight, it is the crowd that hails Jesus as he enters Jerusalem (21.9), the blind and the lame who come to him in the temple (21.14), and the children who cry out, 'Hosanna to the son of David!' (21.15). These are the *nepioi* (babes) of whom the Psalmist speaks and Matthew quotes: 'Out of the mouth of babes and sucklings thou hast perfected praise.'[15] The *nepioi* referred to at 11.25, where Jesus gives thanks to his heavenly father for hiding these things from the wise and intelligent and revealing them to babes, includes the disciples, but as the Gospel proceeds the adult disciples are those who are seen to slip over on to the side of Satan, betraying, denying and abandoning the son of man. Instead, the child becomes a model of the humble: the insignificant yet insightful are offered by Jesus as an example of true greatness.

There is more that needs to be said on all this with regard to

the place 'the little ones' have in Matthew, both their relationship to mystical themes and to the narrow ecclesial setting
which is so often used to interpret Matthean themes. In saying
this it would be naïve in the extreme to deny that I have an interest in a more inclusive interpretation of 'the least of these my
brethren' in the Last Judgement. Prejudice and exegesis often
overlap, and each particular interest needs to be acknowledged.
What I am not convinced of, however, is that the assumptions
brought to the text need necessarily mean an imposition, for the
experience of contextual theology has been that a fresh perspective on conventional ways of interpreting throws up particular
issues which have often been ignored or relegated to lesser
significance by past exegesis.

As a final biblical example of the way in which future time
presses upon the present to create a fresh eucharistic perspective
on the sacrament as a release from the limitations of the present
social order, let us take the case of the Epistle to the Hebrews.
Sobrino's critique of cultic preoccupation was linked to a brief
allusion to the final chapter of the Letter to the Hebrews, where
Jesus suffers outside the camp. The theological critique of ideology which Sobrino's theology is seeking is amply provided for
by this complex epistle. Recognition of an apocalyptic background, brilliantly exposed by C. K. Barrett, helps to rescue it
from the static dualism to which a Philonic interpretation
seemed to confine it.[16] The exposition in Hebrews presupposes
a division between earthly and heavenly. The Levitical priest
serves in a copy of the heavenly shrine (8.5), whereas Christ, via
the cross, has entered heaven itself, not the sanctuary made with
hands (9.24). Even if references to future hope are at a minimum, there is ample evidence to suggest that an apocalyptic
cosmology is used in a creative way to locate the decisive theo-
phanic moment outside the apparatus of the cult: 'outside the
camp' (13.13). It is at Golgotha in his self-offering that the
'priest according to Melchizedek' enters behind the heavenly
veil to the very presence of God.[17] It is a life lived and died
(10.5) in human flesh which ultimately separates him from the
angels (1.3). The author understands the work of Christ as the
decisive moment in piercing the barrier between heaven and
earth. (10.20f). As in the Fourth Gospel the ascent of Christ to
heaven is not an expected glorious progress, for death and
degradation and exclusion are his lot. Yet the goal of the mystic
– the very presence of God behind the celestial veil – is where
Christ has gone as a pioneer. Those who would follow him are
called to share his reproach.

The apocalyptic perspective in the second half of the letter makes possible a critique of the established order. The other-worldly dimension is a temporary refuge pending the terrible consummation which is to come. The fulfilment is only hinted at and the kind of reconciliation between heaven and earth which is such a feature of the soteriology of Revelation nowhere appears. But the heavenly pioneer is to come again (9.28), the heavenly destination is only a temporary stopping place pending the Day that is drawing near (9.25); more directly relevant to our theme, however, is the implication that the place where heaven and earth meet and where the entrance into the divine takes place is in the place outside the camp, just like the Tent of Meeting (Ex. 33.7). But it is a place of shame or reproach where the blasphemers and sabbath-breakers are stoned (Lev. 24.16 and Num. 15.35). The summons to depart is reminiscent of the divine call to leave Babylon in Rev. 18.4, a reminder that the followers of Jesus are citizens of the heavenly not the earthly city. The reproach which is to be shared is clearly of a social kind, as 10.33 makes plain. The community's 'enlightenment' when they accepted Jesus as Messiah led to various forms of harassment. In this they follow not only in Christ's steps but also that of Moses who could be said to have opted for the poor. He denied his status as a member of Pharaoh's court, preferring to share the ill-treatment meted out to a suffering people. According to the writer of Hebrews Moses regarded 'the reproach of Christ greater riches than the treasures in Egypt' (Heb. 11.26 AV).

I realize that I have glossed over a variety of exegetical problems, but all this is potential grist to the mill for a critique of a eucharistic theology which is in danger of lapsing into a domesticated cosiness. Sobrino's brief allusion to Hebrews turns out to be a hunch which repays further exploration. The radical critique of the Levitical ideology is obvious from Hebrews, but its implications for the explanation of what it might mean to serve at the Christian altar are far-reaching in the practice of worship. There is a re-definition of 'sacred space' no less than of 'sacred time' which has obvious relevance for liberation theology.[18]

Liberation as openness to the future

One of the most intriguing themes in eucharistic theology, as we have seen, is the link between Eucharist and eschatology. Let me end by developing one aspect of this. Eucharist according to Gutiérrez is an evocation of human brotherhood, and, according to Boff, a proleptic participation in that new creation which Christ brought about. Those noble sentiments admirably evoke an ideal which regulates behaviour by recalling us to an alternative pattern of existence which contrasts with much of how we live. Liberation theology's realism, however, does not allow such talk to degenerate into utopianism. It recognizes that the character of what we recall in the Eucharist is at once a saving event and a moment of betrayal.

Human fallibility is the mark of human brotherhood from the very start of the biblical story. In the telling of the two brothers' encounter in Genesis 4 the issue of class, privilege, oppression and impoverishment have been features of the interpretation of the story from Josephus to the radical interpreters of the seventeenth century. Liberation theologians stand in this tradition when they make the Eucharist focus not merely on the reality of present human suffering but a future free of oppression and the distortions of the exercise of power and privilege. I have deliberately put the matter in these terms to introduce some illustrations from the German philosopher Jürgen Habermas' 'ideal speech situation'. There's a tension in Habermas' discussion between his refusal to see the 'ideal speech situation' merely as a regulative ideal and his insistence that though it is not a realizable or predictable state of affairs it is the basis of human discourse and the goal of human language. As Nicholas Lash puts it: 'To anticipate the ideal speech situation . . . is at least implicitly to recognize such a situation to be a necessary condition of rational discourse and to act upon this recognition, while neither predicting that any situation will, in fact, be realized, nor speculating as to the form such realization could take.'[19]

In his amplification of Habermas, Lash explores the character of Christian hope as exemplified by the Eucharist. He asserts that as the paradigm of God's Kingdom, the Eucharist fulfils a regulative function 'exhibiting criteria by which all *un*relationship, *un*brotherhood, all domination and division may be judged.' He rejects the idea that the Eucharist is merely regulative, for each celebration is an anticipation of God's Kingdom. Borrowing Habermas' words, he sees it as having the significance of a 'constitutive illusion' which is at the same time the appearance of a form of life. 'Our true future in God,' writes Lash, 'finds fictional appearance'. Thereby he stresses 'the more than regulative function of this acted parable': it becomes, announces, celebrates the fact that in God's time and way 'all shall be made well and all manner of things shall be well.'[20] But it is fictional in that such an anticipation is not a precise preview of future events for 'our true future in God finds, in such parables, *fictional* appearance [and] is intended to remind us that not even the best and truest and most appropriate of the stories that we tell lifts so much as the smallest corner of what Newman called the curtain hung over our futurity.'[21]

Here there are at least two major resonances with liberation theology: first, the links, however tenuous, between present and future and the way in which fellowship in the Eucharist is shot through with anticipation of an ideal communication; and second, the shared meal as an acted parable of another way of being, intended to right distortions in human relationships. Is it too simplistic to see the Habermasian ideal as a secularized eschatology in which relating with God face to face or with brothers and sisters bearing the same divine name is replaced by a human consensus in which Reason alone prevails?

For the Christian at any rate it is the Eucharist which provides this openness to the future, an openness which by bringing judgement from the future liberates the present. Admittedly, the eschatological preoccupation can sometimes drift into utopianism, but perhaps the shock of Matthew 25 may help prevent that, as also the Spirit who convicts in the present in John 16 and the demand 'to move outside' in the latter half of Hebrews. It is puzzling that liberation theologians do not discuss the Eucharist more extensively than is in fact the case,[22] but as I hope I have shown, they leave us in no doubt of the degree to which it requires of us a transformation of our present condition preeminently in the case of the poor. At its heart lies the mystery of the encounter of the Lord in the poor. As I hope I have shown, through the impact of God's future on each and every eucharistic celebration we acquire a new (sacramental) sense of time and with it a new sense of our solidarity with the poor.

Notes

1. G. Gutiérrez, *A Theology of Liberation* (London, SCM Press, 1974).
2. ibid., p. 264.
3. cf. 1 Cor. 11.17–34 and Jas. 2.1–4.
4. L. Boff, *Jesus Christ Liberator* (London, SPCK, 1980).
5. Here there are obvious echoes of Matt. 25.34ff to which we shall return later.
6. Boff as above, p. 219.
7. J. Sobrino, *Christology at the Crossroads* (London, SCM Press, 1978).
8. ibid., p. 304.

9. J. Sobrino, *The True Church and the Poor* (London, SCM Press, 1985).
10. cf. A. Pieris, *An Asian Theology of Liberation* (Edinburgh: T & T Clark, 1988).
11. See for example S. C. Barton, 'Early Christianity and the Sociology of the sect' in F. Watson (ed.), *The Open Text* (London: SCM Press, 1993), pp. 140–62.
12. D. Rensberger, *Overcoming the World: Politics and Community in the Gospel of John* (London: SPCK, 1989).
13. Gutiérrez, *Theology of Liberation*, p. 263.
14. *Sollicitudo Rei Socialis* (On Social Concerns), Encyclical Letter of John Paul II (London: Catholic Truth Society, 1988).
15. Matt. 21.16 quoting Ps. 8 RSV.
16. C. K. Barrett, 'The Eschatology of the Epistle to the Hebrews', in W. D. Davies and D. Daube (eds.), *The Background of the New Testament and its Eschatology* (Cambridge: Cambridge U. P., 1964), pp. 363–93.
17. cf. Heb. 6.19; 9.24; 10.19f; 12.2.
18. M. Isaacs, *Sacred Space: an Approach to the Theology of the Epistle to the Hebrews* (Sheffield: JSOT, 1992).
19. N. Lash, 'Conversation in Gethsemane', in W. Jeanrond and J. Rike (eds.), *Radical Pluralism and Truth: David Tracy and the Hermeneutics of Religion* (New York: Crossroad, 1991), p. 57.
20. Alluding to Julian of Norwich *Showings* as, e.g. E. Colledge and J. Walsh (eds.) (New York: Paulist Press, 1978), p. 229.
21. Lash, op. cit., p. 59.
22. G. Gutiérrez, *The Truth Shall Make You Free* (London: SCM Press, 1993).